POPES FROM THE GHETTO

DATE DUE

POPES
FROM THE
GHETTO

A View of Medieval Christendom

by JOACHIM PRINZ

Schocken Books · New York

For my children

CONTENTS

ILLUSTRATIONS

Prelude

This book was conceived more than thirty years ago during tragic times. With Hitler's advent to power, the Jews of Germany, who had adhered to their faith for so many centuries, were suddenly being subjected to degradation, injustice and the threat of death. Although it was difficult enough for the *practicing* Jews to understand why a community which had lived in Germany for sixteen hundred years should now be singled out for ruthless persecution, the question was even more perplexing to those others whose Jewish parents or grandparents had embraced Christianity and who themselves had been brought up in the Christian tradition. Suddenly they found their lot cast with that of the unconverted. For Hitler did not recognize conversion. One Jewish grandmother, converted or not, was enough to contaminate the blood and render the resulting "non-Aryan" unfit for government service, the professions and an honorable life. Somehow these "non-Aryans" who could be neither Christians nor Jews came to envy those Jews who were able to accept the new burden with pride, secure in the knowledge that suffering had been the "badge of their tribe" since time immemorial. The assimilated Jew began to contemplate the futility of conversion. He had tried to escape by fleeing from himself. He had denied his Jewishness, changed his Jewish name, betrayed his faith, intermarried, but all to no avail. He now found himself in a huge trap. The letter "J" stamped on his passport said clearly that he was a Jew and would remain a Jew should he go to the ends of the world. And he asked this question: Was Jewish fate *still* inescapable, even in the twentieth century?

13

It had fallen upon me to speak with many of these perplexed people as they suddenly came flocking to Jewish services and meetings in the hope of satisfying their curiosity about themselves and learning why there was no way out. Their very existences were now intrinsically and dangerously bound up with those who had always said, frankly and even proudly, that they were of the seed of Israel, Jews pure and simple.

I began at that time to look into the problem of Jewish inescapability. I was struck by the story of Heinrich Heine, the great German-Jewish poet who had embraced Christianity as a young man but lived his later life in the twilight zone between Judaism and Christianity, belonging to neither. He continued to write flippantly and at times with sentimental self-deprecation about Jews and Judaism, never able to return but never willing to renounce. Lying on his "mattress grave" for months on end—paralyzed, forsaken and miserable—he asked that a Jewish cantor come to his bedside and sing to him "the desert songs of my people." After he died, a sculptor made a death mask of the great and tragic man which, during those days of Hitler, I saw for the first time. It was the face of an old, sick, bearded Jew. He who would not return to his people during his lifetime had come home to them in his death. I spoke of Heine with those people who were so much in doubt about themselves. There was no sense in struggling to escape. They would remain Jews in spite of themselves and in spite of their wills, their convictions and even their faith.

It was also at that time that I came across a little book by Gertrud von le Fort, a German writer, herself a convert from Protestantism to Catholicism. A work of fiction based on interpreted historical documents and written in the manner of a medieval chronicle, it dealt with a family of Jewish converts one of whom had become Pope Anaclet II. The family were called the Pierleoni, a name I had previously seen dealt with in a cursory fashion in a history of the Jews in Rome. The story of a Jew who became Pope fascinated me, supplying as it did historical confirmation of the old medieval legend of a Jewish Pope. There was a scene in the book which I shall never forget, one which provides another dramatic illustration of my theory of Jewish inescapability. In it, Petrus Leonis, the head of the Pierleone family, lay dying in the large hall of his Roman castle. His sons sat silently around his huge bed, but one of them, Peter, had not yet arrived from Paris, where he was serving as Cardinal. It was as if the old man were holding on to life until he could see again his most beloved son. At last the Cardinal arrived in the splendid regalia of his high office—the golden crucifix encrusted with precious stones dangling from a golden chain, the lordly mitre on his head. He went straight to his father, and the dying old man looked with great pride upon the son who had fulfilled his dreams. "Bend down," he said to the Cardinal, "bend down, my son, for I want to bless you." As the Cardinal knelt and leaned toward his father, the old man raised his trembling arm and brushed his son's head. The mitre fell across the bed and onto the mosaic floor, where it lay "like an empty bag." Petrus Leonis pronounced the blessing with regained strength: "May you be blessed, my son, with the blessing of our fathers Abraham, Isaac and Jacob." With this he died. In the hour of his death he had pronounced the Jewish blessing of his ancestors on his son, a prince of the Roman Catholic Church.

Of course the scene was the creation of an imaginative novelist, but to me its tenor was truer than history and more valid than a document. This Catholic writer had understood the problem of inescapability. Deeply impressed by the story, I began to collect every bit of information I could find on the Pierleoni. I soon learned that several historians better versed than I had devoted years of study to the family's role in the history of the Church. Great medievalists in Italy and England and a few American specialists in eccelesiastical history had made astounding new discoveries, fully documented and authenticated. They had found that the Pierleoni had produced not merely Anaclet II, but two of the Gregorys—Pope Gregory VI and Pope Gregory VII. It was difficult to believe that Gregory VII, that giant of the medieval church, the greatest spokesman of Papal Independence and a man universally acknowledged as one of the most important Popes in history, the same Gregory who is venerated today as a saint of the Roman Catholic Church, should have been a descendant of a converted Jewish family of Rome. It is no wonder that this discovery set off heated debate, particularly among German medievalists. But it remains a fact that whether the relationship was by blood or by marriage, the great Gregory was, as the Annals of Pegau put it, "*avunculus Pierleone*"—a phrase which translates as either the uncle or the nephew of the Pierleoni.

I felt that the fantastic story of this family should not be permitted to remain buried in scholastic journals, inaccessible to most readers. I have undertaken to tell it here as best I can. Its relevance to the question of Jewish inescapability will be obvious. For even a hundred years after the Pierleoni had accepted the Cross, Anaclet, the last of the Pierleone Popes, was bitterly attacked as "that Jew on the throne of Peter."

The Legend of the Jewish Pope
As Told by Micha bin Gorion

The ancient story of a "Jewish Pope" was circulated widely in Europe during the Middle Ages. At least four versions survive. In some of them the Pope, having returned home to the fold of his people, commits suicide by flinging himself into the flames. In the Spanish variation, the Pope is named Andreas, no doubt in reference to Anaclet II. The version presented here is translated from Micha bin Gorion's *Der Born Judas—The Well of Judah*.[1]

Once upon a time in the city of Mayence, which is situated on the River Rhine, there lived a famous teacher, and his name was Rabbi Shimeon. In his house there were three mirrors, and everybody could see in them what had happened in the world before and what would happen in the future. When Rabbi Shimeon died, a well sprang up from his grave. This was considered a great miracle, since the water had healing powers.

Rabbi Shimeon had a son and his name was Elchanan. When he was yet little, his father and his mother went to the house of worship and the boy was left under the supervision of a young maid. As usual, a woman from the neighborhood would come to prepare the stove for the family, and when she came, she took the child from the cradle, put him into her arms and left. The maid thought nothing ill of it, for she believed that the woman had gone out to play with the child and would soon return. Yet return she did not, but took the child to a place far away and gave him to the priest of the church.

When Rabbi Shimeon and his wife returned they found neither child nor maid, for she had run out of the house to look for the boy. When she did not find him, she returned weeping and reported what had happened. Then the parents raised their voices and wept and cried out in overwhelming pain. Rabbi Shimeon fasted and chastised his body day and night. He prayed to God that He should return his son to him, but the prayers went unheeded. And the Lord refused to reveal the name of the place where the boy was.

In the meantime Elchanan grew up among the priests and his wisdom and his scholarship grew with him, for he took after his father and had an open and quick mind for learning. He went from one university to the other until his wisdom was exceedingly great, and at long last he came to Rome. Here he learned many more languages than he already knew and acquired a great reputation as a scholar. Soon thereafter he was elevated to the position of Cardinal. His fame soon extended all over the world and everybody wanted to see him because he was so handsome and so learned. It was at this time that the Pontiff of the Roman Church died and nobody was considered worthier to become his successor than the Cardinal. Thus the son of Rabbi Shimeon of Mayence became the Pope of Rome.

There is no doubt that the new Pope knew about his Jewish origin and he even knew that his father was the great Rabbi Shimeon who lived in the city of Mayence which was situated on the River Rhine. But his reputation and the high position which he held forced him to disregard his yearning for his people and his desire to return to his faith. However, now that he had become the Pope his yearning grew more and more insistent, and he was anxious to see his father face to face. Thus he decided to use a ruse to bring him to Rome. He sent a Papal decree to the Bishop of Mayence and asked him to inform the Jews of the city that from now on they would not be permitted to celebrate the Sabbath, to circumcise their new-born sons, and that the women were no longer allowed to observe the law of purity which had been held in high esteem by the Jews. The new Pope thought in his heart: when this decree is read to the Jews of Mayence, they will soon send a delegation of worthy men to ask me to rescind the order, and there is no doubt that the group will be headed by my father. That is what happened. The Jews of Mayence were frightened when the Bishop read the Papal decree to them. They implored him to avert the evil, but he told them that he had no power to do so and advised them to see the Pope. The Jews of Mayence did penitence and fasted and prayed to the Lord, and then they elected two scholars who would accompany Rabbi Shimeon on his mission to Rome.

When the three delegates came to Rome, they went to the Jewish quarter and told their brethren of the purpose which had caused them to come to Rome. At first the Jews of Rome did not believe it, for the Pope had been known to be a friend of the Jews. But then Rabbi Shimeon showed them the Papal decree, and the Roman Jews said: "Woe unto us, for the Lord is wroth at you." And they called a day of fasting and prayed for the welfare of their brethren from Mayence.

After this, they went to a Cardinal who saw the Pope daily and told him about the matter. The Cardinal advised that the Jews from Mayence should put their complaint in writing. He would then submit it to the Pope.

When the letter was given to the Pope, he looked at the signatures and discovered that Rabbi Shimeon, his father, was among the delegates. He invited them to come to the Papal palace. Soon Rabbi Shimeon stood face to face with the Pontiff of the Roman Church. He prostrated himself before him, but the Pope asked him to rise and to sit on a chair. Then he asked him to make his plea. Rabbi Shimeon could hardly speak because of the tears that choked his voice, but he spoke freely about the decree which threatened his community. The Pope did not immediately respond, but he began to engage Rabbi Shimeon in a learned dispute, and the rabbi marveled at the scholarship of the Pontiff. Knowing that the rabbi was a famous chess player, the Pope invited him to play with him, and to Shimeon's amazement he beat him handsomely after only a few moves. But by then the Pope could no longer hold back. He asked everybody present to leave and then told Rabbi Shimeon that he was his son. He explained that the decree had been but a ruse to make him come to Rome so that he could see him. He gave Rabbi Shimeon a Papal letter which rescinded the decree, bade him farewell, and let him return to Mayence in peace.

After many years had passed the Pope disappeared from Rome and clandestinely returned to Mayence. Return he did, not merely to the place of his birth, but also to the God of his fathers. It is said that before leaving Rome he had written a book disputing the verities of the Christian Church which he left in the Papal chambers so that his successors could read it.

There is a hymn which is recited on the second day of the Jewish New Year, written by Rabbi Shimeon, describing the story of the Jewish Pope. Nobody should doubt its veracity for it really happened.

POPES FROM THE GHETTO

I THE EMERGENCE FROM THE GHETTO

As the eleventh century, the most dramatic of all Christian centuries, moved into its third decade, two new families assumed leading roles on the stage of Roman history: the Pierleoni and the Frangipani. They succeeded an ancient nobility which had owned property in and around Rome and dominated the city since the days of the Caesars. These old aristocrats, who exhibited busts of their pagan forefathers about their castles as testimony to their antiquity, were extremely proud to be able to boast of pre-Christian origins. But the two new families were different. The *nouveaux riches* of the era, they represented the moneyed aristocracy which had sprung up recently as a result of the newly developing urban civilization of the century. At least the Frangipani could claim a few generations of acceptance among the nobility; they even had a coat-of-arms. But time would pass before the Pierleoni could acquire a family crest, and when we examine it today as it is reproduced in a seventeenth century history[2] it looks like a belated improvisation. It depicts a golden lion on a purple field. Perhaps it is the Lion of Judah. For the Pierleoni had come straight from the Ghetto.

How long the Pierleoni had lived in Rome and where they came from before that, nobody knows. One seeks their name in vain in the city's six Jewish catacombs, those damp, dark halls where the tombs are decorated with the ancient Jewish symbol of the seven-branched candelabrum and where among the names of the dead, written in Greek or Latin, there frequently appears the word *Shalom*. Most likely, the bones of the Pierleoni rest in the oldest catacombs of the Jews of Rome, those of Montevedere, which lie thirty feet beneath the Villa Torlonia. It was at Torlonia that Mussolini spent many years, holding his most glamorous parties and his amorous adventures and arranging his most private conspiracies. "Did he realize," as the historian Harry Leon asks, "when he issued the anti-Semitic laws against the Jews of Italy in which he branded them as 'foreigners' that beneath the gardens in which he strolled stretched the bleak, grave lines of corridors of an ancient Jewish cemetery?" Perhaps he did, but it did not deter him. To the Italian dictator the Jews were "foreigners" despite the fact that the Jewish community of Rome is the most ancient in Europe. For since the first century before Christ, when there were eight million Jews under Roman rule, Jewish immigrants had been settling in the great capital. And it was in these catacombs that they buried their dead.

We can assume that by the time our story opens, in the year 1030, the Pierleoni had been living in Rome for many generations, if not centuries. Rome was a city so proud of its past and so hostile to foreigners that it was rare even for outsiders from other parts of Italy to establish themselves securely before the passage of several generations. And the Pierleoni were certainly well established. The head of the family, Baruch, was a very rich and powerful banker whose fortune must have been founded many years before by his ancestors. But who those ancestors were we shall never determine by examining the names in the catacombs, for the Italian name Pierleoni had not yet been adopted by the family and we do not know even the identity of Baruch's father.

We do know, however, that the family lived in the Trastevere, that district of Rome on the right bank of the Tiber across from the ancient Roman Forum. The Trastevere was not a Ghetto in the technical sense of the word. The term Ghetto was coined in sixteenth-century Venice, where the Jewish quarter was established close to the *guetto nuovo*—the cannon foundry—and thereafter every *Judengasse* in Germany and *Juiverie* in France was called a Ghetto. But while the term itself did not exist in the eleventh century, it is true that most of the Jews of Rome, aside from a few families in the

Campus Martius and the Suburba, did live in one quarter: the Trastevere.

Trastevere had been a Jewish quarter since the first pre-Christian century. In the days of the Roman Empire, when some fifty-thousand Jews lived in Rome, seven of the eleven known synagogues were in Trastevere. The oldest Roman church, Santa Maria in Trastevere, was also built there, erected in the fourth century on a site where oil had gushed out of the ground. (Instead of a derrick, the people built a church.) The whole district smelled of petroleum, though that smell was perhaps the area's least objectionable. For it was not at all a pleasant neighborhood but, as one historian of ancient Rome describes it, a "district characterized by narrow, crowded streets, towering tenement houses teeming with population. Ancient writers testify to the unsavory character of the area; there were snake charmers, fortune tellers, the noisy vendors of salt fish, hot peas and steaming sausages, the peddlers and petty merchants that thronged the streets. Here were the miserable quarters of the poor, unassimilated, immigrant population, wretchedly housed in vast tenement blocks, perhaps hundreds to a building, as in poorer quarters of Rome and Naples in our day, subject to the perils of fire, building collapse and the not infrequent floods of the Tiber." [3] Yet in the midst of this misery "there were magnificent palaces of the nobles." [4]

By the beginning of the eleventh century, Rome had changed dramatically from the days when it had been the glamorous, teeming capital of the Empire. It was a city in ruins, and only the mystique of the Papacy kept it alive. The Jewish community had gone through an equally striking transformation: though it had dwindled in numbers from fifty thousand to only about one thousand souls, it had also become a highly respected center of Jewish thought. The intervening centuries had dealt variously with the Jewish population. For more than a thousand years, Jews had come from every part of the Empire and maintained their synagogues as autonomous entities within the Jewish community: the Synagogue of the Vernaclasians

—the oldest of them all, where the native-born Roman Jews congregated—and those of the Agrippians, the Tripolitans, the Hebrews and others. But as time passed, the Jews came to say their prayers in Greek, and Hebrew was forgotten. The names they gave themselves were either Greek or Latin, and even the Biblical names of Abraham, Isaac and Jacob were rarely used. The catacombs where they had buried their dead—including the largest one, Montevedere, right in Trastevere—were abandoned. The people were poor and ignorant. There were few scholars.

Thus it is all the more remarkable that the eleventh century saw such a reflorescence of Jewish thought and prosperity. The people began to leave the Ghetto of Trastevere, and a new synagogue was erected in the Rione della Regola, not far from the Church of St. Thomas on the left bank of the Tiber; a new Jewish community began to grow right behind the Theatre of Marcellus (where it can still be seen today). Roman rabbis became world renowned, and Jewish communities as far away as Paris sent messengers to Rome to inquire about legal interpretations. *The Commentaries of the Romans,* a collective work on the Talmud, became a widely acclaimed guide to scholarship. Moses ben Nassi and Abraham ben Jacob, in the beginning of the eleventh century, and their successors, Jacob Gaon and Sabbatai Moses, were the spiritual leaders of the community. Nathan ben Yechiel was the author of the earliest and most influential Talmudic dictionary, the famous *Aruch.*

In time, most of the Jewish community left the filth and stench of the old Ghetto for the left bank. But the Pierleoni did not. Their decision to hold fast was not born out of sentimentality, but was part of the systematic planning of a family which seemed to live by a blueprint on which their every move had been patiently and deliberately determined. And the goal of their plan was the Papacy.

●

There are no documents or autobiographies to tell us just when the conversion of the Pierleoni to Christianity was decided upon and by whom. But we must perforce take up our story with Baruch. Baruch was a tremendously wealthy banker, an important land-owner and a man of great power and respect. He probably held numerous positions of rank among the Roman Jews, and in any event he was the *archsynagogus* of the private house of worship his family had built on an island they owned in the Tiber. (This island was to become a bastion in the future battles of the Church, as we shall soon see.) There was at Baruch's time no Jewish community in the modern sense—no central government of Jewish affairs—but the heads of synagogues, who elected one of their number to act as Chief Rabbi, did meet on various occasions. As one of these, Baruch was almost certainly a leader of Jewish delegations to Popes and senators. Nobody else had such easy and natural access to the authorities as a man of his wealth. He would surely be present at important ceremonies—such as ritual confrontations with the Pope.

Whenever a new Pope was chosen, the *scholae* of Rome, representing the many national and ethnic groups of the city, assembled in festive dress to pay homage to the new ruler of the Church. The Jews had their assigned place along the route of the Papal procession, sometimes in front of the Castel Sant'Angelo. (How ironic that the famous mausoleum-fortress was later to become one of the Pierleone strongholds.) There they stood with the Chief Rabbi and all the other dignitaries of the synagogues, the Elders of the Gerusia, the scholars and the men of means, waiting for the great moment of meeting the man upon whose beneficence they depended.

The rabbi held the Holy Scroll of the Torah, which was dressed for the solemn occasion like a bride, in silk and velvet with many adornments. There were golden crowns and ornaments, some of them encrusted with precious stones, the generous gifts of rich men probably including the richest of them all, Baruch, the banker of Rome. Finally the Papal procession arrived; the Papal litter carried by courtiers was set down, and the ceremony began. After the rabbi had lifted the Holy Scroll, kissed the Papal ring and pledged the Jews' loyalty and support, the Pope would receive the Scroll and address them. What words he used in the time of Baruch we do not know, but we can draw a reliable picture from the formula-speech which Pope Calixtus II inserted in the Papal Book of Homages some decades later. "We praise and revere the Holy Law," it opens, "for that it was given to your fathers by Almighty God through Moses. Your religious practices, however, and your worthless explanations of the Law we condemn. For the Redeemer for whom you wait in vain has long since come according to the teachings of our Apostolic faith, even our Lord Jesus Christ, who dwells with the Father and the Holy Ghost and reigns as God from generation to generation. I acknowledge—but I do not recognize."

If the Pope handed the Scroll back to the rabbi with a benevolent smile and perhaps the assurance of continued protection for the Jews in the Holy City, the Jews sighed with relief. They could not expect more. This was not the place for theological disputations, despite the fact that Jewish-Christian doctrinal debates were the fashion at that time. (Like intellectual bullfights, these debates attracted huge crowds. Christian clergy did not always prove equal to the rabbi. Heinrich Heine later found that "both of them stank.") But here no reply was requested or permitted. The Jews had given the Pope the Scroll of the Five Books of Moses, going through the ceremonial motions prescribed by Roman tradition, and that was all that was expected of them. Not that the ceremony was always so uneventful. Sometimes a Pope would let the Holy Scroll fall into the mud as a token of his contempt for the people who held it to be sacred. The mob would then howl and laugh, while the Jews stood by, powerless to say or do anything but tremble in expectation of the dark days that were sure to come. There was no violence, no physical attack, but mockery by the mob, "those illiterate, uncircumcised brutes," was painful enough.

Was it at such moments that Baruch, the Jew from Trastevere, began to wish for the kind of life for which he prayed in his private synagogue when the Jews consecrated the coming of a new month: *"a life free from shame and reproach"*? So long as he was one of the despised minority, begging for protection, walking the tightrope of permanent insecurity, tolerated rather than accepted, his life would indeed be one of *"shame and reproach."* Was it then that Baruch began to work on that blueprint for his family? Recounting the hundred and eight years from 1030, the year of the Pierleone conversion, until the death of Anaclet II, one cannot help but think of such a master plan.

For the conversion of the Pierleoni was not merely a maneuver to gain acceptance in Roman society. When the ordinary Jew became a Christian, he was from then on in most respects just like the others. But the Pierleoni were not "just like the others." It is interesting that some historians have called them the "Rothschilds of the Middle Ages." Of course, the Rothschilds never converted. Until this day they are Jewish leaders in England and France, and the Hebrew tombstones of their dead and membership in Orthodox synagogues remain *"la tradition de notre famille"*—the tradition of our family. But they, too, had their master plan, first conceived by Amschel Rothschild, an Orthodox Jew who wore his skullcap in the palaces of the great as well as in the little *shul* in the Ghetto of Frankfurt. They pursued their aims as relentlessly as the Pierleoni. The difference is that the "Rothschilds of the Middle Ages" determined to rule with the rulers, believe with the faithful, and fight with the valiant.

Trastevere, the ancient Ghetto, became the Pierleone base of operations. As we have hinted, there were good reasons for this choice. Trastevere was the gateway to Rome, and he who owned it controlled access to the city. In years to come, Trastevere was often opened by the Pierleoni to permit a Pope to enter Rome and seize strategic positions when every other road was held by hostile armies. Furthermore, their island in the Tiber—the Isola Tiberina on which they had built their synagogue—was the site of a bridge leading to the Papal possessions. (Because it connected the left bank of the Tiber with the Ghetto, the bridge was called *Pons Judaeorum*—the Jews' Bridge—and the street leading from it into the Ghetto was called *Rua Judaeorum*—Jews' Street.) So strategic were the island and its bridge that the Pierleoni erected a number of fortified towers in the vicinity to protect them and even purchased the virtually indestructible Theatre of Marcellus on the left bank opposite the bridge to serve as an armed castle. (Long known as Casa Pierleoni, the Theatre now houses poor families in what were once the family's elegant apartments.) Gregorovius, a historian of medieval Rome, saw these towers in the middle of the nineteenth century and described them in mildly anti-Semitic terms: "The Pierleoni Towers are now apartment houses and there today's Jews store secondhand clothes and on the lower floor they maintain their abbatoir for ritual slaughter of the animals. Thus the place where once lived the proud Pierleoni, senators and consuls of the Romans, has deteriorated, and by some curious irony returned to its formerly Jewish origins. On the very spot where the famous Pope of the Crusades [Urban II] had died, and where the Pierleoni themselves produced their own Pope, the Jews of our time sell secondhand clothes as did the ancestors of . . . Pope Anaclet II." [5]

●

With the systematic foresight of a military plan, the Pierleoni had bought up and fortified much of the left bank leading to the Papal City. Now they proceeded to man it with a private militia which could be augmented in times of need by soldiers of fortune ready to serve anyone who could pay. And the Pierleoni could afford to pay well. For they were moneyers.

The moneyers of the Middle Ages were authorized minters of coins, and as such they enjoyed a position to which there is no real parallel in our times. They were not merely professionals, but a caste, indeed one of higher rank and greater importance than most of the nobility. At a time when not merely emperors, but dukes, barons and even bishops minted their own money, when the quantity of precious metals in coins varied from town to town and state to state, when there was neither national nor international regulation of the money market, the minters were of enormous importance. In some cases they even supervised the mining of gold and silver as well as minting. If a king came into possession of a land, he needed his supervising minter as much as his forester or the overseer of his farmlands. Each minter had to be carefully chosen. Bonds had to be posted, unless the man were so trustworthy (and so rich) that his character and reputation were sufficient warranty. Since Jews had been the purveyors of gold and jewels for hundreds of years, a trade which required confidence on the part of the buyer, many dukes and kings had "their" Jewish families, with which they traded for generations. Thus it is natural that so many Jews were known to have been moneyers and minters. In the sixth century, the Jew Priscus was the minter of Chalons. The Jew Gideon was a minter in the Milan of the tenth century. In Winchester there were three Jewish minters in 1181. In London the name of David is remembered, in York it was the Jew Isaac, in Canterbury (a very important Jewish community in the twelfth century) there were Simon and Solomon. Bishop Otto of Wuerzburg in Bavaria at the beginning of the thirteenth century trusted the Jewish moneyer Yechiel; Leopold V of Austria was served by the Jew Shlom. There were Jewish minters even in Poland. The heyday of Jewish minting occurred in the seventeenth and eighteenth centuries, when in Prussia (of all places) Veitel Heine Ephraim was entrusted by the anti-Semitic Frederick the Great to supervise and organize all the mints of Prussia and Saxony; the famous Ephraim Palace, destroyed during the siege of Berlin, was still one of the architectural showplaces of the city when Hitler came to power. The rise and fall of the most powerful of all the Jewish minters, Joseph Suess Oppenheimer, who eventually landed on the gallows, is utterly fantastic.[6]

Of course it must be mentioned that these Jewish minters are singled out here because of their interest in the context of our story. The majority of the minters, bankers and moneylenders were Christians. Lombard Street in London, where all the moneychangers and bankers would congregate, still retains the memory of the Lombards of Italy, the classical Christian moneychangers of the Middle Ages. In spite of strict regulations, particularly in later centuries, even churches and monastic orders were engaged in banking. Yet Jews were not excluded. Even in the days of medieval anti-Semitism, when Church and State had succeeded in restricting Jewish commercial activities, the important minters were elevated to the position of Court Jews. They had easier access to the ruler than most noblemen, and while they usually lived in the Ghetto, the doors of the palace were readily opened for them. They were indeed the rulers' most precious "possessions," the purveyors of their art collections, and often, in times of crisis and catastrophe, their fellow Jews' most convincing spokesmen.

When the Pierleoni appear on the scene of documented Roman history, they were bankers, but there is a strong suspicion that they had begun as moneyers. A banker then, as in our own days, was also a moneylender. It was an important and lucrative business. Although money-changing netted only 8.33%, a personal loan was far more rewarding. The tables of going interest rates in the Middle Ages vary with the country, the circumstance and the personal standing of the recipient, but a prince with large holdings could pay 33% per annum, while pawn shops charged up to 300%. These were legal rates laid down by the authorities and not considered usurious.[7]

There can be little doubt, as we have noted, that the fabulous wealth of the Pierleoni was accumulated over a period of generations. Baruch the banker might have been a genius in his field and we know that his connections were excellent, but it is still improbable that all the family wealth was amassed by one man. Furthermore, since Jews are known to have played other important roles in the economy of the early Middle Ages, the ultimate origins of Baruch's fortune may have been not in banking but in some form of trade.

We read in the report of Ibn Kordadbeh, a postmaster of the Persian Empire in the ninth century, about the role of the famous Jewish merchants called Rhadanites who headed a far-flung business in the Mediterranean trade of the time. "These merchants speak Arabic, Persian, Roman [Greek and Latin], Frankish, Spanish and Slavonic. They travel from east to west, and from west to east, by land as well as by sea. They bring from the west eunuchs, slave girls, boys, brocade, beaver skins, marten furs and other varieties of fur. They embark in the land of the Franks on the Western Sea, and they sail toward Al-Fraya in Egypt. There they load their merchandise on the backs of camels and proceed by land to Al-Qulzum [Suez], twenty-five prangs distant. They embark on the Eastern Sea and proceed from Al-Qulzum to Al-Jar [port of Medina], then they go to Hind [India] and China. On their return they load musk, aloe wood, camphor, cinnamon and other products of the eastern countries. . . . Sometimes they take the route back of Rome, and crossing the country of the Slavs, proceed to the Lower Volga, the capital of the Khazars." [8]

Even in its abridged version this document conveys a picture of the activities of the Jewish merchants. Though it is probably wrong to think in terms of Jewish monopolies in the early medieval economy, it is equally wrong to think of the Jews of the eleventh century in terms of persecution, Ghetto and separation from the Christian world. All this came soon enough, but as we shall see it did not come before the First Crusade (1095), and even then it was restricted to certain areas.

In the eleventh century, little separated the Jews from the Christians save their religion. They spoke the language of the Christians. They often occupied the same quarters, and at times the same houses. Even the differences which did exist encouraged a certain intellectual inter-relationship: Jews taught Christians the Hebrew they used in their liturgy and frequently in their literature, and Christians taught Jews their Latin. Christians went to synagogues to hear the rabbis' sermons, while Jews sometimes assisted at mass. Jewish merchants and Christian customers often partook of one another's family celebrations. [9]

In fact, many towns of the early Middle Ages were eager for Jews to settle in their midsts. The most telling document in this connection is the famous invitation extended to the Jews to settle in the Rhenish city of Speyer. In September, 1084, Bishop Ruediger Huozmann decided that the significance of the town would gain if he invited Jews to live there. For their consent he was willing to grant them certain privileges. In addition to complete freedom of commerce in the town and its harbor, they were permitted to own land, buildings, gardens, vineyards and farms. [10] They were granted their

33

own judges and autonomy in their own social and cultural affairs; the archsynagogus was as powerful in his realm as the burgomaster. They were allowed to own slaves and (contrary to Papal decree) to hire Christian farmhands and wetnurses. They could sell to Christians that part of the meat which they were not permitted to eat. *As a means of protection* they were assigned a certain quarter of the town which had walls to protect the Jews from the rabble. For these privileges they paid an annual tax of three-and-one-half pounds of gold. This decree was later confirmed by the Emperor, Henry IV.

Since the Mohammedan conquest of Spain in 711, the overwhelming majority of European Jewry lived in that land, happy, prosperous and in large numbers. Some Spanish towns had Jewish majorities; Granada was known as a Jewish city, Lucena was almost entirely Jewish, Tarragona was called "Medinat al-Yahud" (the Jewish town) and more than a thousand Jewish families lived in Barcelona. Although no exact statistics are available for France, England and Italy, Salo Baron maintains that up to twenty thousand Jews lived in England, and that the majority of them lived in York, Lincoln, Bristol, Cambridge, Oxford and, of course, London.[11] In Italy, the Jewish community was much smaller. But population figures convey little of the commercial, social and cultural influence of the Jews.

In the early Middle Ages, the Jewish quarters were not always the dingy, filthy places they became later, when the Jews were surrounded by walls, restricted to a certain area regardless of growing population, and locked in after dark. They were often situated in the very center of the town near the city hall or the castle or close to the ancient Roman trade routes. They were the subjects of envy rather than hate. William, the canon of Newburgh, England, describes medieval Jewry in York in these words: "The Jews had built in the midst of the city, at most profuse expense, houses of great size, comparable to royal palaces. Therefore very many men of that province had conspired against them, not suffering that these men should be rich while they themselves were in want."

The Jews were active at that time in almost every phase of the economy. They owned salt mines in Saxony; they cultivated vineyards in France and sold wine; they were highly respected and even protected exhibitors at fairs in the Rhinelands and in France, and some fairs, in deference to the Jewish merchants, were not held on the Sabbath. They were weavers and tanners in Sicily, pearl fishers and merchants in Persia, glassblowers whose products were praised and sold as "Jewish glass," textile manufacturers and dyers in Brindisi, Egypt and Syria, traders in silk between China and the western countries, paper manufacturers in Valencia and other Spanish towns, and importers and exporters of high repute. Jewish merchants carried perfume, silk, jewelry and rare textiles from faraway lands and brought them to the castles and chateaux of emperors, Popes, bishops and dukes. Profits were high, but so were the dangers of piracy on the seas and highway robbery on land; it is said, for instance, that gold bullion could only be entrusted to Jews who transported it safely from Constantinople to Sweden because their fortified houses were built along the old trade routes.[12] No claim can be made that the Jews had no competition in these fields. But it cannot be denied that their fame and success as international traders were based upon the fact that Jews lived throughout the entire world and that there was an understanding between Jewish traders from Spain to India and China (where ancient Jewish communities still exist) and even Korea, an understanding based on Jewish law as well as brotherly trust. Hebrew was the *lingua franca* of these traders.

These Jewish merchants were not merely out for profits alone. They read and carried books. They were indeed representatives of a civilization that considered literacy a prerequisite to piety. In the towns, particularly the university towns, the small Jewish communities played indispensable roles as translators and interpreters. It was a Jew, Isaac, who served as interpreter to Charlemagne's ambassador in his famous mission to the Persian caliph Alrun al-Rashid. Mohammedan Spain, the Mecca of medieval culture, prepared the European revival of Greek and Latin civilization, and it was Spanish Jews who brought the classics to the West; the value of this knowledge to medieval medicine, mathematics and science cannot be overestimated. In the twelfth century, which is often called the century of the early Renaissance, Jews played an important part at the universities of Paris and Oxford.

Such mobility in the commercial world and in the cultural life of the cities precluded, as we have noted, the existence of significant social barriers between Jews and Christians, and even later in the Middle Ages the separation was far from complete. The thickest ghetto walls were not strong enough to hold back the cultural interactions of the times. Linguistically, Judeo-German (which is still preserved in Yiddish) was not far removed from medieval German, and Ladino, the language of the Spanish Jews, is Castilian Spanish. Rashi, the medieval Jewish commentator on the Bible (and, incidentally, owner of important French vineyards), used medieval French to clarify certain points in his Hebrew commentary. In architecture, the buildings of the Jewish quarters were erected in the styles of the era: the synagogues of Toledo, Prague and Worms are fine examples of Spanish, Romanesque and Gothic styles respectively. There was at least one Jewish troubador in Germany, the Minnesaenger Suesskind von Trimberg, and there may have been others. Contact between Christians and Jews was thus personal and immediate, and very often intimate. The final strict prohibition of the Church which in the thirteenth century enforced both the Ghetto and the distinctive Jewish dress are witness and proof of the existing social intercourse between Christians and Jews. Sexual relations were so frequent that Jewish scholars of the fifteenth century explained the expulsion of the Jews from Spain (in 1492) by saying that Spanish Jews "took Gentile women into their houses until they became pregnant. Their children became Gentiles and afterwards were among the murderers of their fathers." The explanation seems too simple, but that the problem of such relationships between Jews and Gentiles did exist is borne out by both Jewish and Christian warnings to the adherents of the respective faiths.

Considering the economic and social role of the Jews, it is amazing to note that there was hardly any voluntary mass conversion. Most conversions to Christianity occurred under duress, and even then their efficacy could well be doubted. From the time of the Visigoths, Jews were forced to embrace Christianity, but the converts, although professing Christian piety in public, often continued their Jewish worship and customs clandestinely. This kind of crypto-Judaism became the main problem of Christianity after the expulsion from Spain. Marranos—the *Christianos nuevos* of Spain—maintain their Jewishness until this very day, and the descendants of those converts live in their own exclusive community on the Balearic Island of Mallorca as though the expulsion had taken place yesterday. A marriage with a *Chueta* girl, a daughter of those wealthy converts of fifteenth century Jews, is still considered a *mésalliance*. The Marranos of Portugal still say Jewish prayers, and wealthy Catholic ladies in Brazil and Argentina, remembering their Jewish ancestry in medieval Spain, still light candles on the eve of the Sabbath. Official Catholicism considers the conversion of Jews a rather doubtful undertaking. In the Cathedral of Cologne there can be seen the relief of a sow, called the "Jewish" sow (it became a medieval pattern and can be seen in other German and Swiss churches as well), under which a caption reads:

So wahr die Maus die Katz nit frisst
Wird der Jud kein wahrer Christ.

(As truly as the mouse eats no cat
the Jew never becomes a true Christian.)

This summarizes the general opinion amply documented in a book written by the German Jesuit Peter Browe and published under the auspices of the Vatican.[13] There were significantly few conversions in the early Middle Ages, Browe says, and conversions based on conviction remained rare. "Usually," he claims, "Jews converted only when material promises were made or when they were threatened. Even the fact that some converts achieved high clerical positions is no proof of their sincerity." Isaac the Convert, who served as Pope Ursinus' councillor and wrote extensively, reconverted to Judaism. During a pogrom in Worms, according to the monk Bernold of St. Blasien, the Bishop promised the Jews asylum if they converted; they asked to be left alone in order to discuss the matter among themselves, and when the Bishop returned he found that all of them, "advised by their own stubborness and the devil," had committed suicide. The Jews of Metz were baptized in 1096 (during the First Crusade), but when the threat of physical danger had passed all of them returned to the faith of Israel. Between 1125 and 1152 there were only two conversions in Cologne. When the Jews of England were forced in 1290 to choose between conversion and expulsion from the country, not a single one out of twenty thousand converted. In Austria, some Jews converted in 1439, but none remained a Christian. In the city of Toledo, where in the wake of the 1391 blood bath of Seville hundreds of Jewish families converted, the Franciscan monk Alfonso Lopez de Espina later investigated their religious attitudes and habits and found that they circumcised their children, observed the Sabbath and worked on Sunday, rejected the cult of St. Mary (calling her a sinner), made only half the sign of the cross, observed the Jewish customs concerning the dead, educated their children in the Jewish faith, and, when in dire need, exclaimed: "May Adonay help me."

It is only fair to note that almost every Pope since Gregory I (590–604) issued solemn warnings against forcible conversions, but these were quite ineffective. Force was in fact applied, and the number of conversions under circumstances of stress and threat was very great. Conversions in Spain were so numerous between the 1391 pogrom of Seville and the final expulsion of the Jews a hundred years later that only 250,000 were living in Spain when the actual expulsion decree was issued. The problem of neo-Christians in Spain was paralleled by the *neofiti* in southern Italy; when, in the city of Trani in 1297, every Jewish convert was offered an award in gold, 310

Jews converted. Nobody knows how enduring the benefits of conversion were in terms of genuine Christian convictions. Salo Baron, in his investigation into the Jewish factors in medieval civilization, claims that Jewish values and Jewish thought were transmitted through such conversions and that "some zealous Christians indeed resented such incursion of 'foreign' ideologies." But this is difficult to measure. The fact remains that mass conversions occurred only when it was a matter of life and death or when expulsion was threatened, and even then conversions were not inevitable. Surely the brutal measures of the Russian czars in the nineteenth century, the Pale of Settlement and the bloody pogroms, did not result in any mass conversions, and the era of assimilation after the French Revolution added only comparatively few. Why force proved so successful in Spain, both under the Visigoths and after the Christian reconquest, remains one of the many unsolved problems of Jewish history.

It follows, then, that the conversion of the Pierleone family was one of the rare events of eleventh century Rome. We know of no other prominent Jewish family of the time, in Rome or elsewhere, which converted as a group. Nor is there any Jewish family in all of history whose conversion has had such far-reaching consequences. Considering the subsequent loyalty of the family to the Church, it is easiest and most natural to assume that it was done out of profound conviction. This is, after all, the best, indeed the only, reason which makes a change from one religion to another understandable and palatable. But since no literature is available, we can only speculate on the reasons which led to this most important step.

•

During the week before Easter in 1030, the Pierleoni assembled for the first step in the elaborate conversion process, the ritual of *scrutinium*. There were many such "scrutinies," for the converting priest had to make certain that the candidates were fully aware of the new faith they were about to embrace. In the presence of their godparents (in all probability, members of the family of the Frangipani), the Pierleoni, each of them, men and women, professed their faith, listened to sermons on the Creed of the Church, and were then solemnly and formally admitted to baptism. The *Competentes* had passed the first test. Two days before this admission, a public announcement was seen at the gate of every church in Rome declaring that Baruch and his family would be present in the Church of Santa Maria in Trastevere "at the heavenly mystery by which the Evil One and the Spirit of the World will be overcome, and the Gates of Heaven will be thrown open."

Baptism, even today, is a ritual of exorcism; the demon which dwells within the infidel has to be driven out before the candidate can be baptized. Since baptism is considered a new birth, a new name is given to the convert. Thus it was that at the final fateful ceremony in the Church of St. Mary, when Baruch was asked for his name he declared solemnly that if he be accepted into the true faith he would like to be known as Benedictus—an exact translation of Baruch, both meaning "the blessed." (Henceforth he is known in documents as Benedictus Christianus—Benedict the Christian.) Subsequently each of the other members of the family forfeited his Hebrew name as he was forfeiting his old Hebrew faith. The new names were duly recorded, and the candidates were then asked to form two rows, the men to the right, the women to the left. The priest approached each of them, breathed upon each of their faces as Christ had breathed the Holy Ghost into his apostles, made the sign of the cross on their foreheads and recited the prayer from the Gelasian sacramentary: *Ad Catechumen Faciendum.* John the Deacon explains that "the breathing is to give the Evil Spirit notice that he is about to be evicted by the Holy Ghost and must prepare for the entry of Christ our God. The unbaptized is the dwelling place of Satan. He must now become the abode of our Saviour. Against the Evil One, now doomed, a mere breath is all that is deemed necessary for this is all he deserves." After the ceremony of breathing, salt was placed in the mouths of the converts. "Salt in the natural order preserves and seasons flesh. We season the spirit of the neophyte with the blessed salt of wisdom and the teaching of the word of God, that he may gain fortitude and health against the corruption of the earthly spirit." Upon the conclusion of this prayer, the Mass of Scrutiny was said. There were special prayers for the converts. Then the significant moment arrived, and the deacon called out: "Let the Catuchemens approach." Baruch Pierleone rose and led the family toward the predella, where the exorcising priest sat. "Pray," said the deacon, "ye chosen ones, bend your knees." *For the first time in their lives the Pierleoni knelt in a church.* In their synagogue on the island of the Tiber they had knelt on Yom Kippur, the Day of Atonement, to say prayers of sin and forgiveness and of praise for the everliving God: "So we bend our knees," they had said with the Hebrew congregation, "to worship and give thanks unto the King of Kings the Holy One, blessed be He. He is our God. There is none else." But now there was someone else; for the synagogue was in the past, and the church in which they knelt, Santa Maria in Trastevere, which they and their ancestors had passed every day, had now become *their* church. Incense, chorales and Latin prayers replaced the voice of the chazan, the ancient Hebrew song and the sound of the shofar. They knelt and recited their new prayers, and again came the voice of the deacon: "Arise, complete your prayer in unison and say: Amen." Baruch and his kin arose, concluded the prayer in unison, and in unison they said Amen. Once again the sign of the cross on their foreheads. Again Satan was ordered "for the future to have nothing in common with the servants of God who are resolved to turn their backs upon his [Satan's] kingdom, but to hand them down over to the Redeemer of the world. May the God of Angels and Archangels, the God of the Prophets and Martyrs, guide the converts to the grace of baptism." Preparing to leave the nave of the church, the candidates were offered bread and wine on the altar by their sponsors. The names of the sponsors were read, then those of the converts. Then the mass. Then Holy Communion.

But the converts were still excluded. The part of the conversion ceremony most difficult to bear was still to come. Anyone of faint resolution would have turned back, but the Pierleoni stayed. This had not been a hasty decision. The family had sat around their tables and taken council with each other. Was it not enough for these Jews in the great city of Rome to have achieved influence, wealth and respect? Could they not go to Pope or bishop, prefect and senator, without fear? Was it not sufficient to own so many of Rome's choicest houses and castles that they never could be removed from this soil which had been theirs for generations? Did it not suffice that their status as members of the moneyed aristocracy made them barons of wealth and property? It did not. Property did give them a place in the social hierarchy, but the nobility of blood would establish them in the Christian brotherhood, and this is what the Pierleoni wanted. This and more: Some day, Baruch, prayed, one of his family will sit on the throne of Peter.

The Pierleoni, who would still be called "members of the Hebrew congregation in Trastevere" three generations after their conversion, now knelt in the church and prayed their new prayers, hoping that some day one of their family would be the Pope of *all* the churches in the world.

Passages from the Gospels were read: Matthew (the Man); Mark (the Lion); Luke (the Ox); and finally John (the Eagle). The acolytes were then asked to choose the language in which they wished to confirm their faith. "Latin," said Baruch, defiantly and firmly. Since the language of the Jews in Rome was Greek and the Pierleoni no doubt spoke Greek in the privacy of their homes, the choice of Latin as "their" language was still another token of conversion.

On the day before Easter, the last act of this drama of conversion was played. Each convert turned to the priest, who symbolically anointed his breast and back with holy oil, then touched his upper lips and eyes with a moistened finger to the prayer of *Epipheta* ("open to an odor of sweetness"). The Pierleoni then removed their shoes and walked barefooted toward the altar, where this decisive question was asked: "Dost thou renounce Satan and all his works and all his pomp?" Together they answered: "I do renounce them."

Under ordinary circumstances, the ceremony of conversion would have ended here. Prepared in the days of Constantine, when Christianity became the official State religion and conversions of pagans were conducted wholesale, the ceremony had come to be taken for granted; the occasional conversions created little stir in the Roman Church or in the community. This case, however, was different. Not only were the converts a prominent family and relatives of the nobility (the Frangipani), but they were Jews. The conversion of Jews was a rare occasion in Rome, and if it had indeed ever occurred there at all, it only involved some unknown and insignificant poor souls. In fact, it was so infrequent that bishops and monks versed in such liturgic matters had to be asked about the proper procedure. Characteristically, the procedures they produced came from Visigothic Spain, where there had been mass conversions of Jews under threats of every conceivable kind.

It is in this liturgy, one of the oldest of the Church, that the unique relationship of Christianity and Judaism is most graphically expressed. In the Church's plan of redemption, the Jews occupy a very particular position—an ambiguous one to say the least. On the one hand, the Jews must continue to exist as living witnesses of the life and death of Christ. (This position was modified by Pope Paul VI in his declaration on the relation of the Church to non-Christians —Vatican Council II, 1965.) On the other hand, the Church still hoped that the Jews would some day see the light and convert to the only true, redemptive religion—Christianity. The inconsistency of these two hopes—continued Jewish existence and Jewish conversion —have never been reconciled, perhaps because the hope of conversion has been so remote and unrealistic that there was no practical need for reconciliation. We have already seen that what results conversion did yield were really pitiful, and additional evidence is ample: During the reign of Gregory I, it was mainly widows who converted. In Sicily, Jewish farmers, forbidden to keep slaves, were promised relief and exemption from the law, but in spite of these material advantages, few, if any, Jews embraced the new faith. In France the Jews were informed that "every Sabbath the law of God will be preached in the synagogues by our friars and preachers." It was of no avail. In Lyon, Agobard, who spent much of his life attempting to convert the Jews of the town, had to give up, exclaiming in desperation: "With all humanity and good will which I have extended on your behalf, I did not succeed in leading a single one of you into the spiritual community." [14] There were exceptions, of course. In Clermont, for instance, the archbishop succeeded in converting some five hundred of the Jewish population. On the evening after their public conversion they marched with torches through the town, while the unconverted Jews left quietly and unmolested for Marseille. But such occurrences were rare. (Some insight into the mentality of the converted, incidentally, survives in the form of curious documents.) [15]

There were, of course, special prayers for the Jews, prayers which hoped for the day when Synagogue and Church would be united, just as Esau had embraced his brother and as Israel itself had returned from the Babylonian Exile. Conversion was to be the great homecoming, salvation and redemption—for as the Church says, although the Jews deserve to die, God preserved them for the purpose of their final conversion. St. Augustine prayed that the Jews "may see the light and accept the mystery of incarnation," and of course there was the famous prayer recited on Good Friday for the "perfidious Jews." In one of his many humane acts, Pope John XXIII ordered the word "perfidious" to be omitted from the prayer, not because it was originally meant to be anti-Semitic, but because the lower clergy and the rabble had so interpreted it. The prayer was often an overture to bloody riots in medieval Ghettos and to pogroms in Czarist Russia. "Omnipotent and Eternal God," the prayer reads, "who dost not exclude from thy mercy even the unbelieving Jew, hear our prayers which are raised for the blindness of

44

this people. May they recognize the light of truth which is Christ. Let us pray for the unbelieving [*perfidia*] Jews and may our Lord and Saviour lift the veil from their hearts so that they may recognize Jesus Christ our Lord."

It was true that the Jews were, as Martin Luther was to express it, "cousins of our Lord." They were blood of His blood, flesh of His flesh. Had He not been circumcised on the eighth day after His birth? Had he not spoken of the Torah, the law of the Jews, the law that He respected and by which He had lived? This was true enough, but Christ was not *merely* a Jew. He had been elevated, by Pauline theology and by Christian faith, as God's only begotten son, to be revered as God Himself. He had been crucified with the help, or at least active acquiescence, of the Jews, the same Jews who lived in Rome, in Trastevere. And the Pierleoni were Jews. They had rejected Christ. In a sinister pact with the Devil, they had refused to do homage to Him and stubbornly they had been waiting for the Messiah to come. They had been so blind as not to see that He *had* come, in all His glory, Christ, the anointed, the true Messiah. But now, here they were professing that they had finally seen the light. Was it really true? Will they, perhaps, accept Him with their mouths, but not take Him into their hearts? Will they not continue clandestinely to believe in their obnoxious Jewish God, a God who had no son because all the children of men were His sons? Will they not secretly observe their customs, invented by the Devil himself, circumcise their children and observe the Sabbath?

It was to safeguard against these possibilities that the Church had added to the regular conversion ceremony a special ritual to be used in the conversion of Jews. The Pierleoni were now required to undergo this particularly painful ordeal required only in Jewish conversion. The priest began to read the solemn oath, pausing after every few words so that the family could repeat them in unison:

"I swear solemnly that the sacrifices recorded in the Old Testament are the forerunners of the great, holy sacrifice of Christ as He suffered on the Cross.

"I swear that the redemption of Man through Christ is announced in the promises which God Himself made to Abraham and the other patriarchs, and which the people of Israel did not heed but crucified the promised Redeemer, Christ Himself.

"I swear that if I ever deviate from the only true faith, the faith of the Catholic Church, I deserve to die.

"I swear that I willingly and voluntarily, with all my heart, and all my soul, and all my strength, accept the Law of Christ, and no other Law. According to my former faith as laid down in the Old Testament, only two or three witnesses are required to establish the truth. But the truth of Christ is established by twelve witnesses, the twelve Apostles of Christ.

"I swear that although my people and I had rejected Christ, I now accept Him in all His glory and power.

"I solemnly swear that I now believe that the coming of Christ is proven by the Testimony of the Torah and the Prophets.

"I swear that I reject the Laws and precepts of the Jews and will no longer refuse to eat foods forbidden by the Jewish Law, unless I do it for natural aversion and not for reasons of the old superstition.

"I swear that from now on I shall abstain from any contact with those Jews who are yet unconverted.

"I swear that I shall surrender to the ecclesiastic authorities all Jewish books that are in my possession, even the Apocrypha, so as to avoid all and any suspicion which might accuse me of lack of faith and loyalty to my new religion.

"I swear that I shall not go near a synagogue and certainly not enter any Jewish house of worship, but studiously walk by another road in order that I may not even see it.

"I swear that what I attested to in this oath is said for myself as well as for all the minors in my family." [16]

The tone was stern. Everybody knew that each transgression called for severe punishment. For the celebration of Passover, the convert would receive a hundred stripes with a whip, his property would be confiscated, and he might even be expelled. For circumcision, the most frequent violation, the father of the child would be castrated and his property confiscated. In early Spain, the fathers' noses were cut off. There, under the Visigoths, the Jewish converts had to serve a period of probation and were assigned to a bishop. If they travelled, they had to report to the bishop of that town, just as a probationed prisoner would have to report to an officer of the court. On the Sabbath and the Jewish holidays, they had to appear before the bishop so that they should not, heaven forbid, observe the ancient customs, nor were they permitted to leave town. The Jewish women who had converted were assigned to pious Christian women who, no doubt, were even more strict than the bishops, for they knew that Christian laymen would be penalized to the tune of three gold pounds if they were lax in their supervision. Converts remained under official suspicion for three generations; only then were they called the "sincerely converted." The severity of these Spanish regulations becomes more understandable if one recalls that conversion under the Visigoths was rarely a voluntary act.

But this was not Spain; it was Rome. And this was not a conversion of threats; it was a voluntary decision by a highly respected Jewish family. In Rome, the Papal decree of the great Gregory I forbidding the use of any threat or coercion was still remembered and strictly observed. The Church of Rome had to be scrupulous in its adherence to the rules. But this scrupulous application would also require that the Pierleoni would receive no special treatment, despite their reputation, their services to the Church (which, after all, they did profit from) and their connections with a respected Catholic family. Therefore the family would now be required to listen to and then sign a document called the *Placitum*. It read:

"I will not profane or abandon the holy Christian faith which I have accepted through the baptismal water. I will not fight it either by acts or words. I will not insult it either publicly or secretly, nor will I evade true baptism either by flight or by hiding, or ever think of returning to the ancient error. I will not try to infringe upon or evade any of the obligations which I have solemnly undertaken and affirmed by my personal signature under this Placitum. I shall not hide anyone who indulges in the prohibited, devilish Jewish customs, and deliver such a person to the ecclesiastic authorities and also inform them of any rumor about such a person in hiding elsewhere. I know that any violation of the obligations which I undertook will be punished by death. I shall not celebrate Passover nor any other Jewish holiday, nor marry any unbaptized Jew, nor reject any food or observe any diet other than that of the Christians."

The family signed: first Baruch, and then a long line, every member of the great family of the Pierleoni, the Jews from Trastevere, assuring the priest that they were binding their minors through their signatures.

Finally the family left the old church, converted and now acceptable to the highest society of Rome. As they passed through the ancient gates, it is likely that the events of the past found significant new meaning both in their eyes and in those of their former Jewish brothers waiting outside the church. There was probably reproach, naked hate, pity, hope for intercession, maybe a little pride, maybe all these in that strange encounter at the gate of the simple church that fateful day before Easter in 1030. The old church of Santa Maria in Trastevere no longer stands today—it was torn down after the death of the last Pierleone Pope in 1138—but some of the old columns can still be seen in the new church. Did Benedictus Christianus, who was once the Jew Baruch of Trastevere, pause a moment to lean meditatively against one of these columns? If he did, what was in his mind?

●

For no one could know for certain then that this family of converts was destined to play such an important role in the most decisive century of medieval Christian history, the century of the great struggle between the Papacy and the German Emperor. Within but a hundred years this family, often despised by the people who could never forget their Jewish origin and even by clergymen who remembered the Jew Baruch when it served their purposes, contributed to the Church three Popes: Ioannes Gratianus (John Gratian), who was Gregory VI (1045–46); Hildebrand, who became Gregory

VII (1073–85); and Peter Pierleone, who as Pope assumed the name of Anaclet II (1130–38). Their lives were turbulent and difficult, but each of them made his contribution to the growth of the Church and the development of the Papacy. Gregory VI, who rescued the Church from one of the most corrupt rulers in its history, was to die in exile. Gregory VII, who was of course the greatest of the three, was the leading spokesman of Papal supremacy and was later to become a saint; he too died in exile. (Even in an official Catholic list of the saints we read under the date of May 25, the day on which Saint Gregory is remembered in the Roman Catholic churches: "His family was not noble and may have been of Jewish origin." [17]) Anaclet II, the brilliant student of the great Abelard, spent his entire Papacy locked in a struggle against the powerful ascetic Bernard of Clairvaux, who was outraged that *"Judaicam sobolem sedem Petri in Christi occupasse iniuriam"*—that a Jew should be permitted to occupy the throne of Peter.

Strangely enough, although the Pierleone family intermarried (even Baruch is thought to have married a Frangipane), they still looked Jewish—"more like a Jew or Saracen than a Christian" medieval chroniclers say of all of them, even of Gregory VII, who might have been related to them only by marriage. The weight of the evidence seems, however, to favor a blood relationship. "No doubt," says Pietro Fedele, the great Italian medievalist who devoted his life to the study of the Pierleoni, "Hildebrand's mother was a Pierleone, if we are to believe the Annals of Pegau in which Gregory VII is said to be a nephew on his mother's side to Peter de Leone [Petrus Leonis, the grandson of Baruch]. But even if these statements in the Annals were not correct, it would always have great weight in our assertion that Hildebrand had the closest family ties with the Pierleoni. It seems that Hildebrand's mother was Bertha. Her brother was the abbot of Santa Maria on the Avantine. We know that young Hildebrand lived with his uncle, the abbot of this monastery, where he was educated and brought up in the monastic discipline. The relationship between Gregory VI [John Gratian] and Hildebrand is well known. When Gregory VI went into exile,

Hildebrand, albeit reluctantly, followed him to Germany. After Gregory's death he inherited his fortune; he felt such gratitude for his master and protector that he took his name, Gregory, when he became Pope. There is no other plausible explanation for this intimate relationship between Hildebrand and the arch priest of San Giovanni [John Gratian] than that they were related to each other. . . . It is because they were both Pierleoni that Hildebrand inherited John Gratian's fortune. It is for the same reason that Hildebrand's parents attached him to John Gratian and that he followed the Pope into exile in 1046."

All three Pierleone Popes were subjected to attacks and calumny because of their Jewish descent. Although it was not fashionable prior to the Crusades (which began in 1095) to make mention of their Jewish origin, there were nevertheless telling innuendoes concerning "ill-begotten money" "connected with usury" directed against the two Gregorys. But in the case of Anaclet, his Jewish origin is mentioned unashamedly in at least five medieval documents and he is attacked directly as the great-grandson of Baruch, a Jewish convert. As Wilhelm Bernardi, one of the leading German medieval scholars of the last century, notes: "If we consider how despised Jews were in those days, we must understand that the main argument [against Anaclet] was that he was a clever Jew who had succeeded [to the Papacy] because of his money. Even those who were ashamed to admit it were inwardly obsessed by their anti-Jewish prejudices, and so they believed all those who maligned him without asking for proof. Eagerly they used every accusation, true or not, in order to overthrow him. All his enemies needed to do was to hint at the fact that Anaclet was a Jew, and everybody understood without having to add anything. Of course, there were those who were glad about the conversion of a Jew; but that one of them should be the vicar of Christ sitting on the throne of St. Peter, nobody could comprehend or condone." [18]

Jews have served as financial advisers to many Popes, and throughout Church history Jews (sometimes converted, often not) have been personal physicians and librarians to Popes and scholars whose advice was sought by the Curia. But no Jews have ever been such active participants in the affairs of the Church as were the Pierleoni. Demetrius B. Zema, a Jesuit professor at Fordham University, acknowledges their intimate participation, noting "that the Pierleoni were a family of extremely wealthy financiers, that John Gratian shared their wealth, that Hildebrand had close ties with John Gratian, his namesake in the Papacy, and that he was reputed to have had business relations with the moneyed house, a thing that Hildebrand's function as comptroller of the Papal treasury and provider both for the Abbey of St. Paul and the Curia renders more than likely. But above all these considerations, in point of evidence, is the fact that throughout the Reform contest the Pierleoni stood squarely and steadfastly on the side of the Reform Popes, affording them refuge, men and money, and always formed a positive counterweight to the Roman aristocracy and German party in the struggles between Popes and anti-Popes." [19]

Thus, even if they had not produced three Popes, the role of the Pierleoni as financial advisers of the Curia and staunch backers of the Reform Popes would have been recorded. No wonder then that their names appear on so many Roman documents during a whole century of medieval Roman history. Many of the old Roman families have disappeared, but the descendants of the Pierleoni still exist in modern Italy and continue to be active as bishops, writers and merchants.

The Pierleone Popes lived at a time when the main issues of Church and State were fought out. It is a strange coincidence that it was Ioannes Gratianus Pierleone, a converted Jew, who as Gregory VI launched the most dramatic turn in Christian history, the great Reform movement in which all three Pierleoni were intimately involved. With him a new chapter of the Church begins. The decay of the Church and Papacy had reached dangerous proportions, and sheer historic necessity cried out for some one who would seize the reins and provide the Church with a new sense of decency and morality. That this man of Jewish descent should also have been the first of a long and almost interrupted succession of Pontiffs of high moral caliber is an interesting testament to the strange and whimsical ways of history.

●

To those familiar with the development of the Church, the idea of a Jewish Pope should not seem strange at all. Was not, Peter, the very founder of the Papacy, a Jew? But somehow the Jewish origins of Christianity do not seem to be generally comprehended and appreciated, and very few Christians are aware of the slow and painful manner in which early Christianity extricated itself from its Jewish moorings. Jesus, the Jew of Nazareth, and Paul, the Jew of Tarsus, are, after all, the founding fathers of the Christian faith and the architects of the Church structure. Therefore, to set the stage for our story we shall proceed in the next chapter to uncover these origins and examine the Judeo-Christian tradition of the Church.

In doing so, we will also be tracing the fascinating origin and growth of the Papacy itself and leading up to the major issues of medieval history. Today the institution of the Papacy is taken for granted and the tribulations of the early Popes are largely forgotten. Although the Roman Pontiff still retains some political influence, he is no longer allied with any great power; he retains merely the role of moral conscience of a world which he admonishes from time to time, but no longer rules. Gone are the days when the Emperor had to be confirmed by the Pope in the solemn act of coronation without which he could not be considered the lawful ruler of his realm. Gone also are the days when Popes fought bloody battles at the heads of Papal armies and exerted an influence which no secular ruler could rival. Nor can we conceive today of the degree of moral decay in the Papacy which brought Christianity to the brink of disaster, nor the illiteracy of the clergy and the clerical immorality which remained unchecked for so long a time.

The era of ecclesiastic supremacy is gone for ever, and the great issues of the Middle Ages, which divided the world into hostile camps and led to so much bloodshed and human misery, are all but forgotten. The Contest of Investitures, which forced Pope and Emperor into dramatic and often tragic confrontation, is today familiar to few. Yet the three Popes from the Ghetto whose story we want to tell were all deeply involved in this great war of ideas. Without some familiarity with the development of the Church from its beginnings to the ascendancy of Gregory VI, the first Pierleone Pope, the fate and destiny of these converts cannot be fully understood.

2 GREGORY VI
AND THE FIRST THOUSAND YEARS

Yehoshua ben Yosef, the carpenter's son, needed no conversion. There was nothing to which to convert. He was born a Jew, circumcised on the eighth day after his birth in accordance with ancient Jewish custom, and died a Jew. The death notice fastened to the Roman cross on Golgotha proclaimed to the little world of Palestine, mockingly, that the one crucified between two thieves was called Jesus of Nazareth and fancied himself King of the Jews. There was no church to sing the dirges of mourning. Dying slowly on the cross, he recited the Hebrew psalm in the Aramaic version: *"Eli, Eli, lama sabachtani"*—My God, my God, why hast Thou forsaken me?

In his short life as a preacher and healer, he had warned his disciples against the conversion of heathens, for his sermon was addressed specifically to the "lost sheep of Israel." Nobody was to leave the country and venture into the crumbling Hellenistic world. His followers, roaming in small bands across the beautiful landscape of Galilee, devoted their ministrations to the sick and sorrowful Israelites who had given up hope for themselves and for their people, harassed as they were by Roman military government and tax collectors. Never once did they think of establishing separate churches: the synagogues were good enough. The law contained in the holy Torah and interpreted by the rabbis was not to be discarded. Every jot of that law was sacred to Jesus. The end of mankind, he believed, would come soon, and the rule of Rome and rabbis would be replaced by the Kingdom of God. Those among his followers who were circumcised in the flesh and in the heart accepted the hardships of the new message with great joy. Those others, the uncircumcised, were not even approached. Jesus died without having founded a new religion.

It is futile to speculate whether the little Jesus sect could ever had superseded the official Jewish tradition in Palestine, but there is strong reason to doubt it. Here was the well organized Jewish community, which traced its prophetic and legal traditions back to the days of Abraham and Moses and even to the creation of the world; they were God's chosen people, who were to love their neighbors as themselves, walk humbly in the ways of God and serve Him by observing the laws of justice and decency. The groups around Jesus were small and poor and concentrated largely around the Sea of Galilee, the original area of Jesus' ministry. Even after Jesus had died they continued to preach in the synagogues of the Pharisees. They had not broken with Judaism at all. They were obsessed with their Messiah's message that very soon the "Kingdom of God" would come, but that message was still conceived in the Jewish terms of Old Testamentarian prophecy.

The lack of organization which characterized earliest Palestinian Christianity is in itself a reflection of the spiritual message of Christ. The hope he offered was in redemption, not in earthly existence. Of what consequence was the oppression of the Roman occupation when it was obvious that the world would soon cease to exist? Every sign pointed toward the coming of a new era which was not of this world, and the old order had to be obliterated if the new society was to be established. In Jesus of Nazareth, it must be stressed, these ideas were focused upon a very real daily expectation of the end of human history. The life which he was living—and to which he attracted the poor, the degraded and insulted, the hopeless and dissatisfied in spirit—was soon to end. Crucifixion, in this context, is neither accident nor catastrophe: it is a spiritual goal. It had to happen. Later it was this very crucifixion which was to become the cornerstone of Christian theology. Without it there would be no Christian creed, certainly not within the spiritually revolutionary system of Paul, the real founder of the Christian Church and the architect of Christian theology.

Early Christianity—which should be called Jesusdom, for it is still intimately connected with Jesus of Nazareth and not with a church or with a set of doctrines—is a religion of the last days of mankind. In such days, so close to the "end of days" (an Old Testamentarian term), that "which was said of old time" could no longer be valid. This is reflected in the admonitions: "Ye have heard that it was said of old time, Thou shalt not commit adultery, but I say unto you, that whosoever looketh on a woman to lust after her hath committed adultery in his heart." Or, even more sternly and unrealistically: "And if thy right eye offend thee, pluck it out and cast it from thee: for it is profitable for thee that one of thy members should perish and not that thy whole body should be cast into hell." And again: "Whosoever shall smite thee on thy right cheek, turn to him the other also; if a man would take away thy coat, let him have thy cloak also; bless them that curse you, love your enemies; take therefore no thought for the morrow, for the morrow shall take thoughts of the things for itself." Where on earth is there a society which could make these the guiding principles of human conduct? But that question was beside the point to Jesus and his followers. They did not think in terms of a "society," for there would soon no longer be one. Those dark clouds we see surrounding the Cross of Golgatha in El Greco's famous Crucifixion would soon envelop the earth, and mankind would be transformed by faith. This is the meaning of the message that came from the rolling hills of Galilee and the synagogue of Capernaum. Even after Jesus' death, his followers were certain in their hearts that he would come again, for he had arisen on the third day—the tomb was empty and the heavy rock which sealed it had been rolled away.

In this atmosphere of early Judeo-Christian existence in Palestine—where the new belief had all the markings of a sect-family, where the leader and founder of the sect was still alive and the immediate witnesses still living with him—no church or formal organization was necessary. The common breaking of the bread, the visitations of the sick, the sharing of a very simple life paradoxically both solemn and carefree, this was more important than the building of a hierarchy. The prayers were those of the Jews. The law was that of Moses. "Think not," said Jesus, "that I am come to destroy the Law or the Prophets: I am not come to destroy, but to fulfill." After his death there were still those who remembered and knew. Christ crucified was an even stronger influence than the one who lived. It was the dead and resurrected Christ, not the living Jesus, who converted the cosmopolitan Saul.

With Paul (the name which Saul adopted after his conversion) begins the new era, the conquest of the Greco-Roman world. With him Christianity was to liberate itself from the geographic narrowness of Palestine and the strictures of Jesus against "preaching to the heathens." Paul, the Jew from Tarsus, the Hellenized and sophisticated capital of Cilicia, was as polyglot and universalist as the city itself. He had, it is true, studied in Palestine under Rabban Gamaliel, but intellectually he had not become a Palestinian. He remained unprovincial, versatile, and charged with the nervous energy that was needed in his work. Tarsus was a little Athens, with a university and libraries. It was in Tarsus that Cleopatra landed in her gilded galley propelled by silver oars to meet and conquer Antony. Located strategically in what is now southeast Turkey, it was the gateway from Asia Minor to the Far East. It was no accident that Paul, who spoke Hebrew, Greek and Syriac, conceived the new idea of a Christianity which would wed the world of the Jewish sect of Jesus to the pagan world of the Roman Empire. He became the first missionary to bring Christianity out of Palestine. Jerusalem was waning in importance anyway—clashes between Jewish patriots and the Roman army of occupation eventually led to the destruction of the city in the year 70—and the small original "church" of Christ could hardly be maintained. Even Jesus could not have objected to the new effort. For the sermon of Death and Resurrection was still preached only in the synagogues.

By the time that Paul began his mission, there were Jews living throughout the Mediteranean. They could be found, as Strabo complains, in every town and city. As citizens of the Roman Empire, they enjoyed freedom of worship. Moreover, their synagogues attracted not merely Jews, but many Greeks and Romans who found their belief in one God more reasonable than paganism and had converted to Judaism. Since the first pre-Christian century, there had been extensive commercial and cultural intercourse between Jerusalem and Rome. The sons of Jewish kings and members of the nobility had made Rome their place of study and play, and the last Jewish kings were more Roman than Jewish. Nero's wife was a Jewish convert and was buried according to Jewish rites. Aquila, who translated the Bible into Greek, had been a Greek pagan before becoming a Jew. There were also the so-called "God-fearers" who rejected the Jewish rite of circumcision (one of the main concerns in Paul's writings) yet attended the services in the synagogues without formally embracing the Jewish faith. It is to these polyglot, heterogeneous, Hellenized congregations that Paul preached. Surely, he remained a preacher to "the lost sheep of Israel" as he set out on his travels through the far-flung Roman Empire.

On his way to Spain, which had an ancient Jewish community, Paul stopped in Rome, where there was a colony of Jews living (together with Syrians and other "foreigners") in the district beyond the Tiber called Trastevere. In Rome he sought out one of the original Twelve, the one singled out by the Master: Peter, whose life and death were to determine the life of the Church until this very day. Peter, the fisherman whose empty nets were filled with fishes by the miracle on Lake Tiberias, had left his boats, nets and fishes and even his wife to become the most important of the apostles. He had become a fisherman of men.

•

We turn to Peter now because in the official list of Popes he is considered the first Bishop of Rome. In the *Liber Pontificalis*—the *Book of the Popes* written in the fourth century—he is listed in this manner: "Blessed Peter, the Apostle, and chief of Apostles, the Antiochene, son of John, of the province of Galilee and the town of Bethsaida, brother of Andrew, first occupied the seat of the bishop in Antiochia for seven years. This Peter entered the city of Rome when Nero was Caesar, and there occupied the seat of bishop for twenty-five years, one month and eight days. He was bishop in the time of Tiberias Caesar and of Gaius and of Tiberius Claudius and of Nero. He wrote two epistles which are called catholic, and the gospel of Mark, for Mark was his disciple and son by baptism." His end is described in these words: "He received the crown of martyrdom with Paul in the year 38 after the Lord's passion. He was buried also on the Via Aurelia, in the shrine of Apollo near the place where he was crucified, near the palace of Nero, in the Vatican, near the triumphal district, on June 29." [20] Thus it is in the Vatican, the ancient *Mons Vaticanus*, where on the tombs of Peter and Paul the Basilica was erected, that the history of the Papacy begins.

Peter was originally called Shimon, an old Jewish name, but his conversion and his new office required a new name. We have already seen how the act of baptism required the taking of a new name, and even in this very day Jewish tradition hallows the name. The name spells destiny and direction. Thus Jacob became Israel, for he had battled with angels and men, and Abram became Abraham, for the added letter "h" was the letter of the Divine. Thus Shimon became Cephas. Cepha, Aramaic for rock, translates into Latin and Greek as Petra—Peter. When, according to the Gospel of Mark, Shimon, the son of Jona, had recognized Jesus of Nazareth as the Messiah, "the son of the living God," Jesus turned to him and said: "Thou art Peter, and upon this rock [petra] I will build my church. And the gates of Hell shall not prevail against it. And I will give to thee the keys of Heaven. And whatsoever thou shalt bind upon earth, it shall be bound also in Heaven: And whatsoever thou shalt loose on earth, it shall be loosed also in Heaven."

Thus was laid the foundation of the Papacy: the rock, the church, the keys to Heaven, the power to bind and to release. The rest is commentary. A long and fascinating commentary, to be sure, a commentary of dramatic triumphs and tragic aberrations, bloody warfare and human folly, gentle wisdom and brutal force, glamor and pomp and many a circumstance, a commentary still being written—but commentary nevertheless. For the main functions of the Papacy were spelled out in the very beginning, and on that foundation was built the most enduring office in all of human history. No royalty, no noble family, no governmental system, no state has maintained itself in such continuity as the office of the Pope, the Bishop of Rome.

There is little point in disputing the accuracy of the official *Book of the Popes* when it lists Peter and his immediate successors as "Popes." It is only natural that during its first three centuries, the Papacy, if we can apply the term at all to the leadership of the Christian Church of that time, should be different from that of the fourth and fifth centuries. After all, the early Christian sect, at first almost entirely Judeo-Christian and later consisting also of pagans-turned-Christians, was an illegal sect, the members of which lived, worked and prayed "underground." In this respect they were unlike the Jews, who, having lived in the Roman Empire for centuries, enjoyed the liberties of an officially recognized religion despite the fact that they would have no part of the pagan Roman cult which hailed the Caesar as divine. The official attitude toward the Jews was well summed up by the whimsical Caesar Caligula; granting an audience to that famous delegation of Alexandrian Jews headed by the philosopher Philo, he showed open contempt for a people who "are not really as bad as they are insane, for they do not know that I, Caligula, am God." Nevertheless, Jews did enjoy freedom of worship and full citizenship; even Paul, when he was arrested by the Roman police, gained his liberty because he claimed to be a Jew, and thus a citizen. The members of the struggling Christian sect had no such status, and their hours of worship were spent in the darkness of the catacombs. Instead of protection by the authorities, there was the constant threat of death. The head of such a group had little of the glamor of later Popes; he was more like the adored head inmate of a large prison. Thus Peter might be reckoned the first Pope—and, for that matter, the first *Jewish* Pope—but the title does not have the same significance as it took on in later times when the Papacy acquired its power and pomp.

Peter is called the first Pope because he was the first head of the Church of Rome. Of course there were other churches in the Empire—at Smyrna and Ephesus in Asia Minor, for instance, at Antioch in Syria, and at Alexandria in Egypt. (Jerusalem, as we have seen, had become unimportant.) In the days of Constantine the Great, the first Christian Emperor, Constantinople, the "new Rome," became a threat to Rome's pre-eminence. But Rome never succumbed. This is a factor of extraordinary importance. There were many bishops and even archbishops in the growing community of Christian churches, but the Bishop of Rome remained the bishop of bishops. He was the Pope. Strangely enough, but not unusual in the development of a cult, the reasons were not merely political or geographic, although these were important factors. The main reason why Rome had become the authentic Church was because it had been founded by the Apostles Peter and Paul, and particularly Peter, who had arrived before Paul and who was, after all, the Rock, chosen by Christ himself, upon which the Church was to be built. By this designation he *was* the Church. Thus there is the "apostolic tradition" which gives authenticity to the Church of Rome and makes its bishop not merely the advisor to, but the legitimate head of the Church. This position was maintained not only by the assertion of doctrines concerning the theological problems which often split the Church—such questions as the protracted fight over the nature of the Godhead and the personal qualities of the Holy Ghost—but also in acts of international (that is, of *catholic*) nature which had become the functions not of the Church as a whole but of the See of Rome. Among these practical matters were the redemption of Christian slaves, the release of prisoners, charitable gifts to churches in distress and other activities which did not respect distances or racial differences. These responsibilities were entrusted to the Bishop of Rome from a very early time in the development of the Papacy.

Of course the pre-eminence of Rome was also influenced by its status as the capital of the Empire, the most glamorous and spectacular city in all the world. It is true that to the early Christians this was more of a danger than a benefit. Living in the very shadow of the Imperial court, their existence was threatened by deprivation, imprisonment, discrimination and very often death by crucifixion. While the danger and secrecy of the sect were in themselves attractions for many thousands of men and women, it was neither pleasant nor easy to be part of a subterranean brotherhood which dared not identify its own members, was constantly open to betrayal and blackmail, and had to bury its adherents in the Catacombs, the underground world of the dead. But after Constantine embraced the very same detested cult and proclaimed Christianity the religion of the State, the Church of Rome stood clearly in the sunlight that shone benevolently from the Emperor's throne. As the official cult of the Empire, with the Emperor himself proclaimed as its temporal leader, the Church enjoyed great status, glamor and recognition. Rome became quite naturally—by an apostolic tradition which guaranteed its authenticity and spiritual continuity and by its geographical-political position as capital—the leader of the churches. And Rome's bishop was the head of the clergy all over the world. Neither Constantinople nor, at later times, Milan and Ravenna were ever able to maintain more than transitory competition.

●

By the end of the first century, the world had still not perished. In fact no spectacular event of any kind had occurred to bear witness to the message of Christ. It is true that a new religion had come into being, that churches were being built and that the sayings of Christ were being written down and interpreted by the early fathers of the Church. But this Church bore little resemblance to that heavenly apparition called the "Kingdom of God" of which Jesus had dreamt. It was also clear that no one in the Church could live up to the expectations of the Sermon on the Mount, that eloquent message of the great human crisis brought about by the expectation of the end. No, the end had not come. The world was still there, and it was

63

an old world with all its old needs, despairs, failing and hopes. Wordly methods, not those of heaven, were necessary to meet the needs of the new religion. This called for organization.

Organization had seemed unnecessary, even out of place, in the very early Church. Christian communities were small and the bonds which united them were so intimate and natural that formal organization would have negated everything that had brought them together, the beliefs, the fears and the hopes. Even in the beginning of the second century, Ignatius, the second bishop of the Syrian Church of Antioch, could write to his colleague in Smyrna: "The last days are here. So let us abase ourselves and stand in awe of God's patience, lest it turn out to be our condemnation. Either let us fear the wrath to come or let us value the grace we have: one or the other." The early leaders were inspired men, not elected officials. They held sway by charisma rather than through bureaucracy, faith rather than the vote. Although they called themselves bishops even in those early days, there was no hierarchy: the bishop was very much part of the people. The times when the clergy would sit in great thrones in the apses of Gothic cathedrals, distantly removed from the congregations kneeling in the vast expanses below them, were far off.

The foundations of Church organization, which were to develop considerably over the centuries, were prepared in Rome and largely influenced by the political structure of the Empire. It may well be that the Old Testamentarian distinction between High Priest and Levites had some early influence, but this was soon supplanted by the immediate daily experience and example of Roman civil life. The *Teachings of the Twelve Apostles* directs at a very early time: "Appoint for yourselves, therefore, bishops, deacons worthy of the Lord, men who are meek and not lovers of money, and true and approved; for unto you they also perform the service of the prophets and teachers. Therefore despise them not; for they are honorable men along with the prophets and teachers." Of course the very fact that this admonition was called for proves that the bishops were not yet firmly established as an institution. The very early Church was still a loose democracy, a "people's movement," and as such it had all the pitfalls of an informal organization. Its male and female leaders, the preachers and "prophets" of the Gospel, acted largely out of personal inspiration, with the inevitable result that there was soon chaos in liturgy, doctrine and interpretation. If it were to continue on its present course, the Church was doomed to become a conglomerate of all kinds of beliefs, undisciplined passion and abuse. Organization was obviously necessary, and in time a monarchic system replaced democracy. Under the new system, each congregation elected by a simple majority vote a man who was called *episcopus*— that is, bishop. Following his election, he was ordained by three bishops from neighboring churches, who used the laying of the hands upon the head of the elected, the ancient Jewish rite of rabinical ordination, as the solemn act of confirmation. There was, of course, no theological training. The man who served as bishop was to be knowledgeable, pure in character and dedicated to the faith. He was usually married. This presented a problem, since the service at the altar was considered in terms of a Biblical sacrifice, and sacrificial service required sexual abstinence. Altogether, marriage to the ancient Christian was often considered more a means of sexual gratification than anything else, a necessary evil, and many of the married laymen took vows to abstain from sexual intercourse, or at least to restrict it. For the bishop not to be as pious as the most dedicated of his flock was an impossibility. He was therefore expected to be abstemious, at least during the days when he ministered at the altar. If at election he was not married, there was a tacit understanding that he would remain unmarried. Here are the beginnings of the rules of celibacy, which were to play such an important role in later centuries, notably as a part of the program of clerical austerity which was to arise under the influence of the monastic orders.

The hierarchy, particularly in Rome, was almost an imitation of the secular Roman civil service. The bishop surrounded himself with a retinue of presbyters, deacons, sub-deacons, and all grades of the *clerici minores*—the lower clergy. The various functions began with that of the sexton—the messenger, the reader of Scriptures, whose role later developed into that of the preacher. There was every possibility of a career within the clergy; the sexton, and certainly the *lector* (reader), could hope to become a deacon some day, a presbyter or even a bishop. Since there was no formal theological training, it was largely administrative skill and, of course, devotion to the cause which counted.

At the pinnacle of the entire Church structure was the Bishop of Rome. Although there were often more learned bishops in Asia or Africa than in Rome, and despite the fact that there were grumblings and objections at this early stage (as again later in the Middle Ages), the general recognition of the special position of Rome came amazingly early. It must be added that such acknowledgment gave the Bishop of Rome no jurisdiction at all over the local clergy, who were under the complete control of their local bishops. But the Roman bishop's position was nevertheless clearly defined in his title: *episcopus episcoporum*, the bishop of bishops—not more, but certainly not less.

Even before the title "Pope" came into use (it is derived from the Latin *papa*, father), there were certain functions far beyond the administration of Church affairs which were accepted as the exclusive prerogatives of Rome, prerogatives which would lead centuries later (in 1870) to the dogma of the Pope's infallibility. The bishops agreed (it was a tacit agreement, not formal acceptance by a bishops' conclave) that the doctrine of the Church could be defined only by the Bishop of Rome. The importance of this power is not easily appreciated by people of the twentieth century, who care little about doctrines, but the people of the Middle Ages fought bitterly over Christian dogma, at times over a single interpretation or even a single word. Wars were waged over religious doctrines, people died, families separated, sects arose, and the unity of the Church was threatened from the first centuries until far beyond the age of Reformation. The right to determine the authoritative, the only acceptable doctrine was therefore not merely Papal *privilege:* it was the beginning of Papal *power*.

The second prerogative of the Bishop of Rome was to exclude

from communion all those bishops who disagreed with Papal rulings on religious essentials, a logical extension of his power as sole judge in matters of doctrine. Once he had ruled a doctrine in its properly approved wording to be the only acceptable belief, those bishops who refused to recognize it had to be removed. This was done without timidity and in language neither pious nor polite. We read in a letter from Pope Damascus I (366–384) to the Eastern bishops, who were often rebellious and whose churches later seceded from Rome, the following: "Be hereby informed that we have sometime since condemned Timothy, the unhallowed disciple of the heretic Appollinarius, with his impious doctrine, and we believe that what remains of him will obtain no consideration whatever henceforth. But if that old serpent, who has once and again [to] be smitten, revives for his own undoing and continues without the Church, ceaselessly endeavoring to overthrow the faithless with his deadly poisons, do you still avoid him like a pestilence . . . and permit hereafter neither your clergy nor your laity to listen to vain reasonings and idle speculations. . . . Here by judgement of the Apostolic See, in the presence of Peter, bishop of the city of Alexandria, he has been condemned, along with his teacher Appollinarius, who also in the day of judgement will undergo his merited punishments and torments. And if, acting like a man with hope, he is still deluding some unstable persons, although by demolishing his creed he has demolished his true hope in Christ, then *there will perish with him in similar manner whoever wills to withstand the rule of the Church*. God keep you in health, most honored sons." [21] The passage I have italicized constitutes nothing less than anathema, the grave and dangerous weapon of excommunication. Although in Damascus' time it was used only against bishops, it was in centuries to come to be the most formidable weapon in the hands of the Pope and it was used against princes and emperors and even anti-Popes. No other weapon was so dreaded, because excommunication excluded the victim not only from the Church, but from society itself.

But Papal power, which was to play such a great role in international political affairs, particularly during the struggle for Papal dominance during the Middle Ages, was at first overshadowed and dwarfed by the power of the Roman Emperor. Not until the fourth century did a new chapter in Church-State relationships begin.

Flavius Valerius Constantinus, the Roman Emperor, embraced Christianity after the battle at the Milivian Bridge in 312; only a year later, the Edict of Milan restored confiscated Church property and proclaimed religious freedom for *all* religions, including the persecuted Roman Church. Nobody can rightly claim that Constantine had truly become a Christian. He withheld his baptism until a few months before his death in 337, and it is not known whether he ever gave up his former beliefs or even understood Christian doctrines. His motives were largely political. For while pagan cults were apparently no longer able to unite the diverse population of the Empire, Christianity, which had made great headway in the second half of the third century, seemed to possess those unifying elements which could embrace the whole of the Roman world, East and West, Europe, Asia and Africa. Under Constantine, there was to be one Emperor, one Empire and one official church. Christianity did not immediately become the official religion, but a statue of the Emperor erected in one of Rome's great squares showed him holding Christian emblems, and that was good enough. It made Christianity not only acceptable, but fashionable. Constantine and his wife, Fausta, began to make the most lavish gifts to the Roman Church. Sylvester I (314–35), then the Bishop of Rome, recorded in detail the gifts of money, art works and real estate in every part of the Empire (the basis of the Church possessions, the largest holdings of any organized group in the world.) The gifts included silver and gold, candelabra, chandeliers, jars, goblets, statues and every other conceivable object of art. Among the long list of real estate holdings —the income from which, according to Sylvester's records, added up to a considerable fortune—we find the old palace of the Laterani on the Coelian Hill, which became the official Papal residence. The church built next to it was the original Lateran Cathedral. "At the same time," Sylvester reports, "Constantine Augustus built the basilica of blessed Peter, the apostle, in the shrine of Apollo, and laid there the coffin with the body of the holy Peter." [22] Christianity was now a well established, publicly recognized, publicly protected religion, and the Bishops of Rome became the Popes of a Church so universal in its geographic distribution and doctrines as to deserve the name Catholic.

Peter of Galilee, upon whose tomb the Basilica was erected, would have had little understanding of these radical changes. The Bishop of Rome was suddenly the administrator of properties, wealth and estates so large that much of his time was demanded by mundane business. Here are the beginnings of many of the Papal problems of the future, when administrative, political and military affairs would often outweigh spiritual and theological concerns. The Church was moving toward the time when it was to become big business. The days when the moneychangers were chased from the Temple of Jerusalem seemed far away; Jesus of Nazareth had not dreamt of any Church property.

Despite its new wealth and official recognition, the Church was still experiencing inner problems and was being virtually torn apart by debates on orthodox dogma. To Constantine these disagreements, whether between East and West or simply between two theological schools, were a political threat to the unity of the Empire. The same motives which urged him to accept Christianity now prompted him to assume a new role in Church affairs, that of chief mediator. Sylvester, a man of little influence despite his position as Bishop of Rome, was apparently content with the new wealth and status which made his See the richest in Christendom, for he played a rather undistinguished role in the settlement of the urgent theological problems of the time. Constantine, on the other hand, acted as though *he* were Pope. To settle the problem of Donatism, one of the dissenting sects which had arisen in Africa, he called a council of bishops in Arles in 314, a rather impressive group from Spain, Dalmatia, Italy, Gaul and Africa. (This was the first of the many international gatherings which were to play such a decisive role in the history of the Church.) Although bishops presided, the Emperor was the central figure. His pre-eminence became even more apparent at a subsequent Church meeting held in 325 at Nicaea, now a neglected little village in Turkey.

The Council of Nicaea, the first Ecumenical Council, determined the future of the Church for centuries to come. Constantine, who appeared in a purple robe and addressed the bishops in Latin, acted "like a general bishop, appointed by God." "It was not without reason," reports Eusebius, "that he once, while entertaining a company of bishops, let fall a remark that he too was a bishop, speaking to them in my hearing as follows: You are bishops whose jurisdiction lies within the Church. I also am a Bishop ordained by God to oversee the external business of the Church." [23]

The division between the functions of the Emperor and those of the Pope may have seemed of little consequence in Constantine's day. But some hundred and fifty years later, Gelasius I (492–96), a stronger Pope than Sylvester, wrote thus to the Eastern Emperor Anastasius: "There are two by whom principally this world is ruled: the sacred authority of the pontiffs and the royal power. Of these, the importance of the priests is so much greater, as even for kings of men they will have to give an account in the divine judgment." [24] Later Popes were not to be satisfied even with this definition. They were to speak of *Dictatus Papae*, the dictatorship of the Pope which embraces both the secular and the spiritual, maintaining the Pope is subject to God alone, and therefore could not be judged by any secular court. But for the time being, the role of the Emperor was gratefully accepted.

It matters little now that Constantine had still not been baptized when he called the Council of Nicaea, for the bishops had been called to cope with problems far more basic to the future of the Church. In fact, it is only since Nicaea that we can speak of a Catholic Church with a generally accepted doctrine. The central issue before the Council was the question of the Holy Trinity, a question which had already plagued the Church and was to remain its concern in times to come. The issue had been brought to a head by Arius, a man of learning and a popular preacher at Alexandria, who maintained that the second person of the Holy Trinity, Christ, could not possibly possess the same divine quality as God, the father; Christ was indeed the son, created by and therefore inferior to God. Recognizing the threat of schism which Arius's teachings (known as Arianism) posed to the unity of the Church—a threat which could have caused the end of Christianity—some three hundred bishops assembled at Nicaea, "some by the use of public posts, others by an ample supply of horses for transportation." Only six represented the West; the Bishop of Rome himself was absent. In session from the beginning of May until the nineteenth of June, they concluded by branding as heretics Arius and his followers—thus preserving the unity of the Church—and by adopting the Nicene Creed, which, later slightly amended, still remains the basic doctrine of the Church. Thenceforth, a believer acknowledges the "one Catholic and Apostolic Church."

But Arianism and the Trinity were by no means the only concerns of the Council of Nicaea. For with Nicaea, Christianity leaves the fold of Judaism. The Nicene Creed is one aspect of this break. From Nicaea onward, a believer in what Constantine called "God's own conviction" had to accept the following credo as dogma: "I believe in one God, the Father Almighty, Maker of heaven and earth, and of all things visible and invisible: and in one Lord Jesus Christ, the only begotten Son of God; begotten of his Father before all worlds, God of God, Light of Light, Very God of Very God; begotten, not made; being of one substance with the Father, by whom all things were made." [25]

Neither Jesus himself nor his Apostles could have accepted the new formulation. He had never conceived of himself as God. He had prayed to "my God, my God" in the last hours of his life. Nor would Peter, the first Bishop of Rome, have approved of a Christ who was believed to have existed before the world was created. Those who had followed the simple preacher of Galilee, seen him with their own eyes, broken bread with him, prayed in the synagogues and listened to his Jewish sermons, did accept him as the Messiah and believed that the end of all days had come; but they would not have accepted him as "God of God."

By now, however, the majority of Christians were converted pagans, and the march of Christianity into the pagan world called for many compromises. It sometimes appears that a mere process of *Christening* took the place of *Christianization*. To many pagans, Mary was simply a new name for the Goddess-mother of fertility whom they already worshipped. The whole Olympus of paganism underwent a similar change of names—with or without a corresponding change of heart in the believers. Most of the known world had not undergone even this superficial process of conversion: France, Germany, Britain, the Balkans and most of the East were still unconverted, and the Lombards, the Huns, the Visigoths, the Saxons and the Allemans who were soon to conquer much of Europe and Africa had not yet even heard of the new Gospel. Furthermore to most of the converted the depth of Christian dogma meant little, since they were too unsophisticated and illiterate to understand. The whole struggle over doctrine remained restricted to the clergy, and to the higher clergy at that. The lower clergy—the majority of the ecclesiastic family—was hardly able to read the prayers, let alone theological tracts.

The Jewish origins were soon forgotten in the course of Christian history. The very images of Christ, his family and his apostles, as they appeared in the mosaics of the Byzantines and the Romanesque and Gothic statues and altar paintings, were far removed from their Jewish surroundings. Nicaea was just the beginning of a long process of alienation from the Jewish moorings of Christianity. The Jew in Christian lands lived *a l'ombre de la croix*, and that shadow of the cross was a long one indeed. Events occurred in the darkness of that shadow that would have made Jesus shudder.

The Council of Nicaea, having issued the Nicene Creed, proceeded to remove the last Jewish remnants from the Church. For a long time the celebration of Passover had been a main concern in the Church. It was not merely the most important of Jewish holidays, but one which plays a significant part in the story of early Christianity. It was on Passover that Jesus died. The "Last Supper" was, after all, a Jewish Seder: Jesus blessed the bread and then broke it and distributed it among his apostles in accordance with Jewish custom; he blessed also the wine in the ancient Jewish ceremony of Kiddush, the sanctification of the wine. Passover was commemorated on the fourteenth day of Nisan, the Jewish month of spring, and it remained a custom of the early Church to retain this date, with the Quatrodecimanians, particularly in the Eastern Church, holding most tenaciously to it. The festival was still called Passah. (Later in English it was to be called Easter, for the Anglo-Saxon goddess of spring, Ostara.) However, it was no longer the festival of freedom from the yoke of Egyptian slavery, but of the freedom of the Resurrection. The Paschal lamb was now removed from the table of the Jewish Seder, and Christ himself became the lamb, the eternal sacrifice. At Nicaea, the bishops of Syria and Antioch fought for the preservation of the Jewish date, but they lost.

Constantine, in his address to the church, summed up the issue of Passover in these words: "At this meeting the question concerning the most holy day of Easter was discussed, and it was resolved by the united judgement of all present, that this feast ought to be kept by all and in every place on one and the same day. For what can be more becoming and honorable to us than that this feast, from which we date our hopes of immortality, should be observed unfailingly by all alike, according to one ascertained order and arrangement?

"And first of all, it appeared an unworthy thing that in the celebration of this most holy feast we should follow the practice of the Jews who have impiously defiled their hands with enormous sin, and are therefore deservedly afflicted with blindness of soul. For we have it in our power if we are to abandon their custom, to prolong the due observance to future ages, by a truer order, which we have preserved from the very day of the Passion, until the present time. Let us then have nothing in common with the detestable Jewish crowd; for we have received from our Saviour a different way. A course at once legitimate and honorable lies open to our most holy religion.

Beloved brethren, let us with one consent adopt this course, and withdraw ourselves from all participation in their baseness. For their boast is absurd indeed, that it is not in our power without instruction from them to observe these things. God preserve you, beloved brethren."

Already in 321 Constantine had issued a decree which was to eliminate the observance of the Jewish Sabbath from Christian life. In spite of the attempts of the Church to commemorate Sunday as the weekly memorial of Resurrection, many of the Christian communities observed the Jewish *shabat* on the Saturday. The Imperial decree reads as follows: "All judges and common people of the city and workers in all the crafts are to rest on the holy Sunday. Those who live in the country, however, shall take care of the culture of the fields freely and without restraint, since it frequently happens that the work on the grain in the furrows and the vines in the ditches cannot well be put off to another day, lest the benefit granted by a divine Providence be lost in an inopportune moment." The Council of Nicaea confirmed this decree. Nevertheless, the Jewish tradition proved stronger. A quarter of a century later—at the Council of Laodicea—another resolution had to use very harsh language. "The Christians," it said sternly, "must not Judaize and sit idly on the Sabbath, but ought to work on that day. They must honor the Lord's Day in whatever they can by resting inasmuch as they are Christians. But if they persist in being Jews they ought to be anathema to Christ." With these prohibitions against the Christian observance of Passover and the Sabbath, Christianity severs its last bonds with the mother religion. It is now on its own.

●

We now turn to another development indispensable to an understanding of the growth of Christianity: that disturbing and creative influence known as monasticism.[26] The monastic urge, which began early in the third century, received its first great impetus from an Egyptian Copt named Anthony—the famed St. Anthony of the

Temptations, who was born in Koma in central Egypt. It was probably no accident that monasticism started in the East, and not in Rome. The Orient was long accustomed to ascetic movements and has produced the most rigorous ascetic exercises until this very day. The self-denial of Buddhist monks, Tibetan priests and Indian Fakirs and the solitude and patience of meditation and disciplined concentration are typical of the East. Early Judaism was in this respect very much an Eastern religion, and its later emphasis on life and the affirmation of its values must not obscure the fact that many of Judaism's great creations were derived from "monastic" ideals and ascetic life. The great period of Jewish antiquity is not that of the conquered land, the cultivated soil and the domesticated life, but of the desert. Heat, discomfort, hunger, rebellion, severe austerity and the struggle for water and bread were considered the creative and heroic impulses of Judaism. At least the Prophets thought so, and this in itself is significant; for the Prophetic movement—the most eloquent, the most productive creation of a new Judaism foreign to priestly cult and religious organization—has its origin in ascetic ideals. Its spiritual father is Elijah, who sits at the brook, alone, deserted, disgusted with life in the capital, with the king and the priests and with the whole religious "establishment," fed by the ravens and facing God in the violent desert wind. The early Prophetic "schools" lived together in groups and would roam the countryside from time to time to dance ecstatically to the melodies of fiery and exciting music. Moses himself, the Egyptian court Jew, had become a man of the desert (the burning bush is a desert symbol), and the fact that he was not to pass into the "sown land" was not merely punishment, but also a great hymn to the desert and asceticism; it is the people, not Moses, who complain about the desert diet and long for the fleshpots of Egypt. The monastic tendency, which drove the classical Prophets to leave their fields and families, the security of their "sycamore trees," to become obedient servants and preachers of the Lord, is an integral part of Jewish religious growth. John the baptizer, wearing his loin cloth and living a lonely and bare life by the riverside, is only one of many members of the sect. The Essenes, eating their common meals, digging their own graves, wearing the hairy cloth, and tilling the fields they owned as common property, resembled the medieval monks in many ways. Voluntary poverty and rules of purity were the accepted ideals. Whether or not Jesus had been a member of the sect of Qumran which had its monasteries by the shores of the Dead Sea is still unsolved, but it does not matter here. What matters is that such monasteries existed, and that Judaism was not always the robust religion of life affirmation. The mystic movements from the early Middle Ages to the late Hassidic sect are witnesses to this trend. Some of the greatest examples of religious creativity in thought, song and tale were written in the solitude and loneliness of ascetic men who embraced God more fiercely than life itself. Even Jesus must be considered a monkish man: "I have," he said, "no brothers and no sisters."

The monastic movement of Christianity must be seen as an organic continuation of these ascetic pre-Christian traditions. Its later development toward organization, ecclesiastic offices, administration of property, world conquest and formal worship was certainly a deviation from—and perhaps a denial or even betrayal of—the spiritual world of Jesus and his apostles. To be sure, these harsh terms are used in a historic vacuum. Had the Church not begun to build, to plan, to own and to organize, Christianity would not exist. Such is the fate of all lofty ideals. As soon as they become tangible, they fall prey to falsification and a levelling process. In the process called realization, the greatness of the idea is compromised and shrinks to the small stature of man. Adjustment is often betrayal.

Monasticism, in any event, became the wellspring of developing Christianity. If it is paradoxical to say that those who ate and drank little fed the surfeited and smug, it is nevertheless true. Without the continuing stream of harsh admonitions that came from the monks, Christianity would have perished in the morass of daily compromises. The motives of the tens of thousands of men and women who have chosen the cloistered life from the third century until this very day vary with the biographies of the individual monks and nuns, but there is no doubt that they all stemmed from the unbearable tension between the religious ideal of pure living and the desires of the flesh. In many monastic writings and in the rules of the various orders the battle against physical desires plays an important role. Jesus had contempt for the lust of the flesh. Paul makes abuses of the body a major subject of admonishment in his "Epistles." For the love of God demands the mortification of the flesh. "And so there is nothing but the love of God," writes the famous eleventh century monk Peter Damian, "and the mortification of yourselves. . . . The man who is wise and earnestly intent on guarding his salvation watches always with such great solicitude to repress his vices, that with the belt of perfect mortification he girds his loins and his reins, his belly as well as his flanks, on all sides." Peter demands *complete* rejection of the body: "Come now, brother, what is this body which you clothe with such diligent care and nourish gently as if it were royal offspring? Is it not a mass of putrefaction, is it not worms, dust and ashes? It is fit that the wise man consider not this which is now, but rather what it will be afterwards in the future, pus, slime, decay, and the filth of obscene corruption."

Thus the great monks, the founders of the many monastic orders, left their homes and families, and sometimes their thrones, because they were not able to live with themselves—certainly not within a society that believed in the satisfaction of the body. It is in this conflict that the monastic idea was born. Anthony of Koma became a hermit in his own little village in Egypt, and two hundred and seven of his fellow-villagers accepted his ascetic rule, practically the whole community; at first they lived in caves, then they made the deserts of Nitria and Scetis, with their hot winds and burning sun, their "monastery." Another Egyptian, Pachomius, founded a monastery in Tabennisil which had an order similar to later monastic rule, including a division of time between work and worship and the same dress for all. Since they spoke Aramaic, the "father" of the monastery was called *"abba"*—the origin of the word abbot. There was also a "convent" for women.

Some ascetics, incapable of sharing their despair and loneliness and often unable to conform to rules, went still farther. The call of

the body and the passion of the flesh had to be driven out by imposing *total* deprivation on it. Thus Simeon Stylites lived for thirty long
years on the top of a pillar east of Antioch. As Crane Brinton observes, he lived "up there on his pillar sixty feet high in the Syrian
sun (the top does appear to have been railed in), eating, drinking,
sleeping, defecating—all very little—and preaching a great deal year
upon year." [27] But for most ascetics it was soon clear that living together and influencing each other, praying together and working
together would make their exercises more meaningful than a solitary
and ridiculously precarious existence on top of a pillar. The fourth
century monk Basil called upon his fellow monks to work the fields
together, to adhere to a strict schedule of prayer and—very significantly—to leave the monastery to join in the charitable work of the
community. It was not long before the Eastern idea of monastic life
conquered the West, where it was to become the most significant
movement of the Church, at times, as we are going to learn, rescuing
Church and Papacy, indeed all of Christianity, from the abyss of
failure and destruction. Martin of Tours founded the first monastery
in France. A short while later Eusebius, the bishop of Vercelli in
Italy, demanded that the clergy of his cathedral were to live monastic lives. For the clergy to spend some years in the monasteries was
like a spiritual refresher course both in learning and piety.

A very serious monastic chapter was written in Ireland. Columban, an Irishman who suffered from pangs of conscience for his all-
too-frequent indulgences in the passion of the flesh, met a recluse
who addressed himself to the problem in this manner: "Do you believe you can resist the seductions of women so long as you listen
willingly to their voice? Have you forgotten Adam conquered by
Eve, Samson seduced by Delilah, David by the beauty of Bathsheba,
Solomon, notwithstanding all his wisdom, led astray by the love of
women? Young man, you must take flight if you would avoid a
fall." [28] The anonymous recluse could not possibly know that his advice, eagerly accepted by Columban, was to lead to the beginning of
a monastic movement in far-off lands. Columban indulged now in
fasting and prayer instead of bodily pleasures, but he found the cure

insufficient. He left Ireland for the forests of France, where, together with twelve men equally tortured by the torments of the flesh, he fed on "barks of trees, roots and wild berries." By chance, the story of the strange, unkempt but sincere band of men was brought to the attention of the King of Burgundy, who placed an ancient Roman castle in the Haute-Sâone at their disposal. This primitive monastery, headed by the simple but learned Columban, began to attract so many people that the King added two more, Luxeuil and Fontaine. Luxeuil became known as the "nursery of monks"; after serving their apprenticeships there, they left to become missionaries and founders of monasteries in Basle, Normandy and the Rhineland.

In Columban's monastic movement we find a fully formulated monastic rule: "Let the monk live in the monastery under the land of one father, and in the company of several, to learn humility from the one and patience from the other; from the former, silence; from the latter, meekness. Let him not do as he pleases. He should eat what he is ordered to eat; he should not possess except what he receives; he should obey commands that he does not like. He is not to go to bed until exhausted with fatigue; on falling asleep he should submit before his sleep is finished. If he has suffered an injury, let him keep silence."

It might be well to remind the reader that the monastic movement began as a laymen's movement, neither stimulated nor attended by the clergy; clericial participation is a much later development. At any rate, the simple Irishman had succeeded in popularizing it. Almost two hundred years after Simeon Stylites sat in his filth on a pedestal over Antioch—a heroic but rather silly exhibition of ascetic resolution, little more than a stunt—the monastic movement had become a respectable institution.

During the years in which Columban's missionaries were establishing themselves north of the Alps, the most important of all monastic orders was meeting with great success in Italy. In 529, the first monastery was built on Monte Cassino, a community southeast of Rome. It was to become the birthplace of the great monastic movement of Benedictine monks. Their founder, Benedict, came from the town of Nursia in Umbria. He had been a student in Rome, but he forsook the great capital, not because he was unable to master his body's desires, but because he was appalled by the life of a city which had not forgotten its pagan origin, understood little of the spirit of the new Christian faith, and developed a life so "normal" that he found it both disgusting and insulting. Consequently he took up a new life, first in a wild grotto in the mountains of Subiaco, east of Rome, and later at Monte Cassino. He was to be beatified in due time and is today considered one of the great saints of the Roman Catholic Church.

Benedict was blessed with a combination of monastic zeal, a sense of organization extraordinary in a monk, and unusual insight into the tremendous potential of the monastic orders in the growth of the Church.[29] He based life at Monte Cassino on the old ideals of voluntary poverty and complete chastity, apportioning the day into periods of hard work and four hours of pious devotions. But he also added something extraordinary—*the reading of books*—and thereby made Monte Cassino the first important monastic library. Benedictine monks were not satisfied with mere blind obedience, which they took for granted; they were to go beyond the rudimentary level of most monastic existences to become the educated elite in an era of hopeless illiteracy among most of the clergy and laity. The writing and reading of manuscripts, the art of illumination, and the skills of translation and interpretation were among the most far-reaching functions of the order as it spread through many parts of Europe, particularly in France and Germany.

The nobility, too, were to play a significant role in the monastic movement. In England, where Augustine (not the St. Augustine of the *Confessions* but a later one) had built the monastery of Canterbury, thirty English kings from the many small royal families of early medieval Britain became monks. German nobility flocked in large numbers to the monasteries of Fritzlar and Fulda in the Rhineland and Alsace. It became almost fashionable to spend the last years of a disappointed and often dissipated life in the serenity of the cloister: Bathilde, a Queen of France, fled from her troubles to spend her last fifteen years in the monastery of Chelles, and Carloman, the brother of King Pepin the Short, left the security of the throne to become a Benedictine monk in Monte Cassino. The noble and royal families were not merely easing their consciences by placing castles at the disposal of the orders. Many of them were deeply caught up in the all-pervading mood of penitence and guilt which was an enormously important aspect of life in the Middle Ages.

Christianity even succeeded in civilizing the barbarians. The Franks, the Germans and the English, whose first contacts with Mediterranean culture had been with Roman armies representing a dying and unconvincing civilization, now became the tardy heirs of the Greco-Roman legacy. Although much pressure had to be exerted to convert the Saxons and the Slavs, the message of the new faith was not preached in vain; while the serfs and the peasants continued to cling to the old pagan beliefs, the educated nobility was soon won over. Constant wars, plagues, highway robberies and the general insecurity of life stirred a yearning in the best of men for some more meaningful existence. The wrath of God, Purgatory, Hell, the Last Judgment and the retribution in the life to come were among the very real fears of the medieval man. Later, in the eleventh and twelfth centuries, every Romanesque and Gothic cathedral would warn of the impending damnation in the stark sculptures above its portals. It was not a polite sculpture. The falling, tortured bodies in these Last Judgments, executed by the master craftsman of the Middle Ages, the late descendants of the Greek sculptors, inspired a sense of identification in the pious worshipper which the modern sightseer in Rheims, Chartres and Bamberg does not possess. The medieval man who looked upward as he entered the church saw *himself* perishing in the flames of Hell. And his desire for forgiveness was very real.

More and more did the monastery become the only repository of genuine Christian life. The Church developed into a huge worldwide organization with a hierarchy of bishops and priests whose lives hardly differed from those of the laymen. The Christian ideal of the apostolic era was almost lost in the formal service, the perfunctory confession and absolution, the collection of church contributions and the administration of church property. Nor was there much adherence to the ancient Christian ideal of sexual abstinence. The courts of the Middle Ages were fully occupied with thousands of claims by women whose illegitimate children could rightly boast of their fathers being bishops and priests. The ribaldry and debauchery we see in Hieronymus Bosch's grotesque paintings were very much part of the lives of priests who were too ignorant to know better or too immoral to care. "We found that the priest of Ruiville," writes the Archbishop of Rigaud in February 1248, "was ill-famed with the wife of a certain stonecarver, and by her is said to have a child; also he is said to have many other children; he does not stay in church, he plays ball, and he rides around in a short coat, the garb of armed men." He continues with a list of fifteen priests, each of them accused of the most unpriestly behavior. "The priest of Ribeuf," for instance, "frequents taverns and drinks to excess; the priest of Gorray is ill-famed with a certain one; also, Laurence, the priest of Longueil, keeps the wife of a certain one who is out of the land, and she is called Beatrice Valeran, and he has a child by her." Their behavior at the divine services is not less coarse. "We found that the canons and choir clerks talk and chatter from stall to stall, and across each other while the divine office is being celebrated." [30]

Surely, the clergy set a poor Christian example, and the rapid advance of the monastic movement is not at all amazing. The churches in the towns were little comfort to the sincerely pious. The passionate preachers who left the monasteries for a while to spread the Gospel to the people in the cathedrals often found themselves talking to the clergy, who needed it most. The gap between the "official" Christian religion and the practice of the monastic rule had become almost unbridgeable. There will come a time, we shall see, when the monasteries themselves will yield to moral corruption, but by that time new orders will have sprung up and old ones will have been rejuvenated. Even the Papacy will be drawn into the relentless process of decay, and there will be a common cry for a complete reform of the ecclesiastic order. It will be at that time, in the middle of the eleventh century, that all the monastic forces from their crude beginnings in Egypt and Syria to the noble and pure efforts of St. Benedict and St. Bernard of Clairvaux will bear fruit. But before we deal with this, we shall have to retrace our steps to the last decades of the Roman Empire and to the actual beginnings of the Papacy.

●

After the death of Constantine the Great, the Empire of the West fell prey to a multitude of northern barbarians rushing southward in search of land, pillaging, robbing and raping the indigenous population. Vandals, Visigoths, Lombards and Ostrogoths came and took half of Europe and North Africa. The names of their leaders, their origins and patterns of behavior, their success and failure in imposing their ways of life on the native populations, all this is fascinating, but it need not concern us within the context of this book. Our concern is with the fate of Christianity and the Papacy.

The first theological problem created by these migrations of hundreds of thousands of "wild men" was a revival of Arianism in Italy, North Africa and for a while in Spain. The old battle which Nicaea had supposedly settled once and for all had to be fought all over again. In Italy, where Ravenna had become the capital of the Arian Ostrogoths, accommodations between the Nicene Creed and Arianism were sought with varying degrees of success. The Franks, who conquered Gaul, adopted Catholicism after King Clovis and his three thousand warriors embraced the faith at Rheims on Christmas in 496, but though the conversion must have been a solemn act (it was presided over by the Archbishop of Rheims) it had little effect on the morals of the King or his followers. At the slightest provocation, they put people to the sword, and their habit of gouging people's eyes for minor offenses was not discarded after their conversion. Perhaps they took Jesus's admonition to "pluck out the eye that angers you" too literally. In order to assuage his conscience,

Clovis made large donations to the Church—which became a rich and powerful institution in Gaul—but he also insisted on the right to appoint the clergy, a rather high price to pay for wealth and influence.

The Ostrogoths had occupied much of Italy and penetrated almost to Constantinople, the capital of the Eastern Empire, but their fate was sealed a little more than sixty years after their conquest. Justinian, in an attempt to reconstitute the Empire, drove out the Ostrogoths, but instead of restoring Rome as capital he retained Ravenna. Of course this had far-reaching consequences for Rome, which could no longer compete for secular power. Furthermore, the onslaught of the Ostrogoths had reduced the city physically. Throughout the Middle Ages, and in spite of the glamor attending Papal elections or Imperial coronations, Rome remained a rather dilapidated town until at last it was rebuilt during the Renaissance. Once a city inhabited by half a million people, it was now a town of but fifty thousand. Strangely enough, this sorry development proved a boon to the Papacy. Since Ravenna was now the political capital of the Empire (or what was left of it), Rome became known as the capital of the Pope. We say capital rather than residence because we speak now of the seat of Papal government and power, not of mere physical presence. I have already mentioned that Gelasius I, who was Pope from 492 to 496, emphasized the ruling power of the Pope and made clear that this world had indeed two Emperors, the one for secular affairs and the other for spiritual. But the difficulty of maintaining these two rulers on equal footing was to remain the perpetual problems of the Papacy. It is in this context that we should devote a little time to Ravenna and its most illustrious and interesting Emperor, Justinian.

Nobody will recognize his Slavonic origin behind his assumed name of Flavius Anicius Iustinianus, but it is a fact that the great king came from a barbarian Slavonic family and that his original name was Uprauda, which translates as "just." Even the Greek which he spoke fluently is said to have retained a barbaric accent. The various commissions which Justinian set up under the guidance of the most prominent lawyers in the Empire succeeded in compiling and consolidating the entire *corpus juris* (body of the law), which had hitherto been scattered and largely inaccessible. But we are mainly interested here in the part he played in the affairs of the Church.

Being an Easterner, Justinian was concerned primarily with the Church whose seat was in Constantinople, and not with the Latin Church of Rome. In the East, the Emperor was engaged more deeply than any king before or after him in the minutiae of the theological struggle. (He was assisted in his analyses and decisions by his famous wife Theodora, whose past as a dancer—some even say prostitute—did not deter her from theological pursuits.) It is of great importance to Church history that Justinian thought of himself as the *pontifex maximus* (supreme pontiff) of the Church as well as Emperor. To him these two functions were indivisible: he was head of State *and* Church. Since the Pope during Justinian's reign was weak and old, he met with little effective resistance from Rome.

There is no doubt that Justinian was seriously attempting to rebuild the State on Christian principles. There was to be a complete fusion of State and Church, not merely a protection of Church property and rights. His concept of civil rights was a religious-Christian concern. The *Codex Justininanus* is therefore not only a legal, but also a religious, document—the Magna Carta of Christendom. Everything flows from his theological convictions. He was impatient with the remnants of paganism, and although at this stage the philosophical schools of Athens were morally closer to original Christianity than some Christian institutions, he closed them. Jews and even pagans were, nevertheless, to be treated as human beings since they were created by God; and although slavery was not abolished, the slaves were to be treated in accordance with these principles. The contributions of Justinian to Byzantine Church architecture and to art and literature in general are still admired; the famous mosaics of Ravenna are enduring monuments to the man whom history has rightfully called: the Great.

Great he was, so overwhelmingly great and so universal that it would have been difficult even for a strong Pope to maintain his own authority. But Justinian's influence could not live on after him. When he died (in 565), the Roman Empire as such died with him, although the Byzantine Empire continued to live on. Ironically, it was the Pope of Rome who was in reality the successor of the Roman Emperor. It would take a very strong and independent man to assert this position and pave the way for the mighty Papacy of the Middle Ages and beyond. The Church found such a leader in Gregory I (590–604), a man of extraordinary ability, the son of a noble Roman family, a descendant of two bishops, and, of no little impact, a kinsman of Benedict of Nursia, the founder of Monte Cassino. Later beatified, he is known to posterity as St. Gregory the Great.

The election of a Pope was a rather simple matter in the sixth century. Theodoric of Ravenna, an Arian Ostrogoth, had established that it was to be by a consensus of the clergy and people of Rome and was then to be confirmed by the Emperor. (Much later in our story the procedure of election will play a very important role, and we will deal with it in greater detail.) Thus, with little pomp, Gregory, the son of a wealthy Roman senator whose family had owned estates in Rome and Sicily and had occupied important positions in pagan and Christian Rome, became the Pontiff of Rome.

Gregory's education had been that of a Roman nobleman and he was always to remain a Roman; Latin was his speech, and he refused to learn Greek even during the six years he spent in Greek Constantinople. It was not surprising that a man of his background, his family connections, his wealth and his administrative ability should have been called to the highest office in the city. At the age of thirty he had become the *prefectus urbi*, a position which was preserved from ancient Rome into the Middle Ages. It was a post of honor and responsibility, and Gregory, with his impressive figure, high forehead, dark eyes and flowing blond beard, filled it with appropriate dignity. After his first year as prefect, however, his father died, and, whether out of personal grief, an old yearning or the influence of his kinsman Benedict, he abdicated his office and became a monk. He gave his luxurious parental home to the Benedictines and took the monastic oath in that same edifice, which was now called the monastery of St. Andrew's on the Coelian Hill. There he lived a life of prayer, fasting, meditation and writing. His first books were written in the monastery—one on the Book of Job, others on various Books of the Old Testament, including the Song of Songs. He gradually began to relinquish the possessions which he had inherited, placing his large holdings in Sicily at the disposal of the Benedictine order, which had six monasteries built there at his expense. After his mother took the veil and joined him at St. Andrew's, he had no family responsibilities. But he was not destined to be left in peace. When Pope Benedict I (575–79) appointed him one of seven deacons responsible for the ecclesiastic districts of Rome, he had no choice but to obey, for to serve was his main purpose in life. (Even as Pope he rejected all titles and called himself simply *Servis Servorum Dei*, the servant of the servants of God.) He accepted again when Pope Pelagius II (579–90) appointed him as *apocrisiarus* (a post similar to Papal legate) to Constantinople; the diplomatic skill and familiarity with affairs of state which he acquired in the Byzantine capital were to serve him well in later years. Upon his return to Rome, he was happy to learn of his appointment as Abbot of St. Andrew's. At long last, he thought, he would be a simple monk again.

During this time, Rome was experiencing great tribulations. She was continuously threatened with barbarian invasion, with overflows of the Tiber, which turned surrounding areas into marshes, and with plagues which killed thousands. It was during one of the worst bubonic plagues that Gregory led a procession of monks, clergy and citizens through the streets of Rome to the Church of Santa Maria Maggiore, in the drenched quarter near the river. Passing by the black corpses of the plague victims lying in the streets, the stench of death in the nostrils of the pious marchers and the anguished cries of the sick in their ears, the procession made its way to the huge and somber Mausoleum of Hadrian. A legendary account of the incident reports that as the marchers approached, an apparition of an angel could be seen hovering over the ancient bronze chariot which then adorned the top of the monument. The angel was sheathing his sword, a sign that enough people had died. Suddenly and miraculously, so the story goes, the plague ceased. From that time on the gigantic memorial was called Castel Sant'Angelo (Castle of the Holy Angel), and today the statue of an angel can be seen on the monument.

Pelagius was among the victims of the plague, and it is not surprising that Gregory was elected to succeed him—by unanimous vote of "clergy and people," according to custom. The Eastern Emperor's approval was held up by Gregory's insistent pleas to him that it be denied—a unique event in Papal history; after seven months, however, it did come, and Gregory was consecrated Bishop of Rome on September 3, 590.

Gregory was fifty years old at this time and already weak in body. Even as a monk (when he had tried to make light of it) he had suffered from an undetermined disease of the stomach which caused him unbearable pain, and two of the fourteen years of his Papacy he spent in bed. But for Gregory there were more important things than the care of his body. For it was he who laid the foundations of the modern Papacy. It was he who established the Pope as the ruler of Rome and the successor to the Emperor of the Western world. As he had once been prefect of Rome, so was he now prefect of the entire Catholic world. Insisting on simplicity and austerity, he was ruthless in his supervision of the private lives of the clergy and merciless in the prohibition of sexual indulgence, clerical extravagance and episcopal wastefulness. He had little patience with even the slightest abuse of ecclesiastical office and watched jealously over the Church's interests. As a man who had grown up rich (though not extravagant) and knowledgable in the art of administration through his handling of his parents' fortune, he now insisted on a minute inventory of property owned by every church and bishopric, from chalices and candlesticks to the huge Church-owned estates. The Church's richest land holdings were in Sicily, but there were others in almost every part of the known world, including a great many in Rome itself, in other parts of Italy, in Gaul, Spain and Africa. The income of the Roman Curia in those days has been estimated at almost $2,000,000 annually, an unbelievably large sum of money for the sixth century. But to Gregory, money existed to be spent, and if anything in his administration can be criticized it would be the lavishness of his charity. He insisted that the money be used for the poor. Papal carriages could be seen in Christian parishes all over the world distributing food and clothing to the needy. The Pope was, after all, a Benedictine monk, and charity was an important part of the Benedictine rule. He saw to it that the Papal estates produced food. Wheat was shipped from Sicily and carefully stored in the Papal silos for use in the event of famine or other catastrophe.

Although Gregory sincerely believed himself the humble and self-effacing "servant of the servants of God," he was also their master, and his attitude toward the dignity of his office was militant and unbending. When the Patriarch of Constantinople attempted to adopt the title of Ecumenical Patriarch, Gregory responded bitterly; no person was "ecumenical"—that is, world-wide in influence—except the Bishop of Rome. He fought the bishops and the Emperor on every single infringement upon the Papal prerogatives. He had become not merely the head of the Church, but Prince of the Realm. He conducted negotiations with friend and foe. He entered into a peace treaty with the Lombards when they were poised to ransack Rome, paying an annual tribute of five hundred pounds in gold from the Papal treasury. He used military force whenever he deemed it necessary. He was the first of the Popes to assume the complex duties of general, administrator and Vicar of Christ, a formidable combination of functions.

It is said that even while he was the Abbot of St. Andrew's, Gregory thought of organizing a mission to Britain, where Irish (as opposed to Roman) Christianity had already found some acceptance. Thus he now dispatched the aforementioned Augustine, who was then the Abbot of St. Andrew's, and a company of forty monks on a carefully prepared journey to Britain, with military protection along the whole route. Their mission was to win over the king, the nobility and the people to the Roman Church. In 597 King Ethelbert and ten thousand of his subjects did in fact embrace the faith, and

Augustine became the first Archbishop of Canterbury. The conversion of Essex followed a few years later.

Because of the special concerns of this book, it is important for us to mention that although Gregory dealt sternly with the pagans and watched against any kind of pagan intrusion, he was lenient with the Jews. His famous rulings on the Jews remained the cornerstone of the Papal policy which we shall deal with later in another context. When he received word that the Visigoth king of Spain intended to give the ancient Jewish community of that country the alternative of either embracing the Catholic faith or suffering expulsion, he objected. In Gaul and in Sicily, Jews were often coerced into accepting Christianity. The following letter, prompted by the situation in Gaul, illustrates his attitude:

"June 591. Gregory to Virgilius, Bishop of Arles, and Theodorus, Bishop of Marseilles, in Gaul. Though the opportunity of a suitable time and suitable persons for writing to your fraternity and duly returning your salutation has failed me so far, the result has been that I can now at one and the same time acquit myself of what is due to love and fraternal relationship, and also touch on the complaint of certain persons which has reached us, with respect to the way in which the souls of the erring should be saved.

"Very many, though indeed of Jewish religion, resident in this province, and from time to time travelling for various matters of business to the regions of Marseilles, have apprized us that many of the Jews settled in those parts have been brought to the font of baptism more by force than by preaching. Now I consider the intention in such cases to be worthy of praise, and allow that it proceeds from the love of our Lord. But I fear lest this same intention, unless adequate justification from a verse of Holy Scripture accompany it, should either have no profitable effort, or there will ensue further (God forbid) the loss of the very souls which we wish to save. For, when anyone is brought to the font of baptism, not by the sweetness of preaching but by compulsion, he returns to his former superstition, and dies the worse from having been born again." [31]

Gregory died on March 12, 604, at the age of sixty-four. He

was buried in the portico of the Basilica of St. Peter, and his body was later to come to rest beneath the altar of Clement VIII. He and his mother were beatified and their names are so remembered in the Catholic Church calendar. He was the first real Pope. He was actually the first to make the world think of the Papal territory as the Papal State, with the Pope as its sovereign. He established Papal rights and duties within and without the Church and laid the foundations of the relationship between Emperor and Pope. He also established a tradition of aristocratic Popes which was rarely interrupted.

●

Less than two decades after Gregory's death, Christianity was put to its most severe test. In the end it weathered the storm, but only after having suffered great territorial, financial and religious losses. As often in history, the tide was turned by sheer accidents. Had it not been for a new invention of an inflammable missile called "Greek fire," which caused the withdrawal of an Arab fleet about to conquer Constantinople in 842, it is almost certain that our Western world would today be Mohammedan instead of Christian. For after Gregory's death, Christianity was not strong enough to withstand the passionate attack which came from completely unexpected quarters, the dormant, neglected and almost forgotten Arabian peninsula. There, in 622, an entirely unknown man of the Arabian tribe of Mecan Hashimites fled from his pursuers to the town of Yathrib, later called Medina. This Mohammed, who then had only a handful of followers, had come into contact with the large Arabian Jewish settlement and a few Christians who had convinced him of the superiority of a monotheistic faith. Soon he began to preach a religion which was based on simple Judeo-Christian notions and customs: prayer, fasting, alms, the Last Judgement, and the acceptance of a few selected prophets including Abraham, Moses and Jesus. This confused conglomeration, secondhand to boot, would hardly seem sufficient to nourish a minority sect, yet it formed the basis of a world religion, Islam—the faith of the "surrender to Allah," the Almighty God whose only real and superior prophet was now Mohammed. This simple faith, geared to the needs of the Arabs in deserts, villages and towns, was combined with unbelievably brilliant military successes to drive millions of Arabs into ready acceptance of Islam. No religious prophet had ever been more successful. No faith, neither Judaism nor Christianity, can claim comparable achievement in such a short time, for in less than a century a considerable part of the world had surrendered to Allah. A quick look at the map of the eighth century makes one think of the possible consequences for our civilization. And if one considers the role of the Arabs in the development of culture and their tolerant, enlightened attitude toward minorities, the thought might not be entirely unpleasant.

When Mohammed died in 632, he and his new religion were firmly established, accepted and venerated throughout the Arabian peninsula. Under his successors Abu Bakr and, particularly, Omar, Islam was carried into the world beyond Arabia. In quick succession they took and converted Iraq, Syria, Mesopotamia, Persia, Egypt and North Africa. After the fall of Maghreb (Morocco), they crossed over to Spain, defeated the Goths in 711, and conquered almost the entire country. They would have taken France too had it not been for Charles Martel, who defeated them in Poitiers in 738. Where there were Christian and Jewish settlers in their path, they were permitted to worship in peace; since both were subjected to a tax levied on non-believers, their conversion to Islam was literally unprofitable for the Muslim rulers. But the native Arab populations, which had developed their own African brand of Christian faith and doctrine, yielded rapidly. After all, Islam had been created for the Arabs and their specific temperament, their national pride and outlook, and it was more genuinely "their" religion. Conversion to Christianity had been an artificial process to them, only skin deep, and to embrace the faith of the Arabs was easy. Language and national tribal habits also played an important role. Islam was a religion that did not have to be translated; the Koran spoke to them passionately in Arab terms. From the day of Mohammed's death to the battle of Poitiers, only six years more than a century had elapsed, but that period had no doubt seen the most revolutionary change in the history of the world.

The consequences for Christianity were, as we have noted, catastrophic. A vast proportion of the Church's former property was now in Moslem lands, and much of it was part of the Mohammedan loot. Three hundred and ninety-five partriarchates, among them very important ones—Jerusalem, Antioch and Carthage, for example —were under Islamic domination. Compared with the map of Arabian conquests, Christendom looked like a tiny minority stronghold between the sea of Islam on the south and the vast, uncultivated, uncivilized and above all unconverted lands and people in the European north. In as far as the Jews were concerned, ninety percent of their population now lived under Muslim rule. Since the Arabs were often untrained in the skills of government, many Jews—and Christians as well—continued to fill administrative positions in the now-Arab states.

At this early stage of medieval life, the Arabs created an era of cultural rebirth which predated the Italian Renaissance by six hundred years. From Bagdad to Cordova, arts and sciences flourished on a remarkably high level. Nourished by a native talent for poetry and storytelling which had been developed in the desert by their cameldrivers and traders, the Muslims began to develop a civilization of courtly elegance in both living and culture. They founded many academies and libraries throughout their Empire, and it is to these institutions that we owe the fact that much of classical Greek literature has come to us in Arabic translations. (Jews and Christians, incidentally, were freely admitted to these institutions, a fact which accounts for the large number of important Jewish and Christian books written in Arabic. Conversely, even late in the Middle Ages Arab scholars were teaching at the early Christian universities of Pavia, Paris and Oxford.) Architecture flourished within the Muslim Empire from its earliest times. The Mosque of Omar in Jerusalem and many other buildings, both secular and religious, rivalled and often surpassed the Byzantine and Romanesque churches and palaces. The religion which had proclaimed a holy war and found nothing wrong with including the sword among its symbols, now developed a genteel new society which contrasted glaringly with the coarseness of medieval Christian life. (The latter was in fact to benefit greatly from the Muslim heritage.) Surely the Arab conquest, however bloody at times, cannot possibly be compared with the onslaughts of the Vandals and Goths, who devastated so much of European territory. No wonder that both the Greek Byzantines of the Eastern Empire and the Mohammedans of Spain and Bagdad looked with contempt upon the Latin Christians, whose crude manners disgusted them.

●

The Papacy, meanwhile, sought in vain the kind of backing it had enjoyed under Constantine the Great and his successors. The rift between the Eastern and Western Churches widened with every century. With the exception of Nicholas I (858–67), no great Pope arose, and the power of the local bishops inevitably grew as the importance of the Pope as the universal ruler of Christendom diminished. Papal prestige was further weakened by the growing influence of the noble families of Rome, who were in fact to dominate the Papacy until the twelfth century. What the Papacy clearly needed was a new protector capable of providing it with the type of powerful backing it had enjoyed in the days of the late Roman Empire. That protection did come, in the person of Charlemagne, King of the Franks. The creation of the Holy Roman Empire under Charlemagne's tutelage was a phenomenon of great importance to the See of Rome, simultaneously a hope and a problem. The Holy Roman Empire was to last, at least nominally, until the nineteenth century. Beginning from the time of Charlemagne's coronation in Rome, the relationship between Pope and Emperor became the main theme of medieval Church history.

Italy was now in the hands of the Lombards, who had come

from the north and established themselves in a land worn out by plague, famine and Gothic wars. In time they adopted Italian as their speech and Roman Catholicism as their faith, though to the native population, accustomed and resigned to constant invasion, they remained foreigners. Italy had three capital cities: Rome, the seat of the Papal State; Ravenna, the capital of the Byzantines; and Pavia, the capital of the Lombards. While the Byzantines never yielded Ravenna, Venice and Naples, they cared little about the rest of Italy. Byzantine Christianity, too, was growing more and more estranged from Italy, and in a few hundred years the final breach between the Roman and Eastern Churches would take place. In the meantime a vigorous new military and political force had grown in the northern part of Europe. It had proven its prowess at Poitiers when Charles Martel's army prevented the conquest by the Mohammedans, and that victory, so decisive for the fate and the civilization of Europe, had established the Franks as a power with which to be reckoned. When King Pepin died in 768, he left his growing Empire in the hands of his two sons, Carloman and Charles. Both were married, by political arrangement, to the daughters of Desiderius, King of the Lombards, but marital bonds were not strong enough to overcome Frankish political ambitions. After Carloman died at the age of thirty-three, his brother Charles, now in full control, divorced his Lombard wife and married the Allemanian Hildegarde. Desiderius was no longer his relative, and Charles' appetite was for Italy.

Ironically, Charles' chance was provided by Desiderius himself when the latter decided to march against Rome and, he hoped, dethrone the Pope. Adrian I, who had been Pope since 772, threatened the Lombard with Papal anathema (the first time it was used as an ecclesiastic weapon against a secular power), then called for the Roman militia, at the same time sending his delegate to the Frankish king. Charles, who was to be known as Charlemagne, was only too eager to help; the call for assistance coming from the ecclesiastic Lord of Rome was the best possible pretext for the conquest which he had previously planned. After a siege of nine months, he conquered Pavia and proclaimed himself King of Lombardy. On April

2, 774, he arrived in Rome. It was a historic day. The Papacy had long awaited this alliance which would re-establish a Gelasian world governed in all matters of the Church by the Pope, and in all secular affairs by the Emperor. The throne of the Emperor had been vacant for much too long.

Charlemagne asked little for himself, at least for the time being. He enlarged the Papal territory and promised it protection. The old Imperial right to confirm the Papal election was not even discussed, though Charlemagne did ask for the right to hear appeals from Roman noblemen—including appeals against the Pope. Charlemagne's title was to be "King of the Franks and Lombards, and Patrician of Rome;" Italy was in effect now part of the Carolingian Empire. After the submission of the North in subsequent years, Charlemagne also became ruler of a considerable part of Europe, reaching from the Spanish March in the south of France to the territories of the Saxons, the Czechs and the Croatians; in addition, certain agreements with the Byzantines concerning Venice and the Dalmatian coast eliminated threatening conflicts. The consequences of these developments for the Papacy were soon to become very clear.

Adrian I died in 795 and Leo III (795–816) was elected Pope. It was characteristic of the chaotic situation in Rome and the unstable condition of the Papal office that Adrian's adherents, who had apparently selected a different successor, decided to kidnap the new Pope. They took him to the monastery of St. Erasmus and treated him so badly that it was considered a miracle that he was able to speak and to see. But he managed to escape, and after an adventurous journey he arrived at Charlemagne's castle in Paderborn. The Emperor, infuriated by the events and pledged to the protection of the Pope, entered Rome with an army. Leo's opponents, now replacing violence with legal procedure, invoked the right to appeal which Charlemagne had ensured them, and a council was convened at which Leo was accused of immorality and perjury. When Leo's adherents countered with the argument that the Pope could not be judged by any authority since he was the Vicar of Christ, Leo himself rose dramatically, seized the Holy Scriptures and swore that he was inno-

One of the few Pierleone possessions still extant, this tower (today known as "The Tower of Countess Matilda") stands at the end of what was once called "The Jew's Bridge," at the entrance to the *Trastevere*, Rome's medieval Ghetto.

A view of Castel Sant'Angelo which the Pierleoni acquired in 1098, but which was placed at their disposal during the time of Gregory VII (1073-85). It served as a fortress into which the Popes under the protection of the Pierleoni could flee from hostile armies.

This is the sarcophagus in the cloisters of Rome's "St. Paul's Outside the Walls" in which Petrus Leonis, father of Pope Anaclet II, was buried (1128).

cent. Both parties were satisfied. A trial had in fact taken place. The Pope had voluntarily submitted to it, although there were no formal proceedings. An ingenious solution.

Two days later, one of the most consequential dramas in Papal history was played out during Christmas mass in St. Peter's Basilica. As the Emperor knelt at the altar, seemingly deeply engrossed in prayer, the Pope approached him and placed the Imperial crown upon his head. Though it is difficult to believe that Charlemagne was not implicated in this political maneuver, historians seem to agree that it came as a surprise to him. Surprise or no, the fact was that the King of the Frankish realm was thus made Emperor of the Holy Roman Empire. The nobility and the prelates of Rome, witnessing this moving scene, greeted him enthusiastically, and he was thus proclaimed: "Charles Augustus, crowned by God, great and peaceful Emperor of the Romans, long life and victory." He was to become the "God-given Autocrat of Western Christendom, the new David, the Lord's anointed Chosen to guide the Christian people in the City of God on earth" (*Cambridge Medieval History*). In the words of his official chronicler, he was "Lord and Father, King and Priest, the Leader and Guide of all Christians." Thus began a new era.

By modern standards the great king seems to be composite of inconsistencies. He inaugurated an epoch of learning known as the Carolingian Renaissance, yet he could not read until late in life, and then only haltingly. He was a completely devout Christian, yet he did not hesitate to enforce conversion by the sword. He was mild mannered, yet on one single day at Verden on the Aller he caused forty-five hundred Saxons to die as traitors. But to the medieval man these inconsistencies did not exist: to him the saint and the knight, the monk and the warrior were equally revered. To the more sophisticated, it seemed repugnant that Saxons and Scandinavians should have been coerced into accepting the faith of the Cross—the preacher rather than the henchman, persuasion rather than brute force would have been preferable—but to Charlemagne, all this did not matter. As Constantine had considered Christianity a means for holding the Roman Empire together, so did Charlemagne use it to solve his military problems with the unruly Saxons by simply converting them to Christianity. The Holy Roman Empire was not born merely in the solemnity of St. Peter's, but also on the battlefields of Europe.

Charlemagne also became a significant organizer and even reformer of the Church. (Although in the end the Church's reform had to come from within, the beginnings were made in Charlemagne's day and at his insistence.) For one thing, the property of the Church, already considerable in the time of Gregory the Great, had now become overwhelming, and it needed more than a good housekeeper. Without asking the Pope's permission, Charlemagne appointed himself to the position of ecclesiastic overseer. But of even greater urgency was the internal corruption of the Church. Since the bishoprics had been permitted to develop their own autonomy in internal affairs, they were eager to increase their incomes, and some of them had resorted to scandalous means of doing so. Many avaricious priests and bishops took blatant advantage of the fanatical adoration of relics, which were believed to cure every disease, and encouraged poor families to sacrifice their last pennies to purchase whatever "holy" remains they had in their possessions. The poor were neglected. Fees for personal services were mercilessly extracted. Ecclesiastic incomes of all sorts found their ways into the pockets of the clergy rather than the poor. The divine service was neglected. Meaningless phrases were mouthed, and nobody cared whether or not the worshippers understood; in fact, since literacy among the clergy was not common, it is to be doubted that even many of them understood. Under Charlemagne, the *Imperial* law (and not the *Papal* decree) reached into every one of these spheres. Exact accounting to the Court became the rule. Monasteries, often richly endowed, had to erect hospitals and poorhouses on their property. The clergy was to share with the poor. The Benedictine rule, by now terribly neglected, was renewed. Charity was to be a commandment not merely for the layman, but for the clergy as well.

Effective as Charlemagne's efforts may have been, the Church was in need of still more stringent measures. It needed *spiritual* as well as administrative reform, a moral affirmation of Christian values and virtues, and this was to be its constant worry. Evidence abounded all over Christendom. (Although the Papacy itself had not yet been corrupted, that would come soon enough; for the See of Rome was about to become involved in a process of moral decay which would carry the Church to the very brink of its defeat.) That the Frankish Church, of which Charlemagne had the most intimate knowledge, was in a particularly sorry condition, is amply documented. "Nowadays," the English missionary Boniface writes in a report to Pope Zacharias (741–52) about the Frankish Church, "among the majority of the cities, the episcopal sees have been given over to the possession of greedy layfolk or adultering clerks, fornicators and publicans, who enjoy them in secular fashion. If among these I find deacons, as they are called, who from their boyhood onward have been always in fornication and adultery, leading their lives continually in all uncleanness, who have come to the deaconate by that token and who now, with the deaconate, keep in their bed four or five concubines or more, yet neither blush nor fear to call themselves deacons and to read the Gospel at Mass, and who, coming thus in such unchastity to the order of priesthood, persisting in the same sins and adding sin to sin, perform the priestly office and claim the power of interceding for the people, and offering the holy oblations, and in these latest days (what is worse) by the same token they rise from step to step and are ordained and created bishops—if (I say) I find such men among them, I beseech Your Holiness that I may have your precept and your written authority in judgement upon such things, that the sinners may be convinced and rebuked by your Apostolic answer. Moreover, bishops are found among them who, though they say that they are no fornicators or adulterers, are yet drunken and quarrelsome, or hunters, and men who fight under arms in battle and shed men's blood with their own hands, whether of heathens or of Christians." [32]

As for women wearing the habit of the nun, the same Boniface writes, "It would be some relief from our shame if your synod and your princes would forbid to women and to veiled nuns that frequency of pilgrimages that they make, going to the city of Rome and back; for the greater part of them come to ruin, few remaining intact. For there are very few cities in Lombardy or Franconia or France wherein is no adulteress or harlot of English race."

Charlemagne's reforms were almost Prussian. He demanded strict supervision of the clerics' private lives. He ordered special cloaks to be worn by them, both in the Church and in the streets, so that if a priest indulged in pleasures reserved for the layman he could be more easily detected. This ruling has particular relevance in our context because a similar system was to be adopted later on regarding the Jews. When the Church under Innocent III (1198–1216) noticed with displeasure that there was frequent social, and sometimes even sexual, intercourse between Jews and Gentiles, it prescribed a special distinguishing dress for the Jews, who could then be more quickly arrested for their "crimes." "Therefore," decreed the Fourth Lateran Council (1215), "that they may not, under the pretext of error of this sort, excuse themselves in the future for the excesses of such prohibited intercourse, we decree that such Jews . . . of both sexes in every Christian province and at all times shall be marked off in the eyes of the public from other peoples through the character of their dress." [33] Thus, ironically, the cassock of the priests came into being for the very same reasons as the pointed Jew-Hat and the yellow badge.

It is unnecessary for us to go into greater detail here in describing Charlemagne's role in Church organization and reform or to relate his extraordinarily effective intervention in matters of Catholic liturgy and music, as well as in Christian education on both the secondary and higher level. What must interest us in our particular context and in order to make the reader conversant with the problem itself is the question: Why was all this done by the Emperor and not by the Pope? Did the act of the Emperor's coronation, however casual (and even comical) it might have looked on that fateful Christmas day in the Holy Church of St. Peter, transfer Papal authority and functions to the Emperor, who, according to the Gelasian formula, was to take care of *temporal* matters only? Did the

Pope, by the act of coronation, forfeit his sacred rights as the head of the Church?

These questions have little importance if we restrict them to an investigation of the relationship of this particular Emperor, Charlemagne, to this specific Pope, Leo III. It is evident that Charlemagne was a great and strong-willed king of unusual imagination and power, and it is equally true that Leo was not a great Pope. Had Leo crowned Charlemagne after an analysis of the Christian situation in the ninth century, and had he the realization that the Byzantine Empire could no longer be relied upon (the throne of Constantinople then being occupied by a whimsical woman, Irene), then it would betray a trace of greatness in the Pontiff. But it was either a momentary flash of genius, not in character with the mediocrity of the man, or it was altogether Charlemagne's idea, conceived, maneuvered and carried through by the great king.

●

Charlemagne died fourteen years after that Christmas day of 800, and for all practical purposes the Carolingian Empire perished. It is true that the year of its final demise is 887, but the intervening years between Charlemagne's death and that of Charles the Fat, the last of the Carolingians, were years of Imperial decadence. It was during and for some time after this interval that Papal authority began to reassert itself. A new period, which began in 962 with the coronation of Otto I as Emperor of the Holy Roman Empire of the German nation, would bring into focus once again the relationship between Pope and Emperor. Since, as we have said, this relationship becomes the most dramatic and bothersome problem of the Middle Ages, or at least the ecclesiastical aspects of that period, it needs our special attention. The struggle was to culminate in the eleventh century, when the greatest of the Popes from the Ghetto, Gregory VII, resolved it with uncompromising vigor, mercilessly severing the umbilical cord which bound Emperor and Pope in mystical union and substituting a Papal dictatorship. This struggle, generally referred to as the Contest of Investiture, will be fully described later, but first we must turn to the very root of the conflict, the basic theological and political theory which defined the relationship.

Using the terms "theological" and "political" to describe the same theory might puzzle the modern reader. During the Middle Ages, however, much of the political thought *was* theological; the secular idea rarely stood alone. (It might be added that even in our twentieth century the two disciplines are not always clearly separated.) Under the Gelasian theory, as the reader will recall, God had created the world as a unity to be governed by the Bishop of Rome, who would voluntarily concede the administration of secular affairs to the ruler of the Empire. The superior role of the Pope was always emphasized: the Pope *concedes* because it is his pleasure to do so and because God Himself had decreed that two such powers should exist in this world, the *sacerdotum* and the *regnum*. The power of the ruler, although God-given, is "mediated" by the Pope, for he alone is the Vicar and he alone can confirm the Emperor's right to govern. Since temporal power can be traced to bloodshed and cruelty, the Papal act of coronation is required to purify and even purge the blood of the battlefield. The two swords God gave to Peter, one of temporal and the other of ecclesiastic power, are in the possession of the Pope, and it is only by his consent that one of these symbols of divine right is entrusted to the Emperor. In this sense, the Pope is the over-lord and the Emperor is merely the highest of his feudal vassals. The Imperial oath, sworn by the Emperor on the day of his coronation in St. Peter's and witnessed by the Curia and the Roman people, is an oath of allegiance to the Pope. Therefore—and this is of great importance to our story—just as it is the Pope who gives the Emperor the dignity and office of a temporal ruler, so it is that the Pope may also take it away—depose and dethrone him. It is this theological-political theory which dominated the Middle Ages. The practice varied with the circumstance. Some Popes were stronger than others, the Papacy itself underwent changes, and its mystical power was often sullied and diminished by the conduct of the man who held the office. But the validity of the theory remained undoubted.

The Pope was the Vicar of Christ on earth; there was none other.

The events of the last Carolingian years will show how this theory worked in action. Although Charlemagne himself had established the precedent under which the succeeding Emperors required Papal coronation, only a few years after his death Pope Gregory IV (827–44) found it necessary to remind the German bishops of the superiority of the Pope's spiritual power to any temporal power, including that of the Emperor. Charlemagne's son Louis the Debonair had been duly crowned by Pope Stephan V (816–17) in Rheims and Louis' son Lothair was crowned in Rome. With Lothair the problem came to a head. When Sergius II (844–47) had himself elected Pope *without* the Imperial consent which had heretofore been part of the agreement, Lothair sent his son Louis to Rome to force the Pope to make proper obedience to the Emperor. The Pope refused Louis entry into St. Peter's and told him sternly: "This door will not be opened to you until you come with an upright intention and for the good of the State." Louis yielded, and the Emperor's representative at the Roman Curia proved to be little more than an ambassador.

In 876 the Council of Pavia spelled it out with perfect clarity in a declaration to Charles the Bald, who had recently succeeded Lothair's son Louis as Emperor: "Since the divine benevolence through the merit of the Holy Apostles, and through their vicar John [John VIII (872–82)], sovereign Pontiff, universal Pope, and our spiritual Father, has raised you to the Empire, according to the decision of the Holy Ghost, *we elect you unanimously* as our protector." (My italics.) When the first of the Saxonian Emperors to be crowned in Rome finally received the Pope's approval, the offer was accepted in these words: "If by God's help I enter Rome, I swear to exalt with all my power the Church and John XII [955–64], its head. From him to whom I may commit the kingdom of Italy, I will require an oath to defend with all his power the State of the Church, the lands of St. Peter."

It is true that the immense possessions of the Church in many lands added physical and financial strength to its theological claims, but without the mystical power of the "apostolic tradition" the Papal position would nevertheless have been untenable. Even in the days of Papal decay, immoral and corrupt Popes retained enough of the mystical aura about their office to impress kings and emperors. What was true of the mystical ties of the Papacy was equally valid of the city of Rome itself, which seemed to possess imponderable innate powers although it had long ceased to be the jewel in the crown of cities. Although there was no Piranesi of the Middle Ages to preserve for us tenth century Rome as that great engraver did for the Rome of the eighteenth, we do know enough about medieval Rome to describe it. It is amazing, considering the burning, looting and pillaging to which Rome was subjected, how much of the old Imperial city has survived. Gregorovius' marvellous eight volumes on the *History of the City of Rome in the Middle Ages* still remain the chief source for those who are interested. We can only permit ourselves a quick glimpse at medieval Rome, but we cannot forgo it completely. The Popes from the Ghetto who are the main concern of this book were members of a family of noble realtors in Rome, and their houses and castles were part of the city's most precious architectural possessions. As we will follow them moving about in the city of their birth, we must know what kind of city this medieval Rome was.

"Sentimentally, Rome was still the heart of Europe," writes R. W. Southern, "but from an economic and administrative point of view it was a heart which had ceased to beat. The countryside in which the town lay had, through lack of drainage, lost much of its old fertility. The town was the centre of no large commerce. The greater part of the area of the Seven Hills was—as it long continued to be—a place of gardens, vineyards, ruins and emptiness. Within the walls which had once housed over a million people, a small population was gathered in clusters in the lower town, along the banks, and on the island between the banks, of the Tiber. It was a town of churches—over three hundred at the end of the twelfth century, and probably not much less two centuries earlier. . . . It was these churches which were the basis of Rome's life. The pilgrimage to

Rome was the city's staple industry: everyone depended on it to some extent, from the clerical population which served the churches, and the lodging-house keepers, moneylenders and the middlemen of various kinds, to the small aristocracy who carved out impregnable fortresses for themselves in the ruins of ancient buildings. This last class drew its revenue and supported its dignity in part from country estates around Rome, but it also aimed at controlling the ecclesiastical, as well as temporal, fortunes of the city. Its greatest prize was the Papacy." [34] The Pierleone family, from which the Popes from the Ghetto descended, belonged to this group of nobility.

In spite of the fact that so much of antiquity had fallen to scavengers (heads of marble statues were used for commercial displays, butchers used ancient vases for their trade, others picked up marvellously decorated sarcophagi to store merchandise), the great buildings of Caesarean Rome were still relatively intact. Among these were the Coliseum, the Tomb of Hadrian, the Theatre of Marcellus, the beautiful Triumphal Arches of Titus and Constantine and the Baths of Caracalla. Of course there were also many of the early churches, including Santa Maria in Trastevere, Santa Maria Maggiore and St. Peter's. Though the roads were often impassable, hundreds of visitors from all over the world could be found milling about, gazing in amazement at the ancient monuments, their hearts longing for the great experience of worshipping with the Pontiff and receiving from him the absolution of their sins, the great goal of guilt-ridden medieval man.

The Roman population, loosely governed by a Senate which retained its ancient name without exercising its functions as a parliament, consisted largely of old families which had stayed on for centuries. The city was divided geographically into thirteen districts and economically in accordance with the ancient system of guilds. The latter, one of the earliest forms of protection, served roughly as equivalents to today's trade unions, providing sick benefits, burial, a guild cemetery and trade agreements. These groups of artisans and professions were self-perpetuating social entities, with fathers training their sons in the old family trade and marriages staying very much within the group. These *scholae* had their counterpart in the *scholae peregrinorum*, the guilds of the "wayfarers." Wayfarers is indeed a rather strange term to describe groups which had lived in Rome for generations—some of them, the Jews for instance, having resided there since the days of Roman antiquity, long before Christ —but the term conveys the fact that each of these groups, although indistinguishable in dress, speech, habit and political allegiance from the other Romans, preserved its ethnic identity as well as its relations to a country other than Italy. Thus there were separate *scholae* for Greeks, Anglo-Saxons, Franks, Lombards, Frieses, Syrians, Egyptians and, of course, Jews, and each of these groups lived in its own "neighborhood." (It might be well to point out that the popular name "shul" for an Orthodox Jewish synagogue is a late reminder of the term *schola* and has nothing to do with the Yiddish word for "school.")

The real power in Rome lay in the hands of the noble families, who often traced their origins to the Empire. They were landowners on a grand scale; some of them, like the Crescenti and the Counts of Tuscany, owned considerable lands in the vicinity of Rome, and the Tusculan family had a fortress-chateaux in the mountains fifteen miles from Rome, a fact of great military importance. It was the nobility which was put in charge of the administration of the city— its judiciary as well as its militia. The power-structure of medieval Rome was headed by the prefect of the city (appointed by the Pope), the chief justice and the head of the militia. Until the great Church reform began, these three offices were frequently in the hands of the same family. Family feuds, complicated by the participants' respective attitudes toward the German Emperor, were fought out on the backs of an impoverished and utterly powerless bourgeoisie. The winner came into possession not only of the three top political offices, but also the Papacy. For much more than a century the Popes were members of the ruling families and mere puppets in the hands of their rich brothers. They had no theological training whatsoever, and very few of them changed their ways of life after assuming the duties of the highest office in Christendom.

Some became Popes while yet in their teens; others continued their lives as noble playboys in the sacred halls of the Lateran Palace, making a mockery of the high office of the Holy Father. Mistresses, children born out of wedlock, bribery and even murder entered the Vatican.

●

Only if we understand the depths to which the Papacy had sunk will we comprehend the greatness and necessity of the Reform movement which finally rescued the Church and Christianity from the morass. "What a condition of society," writes Gregorovius about this disgraceful chapter in the history of the Papacy, "when nations submissively accepted a child as ruler of the Church, when kings acknowledged him and when bishops were not ashamed to receive consecration and the symbol of their dignities or bulls at his hands. The Papacy appeared to have lost its ecclesiastical ideal, the episcopal chair of Peter seemed to be transformed into the seat of a count. Nothing, at least any longer, distinguished it from the narrowed conception of the bishoprics in every country to the seats of which the powerful princes and noble families raised their relatives, and occasionally even mere children. A moral darkness fell upon the Church. If in earlier times Christ had slumbered in the Temple, he now seemed to have completely abandoned his desecrated sanctuary, and to have surrendered it into the hands of the insolent Simon Magus [that is, simony]." [35]

This tragic period began, indirectly, with Formosus (891–96), a former Papal legate to Bulgaria who proved to be a strange study in contrasts. Austere and ascetic in his personal life, given to frequent fastings and devout prayers, jealously watching over ecclesiastic prerogatives, he surrounded himself with the best known scoundrels and schemers of Rome and himself became a political intriguer. Formosus took it upon himself to crown Lambert, the Duke of Spoleto, as the Holy Roman Emperor, only to depose him a year later and crown Arnulf, the King of Germany, with the same solemnity and in the same Church of St. Peter. Neither of these two actions made any sense other than that they satisfied his strange political ambitions, but they were to have the most remarkable repercussions. Formosus died in 896 and was buried with the honors due a Pontiff of the Roman Catholic Church. He was succeeded by Stephan VII (896–97), a Pope of whom we know little more than his role in a Goya-esque scene which took place in the sacred halls of St. Peter's, a scene so utterly shocking that it serves well as a weird prelude to the period of depravity which was to follow.

Lambert's mother, Algitrude, could never reconcile herself to the humiliation of her son's deposition under Formosus. Consequently, she conceived of a plan so incredible that we would probably not even believe it today if it were not so well documented. Nine months after the death of Formosus, members of the clergy and the nobility were invited to attend a trial at St. Peter's—the trial of Formosus. Stephan VII, wearing the robe of the Chief Justice, sat in his tall, regal chair surrounded by the members of the Curia. As the proceedings were opened, the body of Formosus, which had been disinterred from its sepulchre and dressed in the crimson of the Pontiff, was ceremoniously carried into the hall and seated on the chair of St. Peter. The stench of death hovered over the courtroom. The hollow eyes of the cadaver, whose Papal crown sat awkwardly on the skull, seemed to stare at the presiding judge, who read a long list of accusations against his former ecclesiastic colleague and predecessor, charging him with high treason, conniving and immorality. No courtroom had ever been put to such outrageous use. To make the mockery complete, a defense lawyer had been appointed to stand by the side of the Papal corpse. Many witnesses were interrogated, but the defendant was obviously not able to defend his actions. Lambert's mother sat in the witness chair trembling with passion and revenge.

The verdict was then solemnly pronounced, declaring Formosus guilty. His decrees and Papal bulls, as well as all the appointments he had made during the five years of his reign, were nullified. The presiding judge announced that as a symbol of his guilt the three fingers which the former Pope had used to pronounce the sacred Pontifical blessings were to be publicly severed. There in the holy Church of St. Peter, the temporary courtroom, the three fingers of the Pope were cut off from the decaying body. Thus humiliated in death and shamefully mutilated, the crimson robes torn from the body, the Papal crown removed, what was left of the corpse was flung through a window to the howling mob of Rome who had been promised this macabre fun. The masses lurched forward by the thousands in front of the most sacred house of worship in all of Christendom, their eager hands outstretched, shrieking jubilantly, anxious to carry the maimed body to its final destination in the Tiber. This was a veritable Roman holiday, and Algitrude had prudently provided sufficient money for the wine which even the most insensitive must have needed after this unholy feast of desecration.

Could there have been a more fitting overture for that Papal period which knew no decency, turned the Lateran into a place of shame and depravation and permitted women to rule Rome, both the city and the Vatican? Theodora, wife of the powerful Senator Theophyclat, together with her two daughters, took possession of Sant'Angelo, and there they established their rule over the city—a regime of cruelty and lewdness which knew no limitations. Marozia, the more beautiful and passionate of the daughters, gave birth to a child out of wedlock. He later became Pope John XI (931–35). Alberich, another member of the family, had himself elected Senator of Rome and ruled for twenty-two years. It was of no consequence who sat on the Papal throne, for these women were the true power of the city. The Papacy, for all practical purposes, had ceased to exist; the ritual, the Papal bulls, the homage and pomp, the prayers and the faith, all had become meaningless. Satan sat on the throne of Peter.

Within the sixty years following the death of Steven VII in 897, seventeen Popes ascended the throne of Peter, very few of them deserving either the title or the honor. An example among these is Octavian, grandson of Marozia, who became known as John XII (955–64). (He was, incidentally, the first Pope to change his given name when he acceded to the Papal office.) He was sixteen years of age when the Papal robes were put upon him and the people of Rome willy-nilly acclaimed him as the spiritual ruler of the Church. It is said that he never entered the church unless he had to officiate, and although his official pronouncements of faith were faultless, his life was not; he lived the life of a playboy, as did so many of his colleagues before and after him in this period of humiliation and disgrace. Nevertheless, the German Emperor Otto I knelt before him, doing homage to the office rather than to the person who held it, and received in return the crown of the Emperor blessed with the coveted Papal benediction without which no Emperor could have ruled. Such was the power of the Papacy even in the era of decay, and so deep were the mystical beliefs of medieval man. John was later deposed and eventually assassinated.

There were, however, some Popes of a different calibre during the period. Gregory V (996–99), the first German Pope, Otto III's cousin and a young man of twenty-three, was a Pontiff of pure intentions and personal integrity. But he had only three years to prove these qualities; he was poisoned at the age of twenty-six. His successor was the first French Pope, Gerbert of Aurillac, the archbishop of Rheims, who took the name of Sylvester II (999–1003). The tenth century had not produced any other man so versatile and creative: he seems like a Renaissance man born prematurely into a world of turmoil, stagnation and moral corruption. He was an old man when he assumed his Papal duties, which he considered an unbearable burden. He had known three Emperors, and was particularly close to Otto the Great, whom he inspired with a vision of a renewed Empire in all its Carolingian glory. (Otto journeyed to Aachen, had Charlemagne's sarcophagus opened, and in the presence of the great Charles he swore a solemn oath to continue and even enlarge the Empire; but he died too soon to fulfill his promise.) As Pope, Sylvester ruled as a statesman and judged as a scholar. His agile mind was engaged in logic, mathematics, theology and philosophy, and he dabbled in chemistry, medicine and astronomy. He constructed a globe of the Earth and a wondersome clock at Magdeburg and built an organ in Rheims. He had scholastic friends and correspondents all over the known world. He was even reputed to be an alchemist. His writings, letters, Papal decrees, translations, disputations, mathematic works, philosophical dissertations and sermons, many still extant, reveal an enormous knowledge. No wonder he was considered the original Faust of the later legend and Goethe's dramatic poem.

●

So toward the end of the tenth century there was a glimmer of hope for the Church. It was soon to be fanned into a mighty flame by a small group of people assembled in a now almost forgotten community near Mâcon in Burgundy, a place called Cluny. Little is left of the Romanesque abbey which was the seat of the most intensive and productive reform movement of the Church. Nowadays people go there mainly to taste the famous wines of the region, and most know nothing of the great revolution which began there and which, some say, laid the foundation of the modern state. The abbey had been established by William of Aquitaine, who carries the title "the Pious," a man who longed for a regeneration of the genuine spirit of Christianity and the blessings of its mission. The evil spirit of the decadent Papacy had by now infected almost every monastery and church; when the Lateran Palace itself became a brothel and a gambler's den, little could be expected of monks and nuns. Libraries had rotted away, and in many places prayers were forgotten, bells never rang, the litany was never said, confessions were never heard. To cite just one example, the monastery of Farfa, near Rome, manufactured poison. If the Papacy was in decay, so too was Christendom, and it was evident that the artificially maintained facade of Rome would soon tumble down if a reformation was not undertaken.

Cluny provided the new spiritual impetus. Obviously, it could have come only from such a group of monastic devotees, completely independent from secular powers and dedicated to the holy task of rescuing the Church and Christianity. Asceticism, however laudable in itself, was not enough: a new moral discipline also had to be established, one which would brook no violation, however slight. The Reform of Cluny provided that reassertion of the Christian conscience. "By God and in God and all his Saints," said William in the document which is considered the charter of Cluny, "and under the threat of the Last Judgement, I beg and implore that no secular prince or count or bishop will presume to place over the monks an abbot against their will." The monastery was founded in 909. Its abbots were French noblemen; the first was Berno, the second and more important Odo. Although being French and well-bred (they disdained the frugal food of the monastery), they established an unbending discipline. Dissatisfied with their insular existence in Cluny, they began to travel from country to country, from monastery to monastery, until after an amazingly short span of time some three hundred and fourteen monasteries in France, Italy, Poland, Spain, England, Palestine and Scotland had submitted to the Cluniac rule— a few thousand monks in all. There was but one abbot, the Abbot of Cluny; the heads of the other monasteries were now called priors. Monte Cassino, that first and most important Benedictine stronghold, which had begun to fall prey to the general rule of decadence, was the first to be visited and rescued. The goals of the Cluniac Benedictines were threefold: the fight against simony (the sale of church office), the battle against clerical marriage, and the war against monastic incontinence. The list of crimes of which the playboy John XII was accused illustrates how very urgently drastic reforms were needed: in 962 that Pope of the Roman Church was accused in public trial of having taken bribes for the consecration of bishops, of having appointed a ten-year-old boy to serve as a bishop, of having committed adultery with his father's mistress, and of having had incestuous relations with his father's widow. If we add that marriage was common among the clergy (all priests of the diocese of Verona, for instance, were married), that in Milan a married priest was held in higher esteem because an unmarried one was presumed to have a mistress, and that even high ecclesiastic offices could be bought, the extent of Cluny's work can be easily assessed. Nevertheless, Cluny set itself to its task with vigor, making itself the custodian of *all* Christian morality. For however important and, often, effective was its work in the monasteries and the parishes, its most important goal was the conquest of the Papacy. It was to take Cluny one hundred and fifty years before a Pope was firmly alligned with its movement of Reform and still another century before the Contest of Investitures was ended, but in the end Cluny did prevail.

By the beginning of the eleventh century, the men in the Vatican had become, as we have suggested, mere puppets of the Roman nobility. The Tusculans, one of the most important of the old aristocratic families, had emerged victorious from a violent feud with the Crescenti and had elected Sergius IV (1009–12), one of their kin, as Pope. After his death the Papacy seems to have become a Tusculan hereditary possession. Benedict VIII (1012–24), another Tusculan, succeeded Sergius, and, with the consent of Emperor Henry II, his brother became head of the Roman militia, the Chief Justice, the head of the nobility, and the man in charge of Papal elections—a nice tight package of Roman power. Strangely enough, Benedict, though elected by the evil power of the Roman nobility, proved to be an efficient and pious Pope, deeply concerned with the Cluniac movement. After his death, his brother Romulus, hardly trained for and even less worthy of the Papacy, had himself elected Pope and assumed the name of John XIX (1024–32). He was succeeded by another relative who, according to medieval sources, had just celebrated his twelfth birthday—though the English medievalist Reginald Lane Poole is of the opinion that he had passed his twentieth birthday. Whatever his age, his evil character is so well documented that there is no doubt of it. His name was Benedict IX.

With Benedict, the period of disgrace comes to its sordid finale, summing up in this young, immature and lascivious Pope the whole era of depravity. "It seemed," says Gregorovius, "as if a demon from Hell in the disguise of a priest occupied the chair of Peter and profaned the sacred mysteries of religion by his insolent courses. Protected by his brother Gregory, who ruled the city as Senator of the Romans, he led unchecked the life of a Turkish Sultan in the Palace of the Lateran. He and his family filled Rome with robbery and murder. All lawful conditions had ceased." [36] Although the population of Rome had grown used to immorality in the Papacy and a spirit of ruthlessness in the noble families, the goings-on under Benedict appear to have surpassed the limits of even their patience. While the Pope was kneeling at the altar in one of his rare displays of piety, an assassin, probably paid by the Crescenti, endeavored to kill him. The attempt was unsuccessful, but it provided an excuse for the Emperor Conrad, who was eager to reestablish his good connections with the pro-German Tusculans and little interested in the affairs of the Church, to appear in Rome to reinstate the unpopular Pope. Benedict's miraculous escape from assassination added to the rumors that he was not merely possessed of Satan, but that he probably had the magic powers of Satan himself. (It was said, for instance, that he lured virgins into the forests, and there, under the influence of his spell, they fell prey to his insatiable lust.) In 1044 the people, no longer able to endure this unbearable state of affairs, rose up against Benedict. Benedict yielded, if only for a while, and in 1045 Sylvester III was elected Pope. He was not to last; after only forty-nine days the Tusculan militia drove him from the Papal chair and Benedict was once again in power. He returned without contrition, not in the least ready to alter his way of life.

Toward the end of that same year Benedict made his most shocking move of all: he let it be known that he was eager to marry his beautiful cousin. Among those he discussed the matter with was his godfather, the archdeacon of the Church of St. John at the Latin Gate, a man whose character was "by universal testimony" unblemished, a man who was, according to his contemporary Wilhelm of Malmesbury, *"magnae religionis et severitatis"*—highly religious and sincere. We are very much concerned with this man. For he was Ioannes Gratianus Petri Leonis—John Gratian Pierleone, the first of the Pierleone Popes, *the first Pope from the Ghetto.*

Exactly how John Gratian was related to the Pierleoni we can not be sure. Some modern scholars suggest he was actually Baruch's own son. In any event, there is no doubt that he was in fact a Pierleone.[37] He had probably embraced Christianity long before the other members of the family converted on that Easter Sunday in Santa Maria in Trastevere in 1030. As Baruch's name became Benedictus, so he had taken the name of John Gratian in the act of conversion. His Jewish name must have been Yochanan, since John Gratian is a perfect translation.

At the time we meet John Gratian Pierleone, he was in his seventies. The youthful Benedict, we can presume, approached him as a young man speaking to his aged and experienced godfather about a matter of love and marriage, a matter of urgent concern to Benedict since in order to marry he would have to abdicate as Pope, an act so unusual that even a person of such moral turpitude as he hesitated to embark on it. But abdicate he did, and the circumstances surrounding the abdication were no less extraordinary than the act itself. For it is reliably reported that John Gratian Pierleone paid to have Benedict vacate the Papacy and to be elected to that office in his stead. To some interpreters there was a hint that the Jewish family had bought the highest honor of the Church for one of their sons in order to satisfy their ambitions so soon (hardly two decades) after they had converted to Christianity. The price has been estimated at between 1,500 and 2,000 pounds of silver—an enormous amount in the eleventh century, with the lesser figure equalling, according to Poole's estimate, about 6,000 pounds sterling. Obviously, the archdeacon of a Roman Church could not possibly have been in possession of such a large fortune unless he had inherited it or he was connected with a family of great wealth. To John Gratian, this presented no problem. He was a Pierleone, a relative of "a wealthy merchant established . . . in the region beyond the Tiber which was the Jewish quarter of the city." Whether the amount was paid as a purchase price for the Papacy, or, as some medievalists assume, to reimburse Benedict for money spent, will forever remain a secret. But John Gratian was a man of such character and piety that we find it difficult to grant him anything but the highest motives in the transaction. He had, after all, once been at St. Mary on the Aventine, a monastery known for its Cluniastic tendencies, and he himself was a man of the Reform. Moreover, the Pierleone family, his own flesh and blood, were from the time of their emergence the bankers and financial advisers of the Reform Popes and remained so until their names disappear from historic records. It was therefore not greed which prompted him to pay this amount of money. He became the Bishop of Rome because he considered it his mission to serve the cause of Cluny and to end the era of shame and degradation. Thus, adopting the name of Gregory VI, he became in 1045 the first Pope from the Ghetto.

The "election" of John Gratian Pierleone to the Papacy was greeted by Cluny with jubilation and hailed as a victory for the Reform. Whatever importance the exchange of money was to assume some time later, the men of Cluny took no offence at it. "Great evils require drastic remedies," writes Horace K. Mann about this affair in his *The Lives of the Popes in the Early Middle Ages*. He continues: "He [John Gratian] had hoped that by the gift of a sum of money he would bring about that Benedict would carry out his wish (to marry a relative) and resign the charge which he was so profoundly dishonoring." Odilo of Cluny, a contemporary of John Gratian, asked the Emperor in a letter received in Pavia in October of 1047 "to take the greatest possible care in his dealings with the Apostolic See and to see to it that the one [John Gratian] should not lose because he gave all, while Benedict who took all should not possess all." Another contemporary, Peter Damian, the famous Hermit of Fonte Avellana, was outright enthusiastic. Peter led a life of penitence and self-flagellation. In his day hermits often stayed in their cells for more than a decade, subjecting themselves to the most stringent discipline. They fasted three days a week, subsisted on bread and water for another three and only on Sunday permitted themselves to eat cooked pastry. Such and similar penances were a widespread counterpart of the ethical and religious Reform of Cluny. Peter Damian was therefore not a man to write flowery, congratulatory messages without good reasons. Yet upon learning of Benedict's abdication and Gregory's assumption of the holy office he wrote: "To the Lord Gregory, most Holy Pope, Peter, monk and sinner, presents the homage of his profound devotion. I give thanks to Christ, King of Kings, because I have the greatest desire of hearing only what is good of the Apostolic See. The very eulogistic report of you which many have given me has touched my heart. I have drunk in what they said, as though it were a beverage of some extraordinarily beautiful flavor, and in the midst of my joy have cried out: 'Glory be to God in the highest and on earth peace to men of good will. May the heavens rejoice, the earth leap for gladness and the Church congratulate herself because she has recovered her ancient rights. May Simon the false-coiner no longer strike his base money in the Church. May the Golden Age of the Apostles return, and under your prudent guidance may ecclesiastic discipline flourish once more. The greed of those who aspire to the episcopacy must be repressed, the tables of the moneychangers must be overthrown.' " [38]

It was with such credentials that Gregory began his reign. Elected by the people of Rome, though not confirmed by the Emperor, Henry III, Gregory assumed the duties of the discredited office of the Bishop of Rome. The Papal exchequer was empty. The buildings, a sacred trust of Christendom, were in need of repair; the ancient Church of St. Peter itself had been neglected for so many decades that it was dangerous to hold services there. The fortresses in the neighborhood of the Vatican were in the hands of a nobility whose only interest was to enrich themselves. The roads to Rome were infested with highway robbers and brigands, and pilgrims considered themselves lucky if they reached the city unmolested or had enough money left for their offerings. The offerings themselves, placed upon the altar in St. Peter's, were often snatched away.

Too few documents have survived to describe with any degree of accuracy the short Papal career of Gregory VI. Some letters he wrote to enlist help for the most immediate tasks have been preserved, but no Papal decree, no bull, no encyclical. Perhaps there were none. For what had to be done in the first year was the trivial but necessary clearing away of the debris left by the preceding Popes, attending to household matters rather than to the establishment of high spiritual principles. There was nobody who doubted the new Pope's integrity, and his dedication to the theological principles of Cluny was well known; "Gregory," writes the *Cambridge Medieval History*, "a Jew perhaps by descent, was generally recognized." But the first order of business was the physical restoration of the buildings. Some help came from Aquitania but it was not sufficient, and Gregory had to tap the Pierleone fortune to undertake the repairs and rebuilding of the churches and the Lateran Palace. Some of the fortified castles surrounding the Vatican had been taken over by hostile brigands, and force had to be used to drive them out—quite possibly with the assistance of the Pierleone militia combined with the military resources of the Pope.

The old man must have shuddered at the almost insuperable difficulties before him. Benedict IX, from whom he had received his office, was still in Rome, and since his marital plans had not materialized he was eager to return to the Papacy. Significantly, Benedict had not yet been formally deposed. Furthermore, Sylvester III, who had ruled for a few weeks after the revolt against Benedict, was waiting in one of the castles outside Rome, ready to claim the Papacy again. It may not be correct to say that there were three Popes who ruled simultaneously, but there were in any event two ambitious pretenders waiting for the opportunity to seize the Pontifical throne.

It was at this moment of confusion that Henry III, the yet uncrowned Emperor, left Germany with a large army and crossed the Brenner Pass into Italy. He held a Synod in Pavia and then proceeded to Piacenza, not far from Milan, one of the old Lombardian strongholds and an episcopal seat. (Of all the old buildings of the eleventh century, only San Savino, a Romanesque church, remains.) It is not known where the Emperor held court. At any rate, Gregory reached Piacenza in time to bid the Emperor welcome and offer his Papal benediction. He was received "with honor," a fact which must be emphasized in view of the events that were to follow. Whether the Pope stayed with the Emperor after the formal greetings is not known, but we might assume that he returned to Rome while the Emperor and his advisers stayed on to discuss the "situation in Rome," as it was now called, in his absence. The "situation in Rome" included not merely the Papal confusion following Benedict's abdication, but also the complete lack of control over the rivalling noble families, the general insecurity, the economic and moral decay, and, above all, the apparent lack of recognition of the role of the Emperor. Rome seemed to have forgotten that the Pope was to be elected by the Romans with the knowledge and *consent* of the Emperor, and the election of Gregory had clearly challenged Henry's authority.

It would be unfair to attribute the events which followed merely to Imperial ambition and vainglory. Henry III was a deeply religious man. His wife, Agnes of Poitou, was a devotee of Cluny. He himself was convinced that only a complete reform could save Christianity, and he acted accordingly in his own realm. Not only was he meticulous in the choice of ecclesiastic appointments, but he was even ready to sacrifice the financial interests of his treasury. Although the purchase of Church offices had been accepted, or at least tolerated, under his predecessors as a welcome source of revenue, he embarked with almost monastic severity on a campaign to root out that evil. He was given to fasting and prayer, and at a service of thanksgiving after his victory over the Hungarians he appeared barefooted, clothed in the coarse, hairy garment of the pilgrim. When a vessel supposedly containing a splinter of the Holy Cross, one of the most revered relics, was carried into the church, he prostrated himself in a spirit of self-humiliation and repentance. In the illuminated page of the *Codex aureus* which can be seen in the Escorial, he is shown as a bearded young man reverently holding the sacred book. He was indeed young; he was twenty-one when his first wife died, and just twenty-nine when he crossed the Alps. Yet although he acted like a simple sinner in his dealings with Cluny and

the Church, he insisted upon his royal prerogatives in all other matters. He disregarded the new tendency in Cluny which held that the
monastic oath was irreconcilable with the pledge of allegiance to
the king, and he insisted upon subordination. He was convinced that
the responsibilities of a Christian ruler and those of the head of the
Church should complement each other and that no real conflict existed. Nobody in Cluny dared to contradict him. They had every
reason to be satisfied with a German king so devoutly dedicated to
the best interests of the Church.

This then was the man Henry III, young, vigorous and pious,
who left Piacenza with his mind made up and his plan ready to put
the Papal house in order. Under the influence of the hermit Wi-
precht, Henry grew increasingly indignant of "the ancient avarice
of the Romans which had even put to sale the Apostolic chair itself."
The royal cortege and the army halted thirty-six miles north of
Rome at Sutri, an old town in which much Roman antiquity is preserved to this day. The town nestles picturesquely in hills indented
by deep ravines, its ancient walls undamaged. The Cathedral of Sutri
served as the meeting place of the formal Synod which opened at the
beginning of November. Gregory VI had been invited and arrived
with the customary Papal entourage. Whether or not he had also
been informed of the agenda, we do not know. No complete "Acts"
of the Snynod have survived; only the barest facts are known.

At the opening session Henry addressed the bishops with these
stern words: "It is with grief that I take upon myself to address you
who represent Christ in his Church. For as He of His own free
goodness deigned to come and redeem us, so when sending you into
the whole world, He said: 'Freely have you received, freely give.'
But you who ought to have bestowed the gift of God gratuitously,
corrupted by avarice, have sinned by your giving and taking, and are
cursed by the sacred canons. All, from the Pope to the doorkeeper,
are loaded with guilt."

The speech was clearly addressed to Gregory. What happened
after it was delivered has never been fully understood. Benizo called
Gregory "*idiota et morae simplicitatis vir*"—an idiot or at least a

simpleton; others maintain that he was a man utterly unaware of having committed a wrong act. "But when Gregory arrived there," we read in Migne, "and the matter began to be raised and debated by the Synod, he recognized that he was unable to administer the functions of so great a charge. He rose from his Papal chair, divested himself of his Papal raiment, and asking for pardon laid down the dignity of the great high-priesthood." The point made here is that he was not *deposed*, but that he *resigned* voluntarily; although the Synod of Sutri took place one year and eight months after his elevation to the Papacy, the official record emphasized that he was and remained a lawful Pope to the day of his death, two years and six months after his accession. Gregory, whom the Emperor and the bishops treated with "the greatest respect," made awkward and unconvincing excuses. He said that he had "acquired large sums of money [through his family, as was common knowledge] which he was keeping either to repair the Church or to accomplish other work important to the Church." Then he said solemnly: "Before God I declare to you, my brethren, that in acting as I did, I thought to win grace from God. But as I now perceive the craft of the evil one, tell me what I must do." Thus the old man confessed a crime which he had not knowingly committed. Borino, in the largest available study of the episode, writes that the money paid by Gratian to Benedict was not "a price for the Papacy but an attempt to make good the amount which Benedict had spent for his election." Peter Damian, as we know, hailed his Papacy; he thought that finally "the dove with the olive branch had returned to the ark." Poole says cautiously: "He appears to have been so deeply impressed by that Pope's [Benedict's] unworthiness for his office that he took the daring step of buying him out of it. Whether this act was simoniacal or not, I do not know. Simony is understood to mean the payment of money for a spiritual office which one desires; whether it includes also the payment of money in order to remove a scandalous holder of an office by a person who does not desire it, I leave to those better versed in canon law than I am to decide." At any rate, no one condemned Gregory before Sutri. Everyone had greeted his election with respect and relief, but the nature of the man did not permit him to remain in office under so grave an accusation. He "quietly laid down the insignia of the Papacy" and accepted exile as the appropriate punishment. As for Benedict, he was officially deposed and deprived of honor and respect. Sylvester was not merely deposed, but condemned to do penance in a monastery.

After all this had taken place, the king proceeded to Rome, where he was greeted jubilantly. On the 23rd of December a Synod was held in St. Peter's. The Emperor had already designated a German, Suidger of Bamberg, as the new Pope, but he went through the motions required by the Roman agreement. Addressing the assembled Roman nobility, he said: "Signores, however thoughtless your conduct may hitherto have been, I still accord you the liberty to elect a Pope according to ancient customs; choose from amongst the assembly whom you will." The spokesman for the Romans replied with equal lack of candor: "When the Royal Majesty is present the assent to the election does not belong to us, and when it is absent you are represented by your Patricius. For in the affairs of the Republic the Patricius is not the representative of the Pope, but of the Emperor. We admit that we have been so thoughtless as to appoint idiots as Popes. It now behooves your Imperial Power to give the Roman Republic the benefit of law, the ornament of manners, and to lend the arm of protection to the Church." The ceremonial speeches were over. Suidger, Bishop of Bamberg, was elected Pope, adopting the name of Clement II. (He died less than a year later.)

•

While the ceremonies of the Imperial coronation were held with unparalleled pomp in St. Peter's (a full description of the proceedings has been preserved), Gregory VI returned to the Casa Pierleoni. The first Pope from the Ghetto had ceased to reign. With the deep humility which had characterized his life and his short Papacy, he was preparing for a life of exile in Cologne. The family decided that it would not be wise for the old and broken man to go alone, so they selected a young member of the family to escort him. This twenty-two-year-old—"a young Tuscan relative of Gregory VI," as the *Cambridge Medieval History* describes him, "who had followed his kinsman into exile and there became a monk whose practical ability and force of character soon made their mark"—was named Hildebrand. His journey to Cologne must be considered one of the turning points in the Papacy, as it is indeed in our story.

3 GREGORY VII, HENRY IV
AND THE CONTEST OF INVESTITURE

Shortly after the deposition of Gregory VI at Sutri and the installation of the new Pope, an earthquake shook the city of Rome. Although earthquakes, floods and other natural disasters were not rare in Rome, they were nevertheless interpreted by medieval man as the voice of God saying in awesome and forbidding language that He disagreed with man's recent actions. Everyone had left Sutri with a bad conscience. Judgement had been pronounced by a youthful king over the venerable and revered John Gratian, whose monk-like self-humiliation had brought tears to many eyes. Everyone had good reason to accuse himself of having yielded to the power and glamor of young Henry III, and the hilarities and the glittering solemnities of the Imperial coronation, in which all Romans participated, had not quieted their qualms. Now God had shaken His divine head in protest and disapproval, and *vox dei* was stronger and more convincing than *vox populi,* including that of the king.

The theologians who had protested against the election of a new Pope as long as Gregory lived were right. The decision of Sutri was uncanonical. Gregory had not been deposed. He had renounced his Papacy of his own free will—a naive, pure and profoundly innocent old man who voluntarily confessed his sins rather than occupy the chair of Peter with doubts in his heart. Even in exile, he was not a prisoner. He did not travel to Germany with the Emperor's entourage, guarded by his soldiers, but made the long and arduous trip with his own small group of servants, in the company of his relative

Hildebrand. He did not go to Aachen, where the Emperor held court, but to Cologne, in the Rhineland. The Cathedral which now attracts tourists to that city had not yet been built, but the precious little Romanesque churches were there—the Church of St. Gereon, Maria am Laach and the Church of the Apostles. (All were destroyed in World War II.) These were the images which Gregory and Hildebrand were to see, partaking of the quiet grandeur of the Romanesque period during which Christ was King and the Church was the symbol of spiritual power, regal and superior in its serenity, not yet soaring and jubilantly victorious as in the heavenward spires of the Gothic Cathedral. To this Cologne they went, at that time the stronghold of Cluny in Germany. There, certainly, two Pierleoni, members of a family well known as the financial backers of the Reform and ardent in conversion, would be more than welcome among the monks and bishops of the Rhine.

But why, if the exile was voluntary, did they choose to go to Germany, the land whose Emperor had just treated Gregory so harshly? Why had they not gone to Monte Cassino, or indeed to Cluny itself? The answer to these questions lies in the person of the young Hildebrand—the man who was destined to direct and influence the affairs of the Church for the next thirty-five years, probably the most influential figure of medieval Christendom and certainly the dominant figure of the century. They called him, mockingly, *Prandellus*, the little one, for he was indeed a diminutive person—small, visually unimpressive, ugly and swarthy—a Pierleone. Descriptions of the three Pierleone Popes can be found in medieval documents. They all looked alike: "More like a Jew or a Saracen than a Christian." (That description, incidentally, was applied to Hildebrand not by one of his many enemies, but by the Abbot of Cluny.) That a man so ugly and so unimposing should have exerted so much influence aroused amazement and admiration. Since he was also accused of having the diabolic power of black magic, was it trickery with which he worked? Far from it: it was part of the systematic planning of a family playing for high stakes. Benedictus, the old Jew Baruch, was too old by now to do any planning or acting, but his son Leo de Benedictus had become the head of the family and he was much abler than his father, much more sure of himself. They still called him Leo the Jew, but he was by now very much part of Rome's political and religious scene—not popular, not accepted, but tolerated by the ancient nobility.

Hildebrand had chosen Germany because it was the country of the Emperor, without whom no Papal policy could have been carried out. Later, much later, he would carry the battle for Papal independence back into Germany, and a German Emperor would be his adversary, but that time had not yet come. Henry—young, strong, very pious and dedicated to the idea of Reform—was not particularly well suited as a target for attack. He had just succeeded in naming and electing a German Pope, and others would no doubt follow. (As a matter of fact, there were to be five German Popes in succession. They proved to be rather short-lived—most of them ruled less than a year, some for just a few weeks or months, the longest for less than five years—but of course Hildebrand could not have predicted this.) To Hildebrand, who was not a theologian but a practical politician, it must have seemed prudent to establish a close relationship with the Emperor if he was to have any influence over the election of the new Popes. He was determined to stay in Papal politics. It is possible that he officially joined the monastic order of Cluny, though if he did it was a perfunctory, almost symbolic act, and nobody has yet found proof of a monastic affiliation. But he did have Cluny's blessing, and this should be enough.

It is fascinating to watch the Pierleoni and Hildebrand develop their ambivalent attitude toward the German Emperor. They were clearly with the Papal—that is, the anti-Imperial—party, while the older nobility usually sided with the Emperor. In the development of the ideal of Papal independence, of which Hildebrand was to become the chief architect and most radical exponent, the party lines were clearly drawn. The rule of the five German Popes (1047 to 1058) blurred the issue temporarily, since, selected and nominated by the Emperor and only confirmed by the Romans, they could not be expected to be anti-Imperial. Even some of them, however, did have enough courage and intellect to understand the basic issue of the century: the war of Papal independence which went under the theological-sounding name of the Contest of Investiture. The Pierleoni, together with the Frangipani (who changed sides some eight decades later but remained faithful throughout Hildebrand's Papacy and beyond it), formed the backbone of Roman resistance to German domination. Money and propaganda kept the flame of "public opinion" alive among the Roman populace, but the overriding strategy, based on intelligent and cool appraisal of the changing political conditions, was obvious: to side with the Emperor for the time being and wait until the great moment when a central attack would bring total victory.

Faithfully, Hildebrand bided his time with John Gratian Pierleone, who was still called Gregory VI and whose Papal ring of St. Peter, which he had not relinquished, was still being kissed by respectful priests and bishops. But not for long. In 1048 Gregory died in Hamburg. (What he was doing there, of all places, we are not told; perhaps some Pierleone business interest had taken him to the old trade-port and harbor. His grave is unknown and no tombstone is preserved.) Hildebrand inherited a large fortune from his relative, it being only natural for the Pierleone ecclesiastic to leave his wealth to one he knew would continue the tradition of the Reform Papacy. Hildebrand's critics would later begrudge him his wealth, claiming it was usurously begotten, but his financial independence was an important factor in his career. In any event, now relieved of the burden, however cheerfully assumed, of caring for a bitter and sick old man, Hildebrand was free to pursue his political aims.

In the meantime, Suidger of Bamberg, so solemnly and auspiciously enthroned as Clement II before the great coronation of Henry, had died—probably poisoned. His body was returned to his former Cathedral, making him the only Pope buried in Germany. His successor, a German nobleman who adopted the name of Damascus II, had twenty-three days in which to get adjusted to the high and exalted office before he too died, also by poison. It was clearly not healthy to be a German Pope in those days. Hildebrand

The Theatre of Marcellus was the most formidable fortress in medieval Rome. The Pierleoni owned it for three hundred years, and it was known as "Casa Pierleoni."

Les JUIFS presentant le PENTATEUQUE au PAPE dans le Collisee.

This engraving from Picart's *Religious Ceremonies and Customs*, Vol. I, 1731, depicts the chief rabbi of Rome presenting the Scroll of the Torah to the Pope.

A dilapidated Pierleone tower in the Ghetto of Rome was painted by Franz Roesler in the nineteenth century. (*Museum of Rome*)

was now probably in Aachen with the Emperor. By whatever means we do not know, that ugly, unimposing (yet not unassuming) cleric had succeeded in becoming one of the Emperor's closest advisers, at least in matters concerning the Church and, very important, Roman affairs. For Hildebrand was for all practical purposes a Roman. It is significant that nobody knows for certain the exact circumstances of his birth. "The date of his birth is unrecorded," writes John William Bowden, one of his early modern biographers, "but from the indications afforded by different passages of his history, it would seem probable that the event took place between the years of 1010 and 1020. Nor is it quite clear either where he first saw the light or from what parents he derived his origin. But the most probable account of these points seems to be that which designs as his birthplace the town of Soana, on the southern borders of Tuscany." [39] Wherever he was born, everybody agrees that he came to Rome either as a very small child or as a young lad. "He was soon removed," writes Bowden, "from the paternal roof, to a fitter scene of preparation for the toils and duties which awaited him." He came to Rome. It is our contention that he was—either by his mother's marriage, as Reginald Poole contends, or as Pietro Fedele claims, by blood—a member of the family of Jewish converts, the Pierleoni. At any rate, he was a Roman. He knew the Romans, the nobility and the street rabble, all shades of public opinion, the corruptible and the honest; he knew the mentality of these gullible and sentimental Romans, each of their *scholae*, the suburbs and the various parts of the city, best of all Trastevere. He knew their mood and their reactions to every event, political and ecclesiastic. And above all, he knew the Curia. How at his age he should have developed so much knowledge and such unbelievable shrewdness is uncanny, despite the fact that medieval men often finished their university training at the age of eighteen. Nevertheless, Hildebrand remains one of the great geniuses of all times. He negotiated, maneuvered, cajoled, planned, directed, used people and circumstances at will, and remained in control of it all. The agility of his mind, the ruthlessness which he showed in pursuit of his goals, the single-mindedness of his well defined purpose and, above all, his complete devotion to the Church and its ideals make him one of the most remarkable men of history. His enemies thought him diabolical and devious; he certainly was not an angel, but he was not a devil either. He was a young man bent upon a goal. He claimed that he "unwillingly went beyond the Alps" [40] when he escorted his kinsman Gregory, but this might be just a pretty phrase of exaggerated humility and not at all what he meant. As a matter of fact, "beyond the Alps," which means Germany, is where he belonged and he made good use of it.

Henry III's first appointees to the Papacy were dead, and the circumstances of their deaths had made the position not particularly attractive. No wonder some German bishops declined politely when approached. Upon Hildebrand's advice, the king turned to Bruno of Toul, who was his intimate friend and adviser, a man whose noble, ecclesiastic and military traditions were a rare combination. In the end his versatility was to prove his undoing. At any rate, he accepted. The king announced his appointment and made known to noblemen and clergy alike that Bruno of Toul was to serve as Pope Leo IX (1049–54). He was to become one of the great, if tragic, Popes of the era.

To Henry the procedure was simple. Leo, nominated by the great king, was to lead a large German delegation of bishops, theologians and some military contingents to Rome, and there he was to be solemnly installed as the Pontiff of Rome, the Emperor's trusted friend, a man of great piety and integrity. But to Hildebrand it was not so simple. He had attached himself to the new Pope long before his appointment, and was now with him day and night. For many days he prevailed upon him to consider the physical act of his entry in Rome to be one of his most important steps. He knew that the Germans were not very popular in Rome and that German soldiers seemed particularly objectionable. Every German military unit— and the Romans had seen too many too often since the days of Charlemagne—symbolized a colonial power, obnoxious and degrading to say the least. The Roman street rabble could be very nasty, and the Papal robe was too familiar a sight to be expected to make them solemn and submissive. Furthermore, there was the longstanding agreement under which the Emperor and the Romans should *both* have a voice in the selection of a new Pope. It is true that Henry had been able to install "his" Pope with little difficulty during those turbulent days of Benedict, Sylvester and Gregory. He had presented Clement to the Romans, and they had given their consent; it was not altogether legal and canonical, but it had been accepted. But then the Romans at that point had not cared much for anything but order and some semblance of decency. This time they would remember the agreement which called for the election of a Pope agreeable to the Emperor *and* the Romans. The laws of Papal election were still not written (this was to be done soon enough), but to *impose* a Pope upon the Romans was sheer insult.

Hildebrand's great forte was his ability to convince the most reluctant, but Bruno of Toul needed little convincing. He knew of the great challenge and even danger of the Papal office. The bodies of two poisoned Popes, both good and trusted friends and countrymen, were hardly cold; he had attended the funeral services in Bamberg. This was serious and perilous business. He listened to Hildebrand carefully and accepted his advice. Thus he appeared before the gates of Rome in strange attire. There was no Papal robe. There was not even the ordinary dress of a nobleman or priest. He appeared as a penitent sinner, dressed as a monk, barefooted, knocking at the gates of Rome and begging to be admitted not merely as a pilgrim, but one humbled by his own sinfulness and ready to serve the Church as its Pontiff. The Romans opened the gates and the unarmed retinue entered the city. Among them was a small, skinny, swarthy Roman, a Pierleone. For Bruno was accompanied, as Gregorovious notes, "by Hildebrand, a man more important than King or Emperor, dressed as a monk. He was still unknown, but he was destined to become the genius of the Church." [41] Hildebrand had come home to the city and to the Romans, and also to his family, now firmly in control of Trastevere with their strongholds, bridges, castles and militia. Castel Sant'Angelo was now securely theirs. Leo de Benedicto was in full control, and the family's devotion to the Church had not diminished since that day some twenty years ago in Santa Maria in Trastevere.

Baruch-Benedict was still alive when Hildebrand returned, but he would die soon afterward—in 1051. "Although the tombstones of the Popes of that time are no longer extant," writes Gregorovius, "the mausoleum of the Jewish Crassus was carefully preserved. In the cloisters of San Paolo Outside the Wall is a large marble sarcophagus of the worst Roman period, adorned with the statues of Apollo and Marsias and the Muses: this is the tombstone of Pierleone whose inscription—typically Jewish—boasts that he was a man 'outstanding because of his wealth in money and children.' He was indeed survived by many children and their fortune was so extraordinary that one of them became a Pope, the other a Roman patrician and, some claim, a daughter married King Roger of Sicily. The other members of the family were buried in San Nicola in Carcere and in San Angelo in Prescaria. Before this church was torn down I saw with my own eyes a mosaic coat of arms of the Pierleoni representing a checkered lion with three bars." [42] The tombstone described is not that of Baruch (whose sepulchre is now lost) but that of Leo's son Peter, Baruch's grandson. I quote the passage here because the comments apply equally well to Baruch.

The Pierleoni's great hope, Hildebrand, had thus arrived in Rome as the trusted chancellor of the new Pope. The Romans, overwhelmed by Bruno's humility, carried the pilgrim to St. Peter's. There he spoke to them about his Emperor, the great Henry who had asked him to serve as Pontiff. But the Imperial nomination, he added, counted for naught if it was not confirmed by the people of Rome—the noblemen, the clergy and the ordinary men in the street. The Romans, flattered by such consideration, acclaimed him jubilantly as Leo IX. The principle of Roman consent was now fully established. How much Pierleoni money had helped in the preparation of this "spontaneous" acclaim we do not know; what is of concern to us is that Leo had in fact been elected, and a good, and even great, Pope he was. Grateful for Hildebrand's advice and acknowledging his rare gift, he made him Secretary of State of the Roman Curia, which began to look for the first time like the Cabinet of a monarch. Rome had not seen such an assembly of able and dedicated men in a long time. Leo himself conceived of his office as that of an Emperor, ruler of a far-flung realm. In the five years of his incumbency, Leo spent only six months in the Holy City, leaving Hildebrand in complete charge of Papal affairs during his absences. In effect, Hildebrand was "acting Pope" while Leo was abroad holding councils in Italy, France and Germany aimed at solidifying his rule.

Leo was adamant in his judgments of clergymen, high and low, who lived with their common-law wives unashamedly. From time to time he would consult the *Liber Gomorrhianus*, a book which was dedicated to him and which contained the most detailed descriptions of the moral deprivation of the Christian clergy. The author of that book was the zealous, austere and uncompromising Peter Damian, the same Peter who had lauded Gregory VI's ascension to the Papacy and who, against his wish, had been appointed Archbishop of Ostia, a city not far from Rome. That Peter and Hildebrand should both have been such influential figures during the reign of Leo provides us with an interesting commentary on the dichotomy of the medieval Church. Peter, living in his episcopal palace, not at all happy over his new existence of respectability and opulence, felt like a country boy forced to wear formal attire. His ideal was ascetic in the extreme, and with all the honors that had come to him he still longed for the solitude of the monastic cell and for the flagellations which punished his body for the very thought of sin and even for the sins which others committed. Hildebrand, on the other hand, lived in a world of expediency, of political calculations, clever diplomacy, shrewd speculations and financial wizardry involving wheelings and dealings with Peter's Pence and the variety of currencies that came into the empty coffers of the Papacy. He also knew how to use Damian. While Hildebrand was the administrator and secretary of foreign and domestic affairs, Peter was the preacher and propagandist. He was so much more convincing than Hildebrand when he admonished and cursed the clergy and the masses that flocked to the churches to hear him. He was a medieval Savonarola, and from him came the great indictment of the Christians of the eleventh century. Hildebrand could never have competed with him; he was to speak later like a Hebrew prophet, but even this became merely an instrument in the great struggle which was to come. For the time being, Hildebrand had to lead the Curia while his master Leo travelled, as though he were his own Papal legate, throughout all the lands of Christendom. I use "master" in its literal sense, for although Hildebrand was Leo's adviser and trusted archdeacon, the Pope was very much Hildebrand's teacher, and the five short years of his Papacy left their mark upon Hildebrand. Later, in the days of his own Papacy, he was to remember "our father Leo IX" [43] or "our beloved master," and he meant it. Leo's concept of the Church as an Empire, catholic and ecumenical, to be governed by the Pope, the ecclesiastic Emperor, made a deep and lasting impression on Hildebrand, who after all was not yet even thirty.

Nevertheless, if Leo is to be credited with building the international organization called the Roman Church, it was mainly due to the financial and organizational genius of Hildebrand. Again we turn to Gregorovius for a description of this man's stature and duties. "Hildebrand was now not merely the leading figure in Rome, but one of the greatest political leaders of all times. As a leader of the Reform movement, he made other people tools in his battle: the saints and the monks whose fanatical zeal he enflamed; the Popes to whom he gave direction; the Lombardians whom he asked to battle the old nobility, and all the time using demagogic methods, taking advantage of the romantic adoration in which the wealthy and powerful countess of Tuscany indulged and whom he obligated through the bonds of friendship. The major ills of his time were concubinage and simony. He fought them vigorously. But instead of despairing of them, he made them into weapons used by the Pope which finally helped to make the temporal power succumb to that of the spirit, depriving the German Emperor of his influence in Rome and thus establishing the spiritual rule all over the world." [44] (The "romantic" countess of Tuscany mentioned here is Matilda, about whom we shall soon learn a great deal more.)

Another significant, if less dramatic, accomplishment of Hildebrand was the replenishing of the Papal treasury. This was particularly important because the people of Rome actually lived to a large extent on charity. When the Pope had nothing to give, they begged in the streets—or simply stole. Pilgrims who had come from afar to worship in St. Peter's and pray at the graves of the first Apostles were shocked to discover that the roads leading to Rome were not safe and that the Holy City itself was a nest of short-change merchants and extortionists. (Not all the pilgrims had to be forced to give: a chronicler notes that in 1050 King Macbeth of Scotland visited the city, saw the Pope and distributed gifts lavishly among the populace.) The exact amounts which the Pierleoni, the Frangipani and other noble families gave the Vatican are not known, but it can be surmised that the largest part of the gifts that made the Papal treasury look more respectable must have come from a small group of the rich. That the houses of Tuscany and Pierleone played the leading roles in helping Hildebrand financially and making him the financial reorganizer of the Holy See is an acknowledged fact.[45] The financial ties between Gregory and the Pierleoni are also borne out by the Jesuit Zema, who has made a careful study of the Reform Popes. Zema accepts as facts that "Gregory VI was a blood relation of the Pierleoni" and that "Gregory VII was connected with them on the mother's side," though he holds with Poole that while Hildebrand's relationship with the Pierleoni was close his Jewish origin is uncertain "despite his allegedly Semitic looks." [46]

●

The two major events in the reign of Leo IX, one of them with consequences reaching into our own time, must now be mentioned. Both spelled defeat and even disaster for Leo and, in a way, for the world. The first, chronologically, was the final and complete separation of the Greek Church from the Latin Church, which occurred in 1054. The second was the startling emergence of the Normans as a world power.

There are some historians who believe that the present-day East-West conflict has its roots deep in the Church conflict of the eleventh century. It was then, Friedrich Heer claims, that the two "worlds" were created. If the Latin Church had succeeded in establishing one Church, truly catholic and all-embracing, the Balkans and Russia would now be part of the Western world.[47] If this is true (and it sounds most convincing), the separation between Rome and Constantinople is not a local event, a mere date in Church history, but a world-shaking incident. Although the consequences could certainly not have been foreseen by Leo or Hildebrand, it is nevertheless true that Hildebrand failed his master, the Church and the world. His advice must have been sought by the Pope. Either it was rejected, assuming that he counselled prudence instead of direct action, or he simply made the wrong decision. At any rate, we must now turn to the immediate cause of it all, the Normans.

Of all the "barbarian" tribes rushing down from the northern countries to rob, plunder, rape and pillage and ultimately establish themselves in the new countries, the Normans, who came from Scandinavia, are the most fascinating. They founded kingdoms in Ireland and in the north of France (Normandy), from which they conquered England (in 1066). But even before defeating the English, they had established themselves in the hopelessly disorganized and fragmented south of Italy, which at that time belonged partly to the Byzantines and partly to the Lombards and also included three tiny republics—Gaeta, Naples and Amalfi. There was constant strife between these factions, with the Emperors of the East barely capable of defending their possessions so far from Constantinople.

The Normans, fierce and fearless fighters richly deserving of the wages which their masters paid them, came as adventurers and soldiers of fortune.[48] As long as they had no political leadership, they had no political ambitions. But leadership soon developed, and within a few decades they became the main threat to the independence of the little republics and to the Byzantine possessions. They were also soon to cross into Sicily. Their great leader at that time was Robert Guiscard, a man completely ruthless in battle and conquest and a giant who towered over his followers. (Interestingly, the Normans were known to be particularly small and dark, not at all blond and blue-eyed Teutons, as might be expected.) Although the Normans were Christians, Pope Leo IX considered their conquest a threat to the territories of the Papal State, which guarded the integrity of its boundaries as jealously as any other state. Leo was, we must not forget, a general by training and tradition, as befits a German noble of the eleventh century.

When Leo received a delegation from Benevento offering him their town as Papal property in return for his military help against the Normans, the general-Pope agreed. Did it ever occur to him that he was fighting not the Saracens or heathens, but a nation of fellow Christians who were loyal to him, their Pope? Later this argument was to be used in polemics against him. Had he been successful, he would undoubtedly have become the example of a heroic Pope, combining piety and soldierly virtues. But alas, he was not.

The opposing forces met at Civitella on June 18, 1053. Leo's army consisted of the small Papal militia bolstered by Lombards and Italians and a few German army units. (Henry III had been asked for military help but he was too busy to respond with a large army.) Before the battle, the Pope received intelligence that the Normans had only three thousand men on horseback. Triumphantly he told his army that the little devils, too undisciplined and unskilled in battle to be taken seriously, would soon be overcome. Soon enough, those "little devils" came, and little though they were, they were clever in battle, undaunted and fearless. The Italians gave up almost immediately; the Lombards and Germans, too stunned by the sudden attack and the fierceness of the onrushing Normans to resist, were killed to a man. Leo and his group of officers, watching the battle with growing despair, were in the city when the Normans penetrated the unmanned fortifications and embarked on an orgy of arson, pillage and rape. When they unexpectedly came upon the Pope, arrayed in his Papal robes with a golden crucifix dangling from his Papal chain, they abruptly stopped, and (in a scene worthy of Cecil B. de Mille) the sweating, bleeding roughnecks fell down upon their knees before their Pope. Christian amenities had to be observed, war or no war; Leo was indeed the enemy who had tried to defeat them, but he was also the Pontiff of their Church and they owed him homage and obeisance. And so they knelt piously and solemnly while their officer, kissing the Pope's ring and speaking in a voice filled with emotion, declared the Pontiff prisoner of the Normans. Treated as the Pope should be, with every possible consideration and even tenderness, he was nevertheless their prisoner and as such taken to Benevento, where he was forced to stay for six months. He was not released before signing an agreement with the Normans in which he yielded to their every demand. He returned to Rome sick in body and desperate in heart and mind. A few months later, on April 10, 1054, the great Pope died.

•

It was only natural that Hildebrand, the man who had conducted the Papal affairs during Leo's reign, should be asked to succeed him. But Hildebrand declined, advising the Emperor to nominate Gebhard of Eichstadt, another German nobleman and cleric. Gebhard was duly enthroned as Pope Victor II (1055–57). At the beginning of the following year, Henry III, who was only thirty-nine years old, took ill, and Victor rushed to his bedside in time to see the great king die. Henry was laid to his eternal rest in a ceremony presided over by Victor and attended by the noble and ecclesiastic elite of the time, and Victor consecrated Henry's son, who was to rule as Henry IV, as the German king. The young Henry was only six at the time, and the awesome task of ruling for him was taken on by his mother, the Empress Agnes. A year later, Victor himself succumbed to the evil spell that seemed to attach itself to the German Popes. The last German Pope, Stephen IX, was installed shortly afterwards, and again the curse worked: Stephen died a year later.

This quick succession of Popes had created considerable unrest in Rome, and the old nobility, particularly the Crescentians, quickly seated one of their own on the throne of St. Peter under the name of Benedict X. It was an unfortunate name. Related to the passionate and impious Benedict IX from whom John Gratian had purchased the Papacy, the new Benedict enjoyed a reign of short duration, for the Pierleoni were determined to oust him. It was "Leo de Benedicto Christiano, a rich citizen, son of a Jewish convert, influential in the Trastevere and in close touch with Hildebrand" [49] who suggested that another Pope be put up in opposition. Hildebrand himself made the selection: Gerard, Bishop of Florence.

It was at this point that Trastevere's strategic position was to prove itself useful for the purposes of the Reform Popes. The Leonine City, that section of Rome which had been fortified by Pope Leo IV, was still held by the old pro-German aristocracy, and certainly no anti-Pope would be permitted to enter through the gates of Rome, the straight road to the Vatican. But the old Ghetto, to which many more fortified towers had by now been added, was in the hands of the Pierleoni. "In the eleventh century," writes Zema, "they commanded the double-bridged island of St. Batholomew [the Isola Tiberina]; the Theatre of Marcellus on the left bank which they turned into a fortress-tower to guard the approach to the island; and also a strong place at the northeast corner of the Forum, near the Mamertine prison. On this part of Rome the Reform Popes could always fall back to safety as often as they were driven out of the Leonine City or the Lateran." [50] Thus when Gerard, Bishop of Florence and now Pope Nicholas II (1059–61), came to Rome in order to serve Christendom, the gates of Trastevere were opened, and the Pope entered the Holy City through the ancient Ghetto of Rome, escorted by Hildebrand, Leo Pierleone and the militia of their family. The news spread quickly and messengers were sent to the castles of the Crescentians to warn them that the Pierleone militia was marching toward the Lateran Palace. For Benedict there was no way out but to end his short career as Pope, and he fled the city before the new Pope took possession of the Papal residence. He was to maintain himself for several years in a castle outside Rome until he finally agreed to abdicate and move, as a private citizen, to his mother's home in Rome.

Hildebrand had prevailed, but the battle lines were now more closely drawn than ever. Almost the entire old nobility was at this time with the Imperial party, some for political reasons, some because of German ancestry and some simply afraid of the growing power of the Pope and, particularly, of Hildebrand. All of them, moreover, feared the Normans, who had moved dangerously close to Rome. Hildebrand was thus almost entirely dependent upon the new nobility. Benzo, Bishop of Alba and Hildebrand's bitter enemy, enumerates Hildebrand's backers, beginning his list with Leo Pierleone, who is called *"Leone procedenti de Judaica congregatione."* (The baptismal water apparently did not wash off his Jewish origin.) Another document, this one dated April 28, 1060, was signed by a larger group of Hildebrand's supporters, including the new Pope, the cardinals and the Prefect of Rome; the noblemen are again headed by "Leo de Benedicto Christiano." [51]

•

No one was more aware than Hildebrand that the War of Investiture would soon have to be fought in earnest. Henry IV was still young, but the time was clearly coming when the conflict between the Pope and the Emperor, that great medieval drama, would come to a head. It was necessary at this time to strengthen the legal foundations of the Papacy. For in spite of all their violence and brutality, the Middle Ages were very acutely concerned with the rule of law, and it was as important to lay a solid legal foundation for the impending struggle as it was to enlist powerful political allies. Acting for Nicholas, who was completely under his influence, Hildebrand prepared the document which is still, although later changed and amended, the foundation of the procedure followed in the election of a Pope. Up until this time, as we have seen, the election had called for Imperial consent and agreement by the cardinals, the Roman clergy and the nobles. But with the Roman nobility divided into two warring factions which did not hesitate to employ armed forces in the election of their favorite Pope, the situation had become chaotic. The time had come to bring order.

Thus Nicholas, "in the year of His incarnation 1059, the Holy Gospel being placed before us and the most reverend and blessed Apostolic Pope Nicholas presiding, while the most reverend archbishops, abbots and venerable priests and deacons assisted in the Church of the Lateran patriarch, which is called the Church of Constantine," read the Hildebrandine document. It is one of the most important decrees in Papal history. We will quote from it here because it plays a prominent part in the election of two Pierleone Popes—Gregory VII and, particularly, Anaclet II.[52] The decree recalls the many times when, after the death of a Pope, the factions of the nobility had tried to impose the man of their choice. "Ye know," said Nicholas, "how much adversity this apostolic chair, in which by God's will I serve, did endure at the death of our master and predecessor, Stephen, to how many blows, indeed and frequent wounds it was subjected . . . so that the columns of the living God seemed almost to totter. . . ." Therefore, he continued, the succession must be regularized so that there be no room for any further "trafficking." Then he spelled out the procedure explicitly:

1. "When the Pontiff of this Roman universal church dies, the cardinal bishops, after first conferring together, shall afterwards call in the cardinal clergy; then the remaining clergy, and the people shall approach and consent to the new election." The power is thus placed in the hands of the cardinal bishops, but the deacons are also included.

2. This new rule, it is said, is not new at all but in accordance with "the decrees of various fathers," particularly Leo IX, who had made an attempt to write a similar document.

3. The choice of the Pope should be made from the best available men, preferably "from the lap of this Roman Church. But if not, one shall be chosen from another church."

4. A rather casual reference is made to the established right of the Emperor: "Saving the honor and reverence due to our beloved son Henry who is at present called king, and will in the future, it is hoped, be Emperor by God's Grace; according as we have granted to him and to his successors who shall obtain this right personally from this apostolic see." Note this sentence: The Emperor is the *recipient* of his rights. The Pope graciously grants them to him. The decree establishes Papal sovereignty.

5. If after the Pope is duly elected "the endeavors of any man who is prompted by the spirit of malignity" prevent him from ascending to the chair, the elected Pope has at his disposal "all the Papal resources." If, on the other hand, someone should be "elected or even ordained and enthroned through sedition or presumption, he shall be subjected as anti-Christ and invader and destroyer of all Christianity." Such a man should be deposed without trial and "condemned with a perpetual anathema." He shall be excommunicated and "feel against him the wrath of Almighty God, the Father, the Son and the Holy Ghost, and shall experience in this life and the next the fury of the holy apostles." All the curses which condemn the pretender to the Papal throne apply to anyone who recognizes him as well. "His habitation shall be made a desert, and there shall be none to dwell in his tents. His sons shall be made orphans and his wife a widow. He shall be removed and his sons shall go begging. The whole earth shall fight him and all elements oppose him." (The spirit is not very Christian: some historians detect in the Old Testamentarian style the tone of Hildebrand, who very often preferred the stern admonitions of the Hebrew prophets to the sweeter sound of "Love thine enemies.")

The new decree also enlarged the number of electors from seven to fifty, thus diminishing the power of the cardinals to the benefit of the deacons and presbyters, and made special provision that no Pope could be elected before his predecessor had actually died and was buried. Though, as we are going to see, the interval between the death and the burial of a Pope could be as short as only one hour, it was considered decent that three days of fasting should elapse between the two events; in the thirteenth century, ten days had to pass before the election of a new Pope, and this is the usual procedure in our own time. Because of the fear that military forces of some noble families might attack or interrupt the deliberations, it was preferred that they take place in a fortified church; it was—at least in those days—not necessary to hold the elections in Rome. The elections themselves were, of course, preceded by discussions of the qualities of the various candidates, including such factors as their character, the length of time they could be expected to rule before they succumbed to old age, and their attitude toward the Emperor. Often the dying Pope would recommend his successor, and such wishes were frequently honored. Of course, in elections in which only one candidate was named, the new election decree would be neither help nor hindrance. Interestingly enough, it was to be in the case of Anaclet II that the document was to be tested at the beginning of a tragic schism in 1130. How ironic that it should have been Anaclet, a Pierleone Pope so passionately sponsored by his family and so vehemently attacked for his Jewish origin, whose election was to be disputed on the basis of the policies established by his kinsman Hildebrand.

But we are getting ahead of our story. Nicholas II died in 1061, and Hildebrand chose as his successor Alexander II (1061–73), who was the first Pope to be elected by the College of Cardinals and in accordance with the new rules. During the new Pontiff's reign, Hildebrand continued to put the Papal house in order. He had already achieved much since the days of Leo IX, who had found the Papal treasury depleted. He had, among other things, appointed his family, the Pierleoni, the official bankers of the Popes. As Georg Caro notes, Benedict and Leo Pierleone "engaged in financial transaction before and after their conversion, which can be called a regular banking business. Thus it is probable that Hildebrand deposited the money of the Church with the Pierleone bank. It is to be assumed that the

Church received interest for these deposits although they might have been in partnership in certain commercial transactions which brought them profit. Since the financial contact between Leo Pierleone and Hildebrand was established, moneys were paid out from the regular account and other sums were advanced against the Papal holdings in the bank. This was particularly consequential during the years between 1059 and 1061 when there were uncertainties about the election of the Pope, and when money had to be distributed among the populace to win them over to the candidate of the Reform party. It is therefore no coincidence that it was with the help of this shrewd business man [Leo Pierleone] that Hildebrand succeeded in putting the finances of the Papacy in order. It is reasonable to assume that Benedict had already been involved in the financial affairs of the Curia and even some time later a Jewish administrator of the affairs of the Papal household can be found." [53]

●

The inevitable happened in 1073, when, after nine years in the Holy See, Alexander II died. Even during his illness, Hildebrand had been approached to succeed him. He was the natural choice, for no other man in Rome or elsewhere could boast of such broad experience. (It is also true that no other had as many enemies.) In matters of Church reform, Hildebrand was as outspoken as Damian, for he knew that the prerequisite of the independence of Church government from the Emperor was the cleansing of its own house. Only a Church morally strong and pure could expect recognition as an independent ecclesiastic Empire. His views on simony and concubinage were also well known: all the Popes in whose selection he had had a hand had made strong pronouncements, either prompted by their own convictions or stimulated by Hildebrand; bishops and priests had been excommunicated by the hundreds, and Leo IX had gone so far as to ban the common-law wives of the clergy from the western cities. Equally strong and well-known were his views of clerical investiture: he strongly opposed the appointment of bishops and priests by the kings, princes and noblemen in whose realms those clergymen lived. Finally there was his political position. The pro-German party had always, and with good reason, been suspicious of his negative attitude toward the German Emperor and German influence in Rome. Of his ability there was no doubt, but no intelligent observer could deny that with the election of Hildebrand to the Papacy a dramatic new period in Church history had begun.

And dramatic it was from the very start. In a letter to the Abbot of Monte Cassino in April of 1073, Hildebrand himself described the events: "Our lord Pope Alexander is dead. His death was a heavy blow to me, and all my inward parts were stirred to their depths. For after he had died, the Roman people, contrary to their custom, placed the conduct of affairs in my hands so quietly that it was evidently done by an act of divine grace. And so, taking counsel, we decided that after a three days' fast and after public funeral services and the prayers of many persons, accompanied by works of charity, we would determine what it would be best to do about a choice of a Roman Pontiff." We might pause here to note two things. First, that Hildebrand, the author of the Nicholene election decree, had to be particularly careful to honor his own rules; he was well aware that at some later time the canonical validity of his election could be doubted—as in fact it was. Second, that the conduct of the elections was entrusted to Hildebrand by "the Roman people," meaning the ordinary population and not the nobility, suggesting the possibility of some undue influence in the form of money. Was it that the Pierleone banker foresaw difficulties for his man—perhaps in the form of an anti-Pope put up by the Imperialist faction? Perhaps. In any event, Hildebrand's description continues: "But then suddenly, while our lord was being carried to his burial in the church of Our Saviour, a great tumult and shouting of the people arose, and they rushed upon me like madmen, so that I might say with the prophet: 'I am come into deep waters where the floods overflow me. I am weary with my crying: my throat is dried' and also 'Fear and trembling are come upon me and darkness hath encompassed me about.' " [54] (Again note the use of Old Testament quotation, which fitted Hildebrand better than the mild sentences of the Sermon on the Mount. Just as he quoted the Old Testament in his first letter as Pope, so his last sentence, spoken shortly before his death was also from the Hebrew prophets.)

The official record of Hildebrand's election as Gregory VII mentions nothing of the crowds rushing "like madmen" described above. We are told in a document dated April 22, 1073, that "the cardinal clerics of the Holy Roman Catholic and Apostolic Church, acolytes, subdeacons, deacons and presbyters, in the presence of venerable bishops and abbots supported by their priests and monks, and amid the acclamations of vast crowds of both sexes and various ranks, assembled in the Church of St. Peter ad Vincula" to elect Hildebrand with dignity and due solemnity. They described Hildebrand, archdeacon of the church, as "a man of piety, eminent for learning both sacred and profane, famed for his love of justice and equity, strong in adversity, moderate in prosperity, and, according to the words of the Apostle, of good character, of pure life, modest, sober, chaste, given to hospitality, ruling well his own house, brought up and taught in noble fashion from childhood in the bosom of his Mother Church, and for his merits raised to the honor of the archdeaconate." It sounds like a nominating speech at a political convention, but it did express the convictions of the assembly.

"Do you agree?" they were asked.

"We agree."

"Do you desire him?"

"We desire him."

Again: "Do you approve of him?"

In unison and enthusiastically: "We approve of him." [55]

•

The election of the Pope was the prelude to great popular festivities. Prior to the election of Alexander II, the remarkably quick turnover of Popes, at times within mere months, had diminished the people's fascination with the traditional celebrations. But in the case of Hildebrand, nine years had elapsed since the accession of Alexander. Moreover, Hildebrand was a Roman and a member of a well-known, influential and wealthy family. His coronation would be a day of special splendor, community pride and, of equal importance to the rank and file, generosity. The enthronement took place on June 29, a rather hot summer day. (The actual election had taken place on April 22, but Hildebrand considered it wise to inform the Emperor, Henry IV, and permit him to send his representative.) The crowd was assembled in the square in front of St. Peter ad Vincula, where the formal elevation to the Holy See took place. Now they waited for the new Pope to emerge from the great church. The organ, which had but recently been recognized as the classical musical instrument of the Church (a relic from pagan Roman days, it was brought over from the Byzantine court), had played the last hymn. The chorus, still singing, appeared in front of the main gate. The clergy and the lay officers of the Curia followed. While the crowd cheered wildly, the Pope himself passed through the gate wearing the red robe with the episcopal mitre on his head. The group came to a halt on a platform high above the staircase as the chorus ended its chorale. The people, suddenly still, waited in awe and expectation as though frozen to the ground by the solemnity of the moment, holding their breaths and straining so as not to miss a single far-off action or word.

Three archbishops surrounded the Pope as his attendants: those of Ostia, Albano and Porto, as prescribed by an old tradition. The archdeacon then removed Hildebrand's mitre, and holding the pontifical tiara in both hands he pronounced the formula of coronation: "Take this tiara and know that thou art the father of princes and kings, the Master of the world, the Vicar on earth of Our Lord Jesus Christ, whose glory and honor thou art bound to guard for all eternity." He then placed the heavy and bejeweled tiara, a symbol of the heavy burden of the pontifical office, upon the head of the new Pope, and the procession formed for the long journey across the city to the Lateran Church, the "mother and head of all the churches in the world." It was the Church of the Lateran, Constantine's church, and not St. Peter's which was then considered the Papal church. In order for the Pope to be considered the duly and canonically elected Pontifex Maximus, he had to take possession of the Lateran Church and its adjacent palace.

The bearer of the golden cross now moved forward, followed by twelve men (known as *bandinarii*) carrying twelve Papal banners. Two riders, holding lances decorated with golden cherubins, and two prefects took their assigned places. The order of the procession was in accordance with long established custom, modeled after similar events in ancient, pagan Rome. First came the advocates of the Papal court, then the judges in their long black velvet robes, then the chorus which was to sing the liturgy prescribed for the occasion. The clergy was led by the deacons and subdeacons, the abbots from cities other than Rome, the bishops, the archbishops, and finally the abbots of the twenty abbeys of Rome. The Imperial Chancellor, Henry IV's official representative, and Henry's mother the Empress Agnes were also in the Papal entourage. The Pope was now being assisted onto a black horse decorated with the Papal tiara, its saddle adorned with precious stones, the leather of its reins crimson like the Papal robe. Its richly decorated bridle was held by the Prefect of Rome, this honor being reserved for the ruler of the city. The college of judges, the corporations of the city, and the heads of the noble families formed the rear guard of the cortege. As the elegant carriages of the nobles, each displaying the family's coat of arms and drawn by four horses, proceeded slowly forward, a coach bearing a golden lion on a purple ground was among them and was duly applauded. It was that of the Pierleoni of Trastevere, Hildebrand's kinfolk.

The city was brightly decorated for the occasion; colorful tapestries and banners hung from the houses of the rich, while the poor festooned garlands of wild flowers from their windows. The bells of the churches, of which there were some three hundred in Rome not counting the abbeys and basilicas, provided a tumultuous musical background. It was deafening at times but often drowned out by the yelling, screaming, cheering crowd which lined the streets, held in some semblance of order by the combined militia of Pope, city and nobles. Special arches bearing the names of the new Pontifex had been erected for the celebration, though they could compete only unsuccessfully with the grandeur of the arches of antiquity, those of Constantine and Titus, of Gratian, Theodosius and Valentine. The scene was made still more grand against the background of the aforementioned ruins of great Roman buildings, such as the Coliseum, the Baths of Caracalla and the ancient Theatre of Marcellus, and the five Imperial forums. There were also the fortified towers of the nobles, the windows and walls of which stared at one another in solemn hostility. The majestic architectural chaos of medieval Rome seemed like a mixed marriage of paganism and Christianity, with the gods and goddesses of Rome standing peacefully beside the statues of the saints of the Roman Catholic Church; this phenomenon was well symbolized in the church of St. Nicolas in Carcere, which was built into the ruins of the temples of Janus, Junon Sospita and Esperanca, using ancient Roman columns to hold up its roofs.

The procession moved at a slow pace toward the Lateran, which was so far away from Mons Vaticanus and St. Peter's that even today sightseers find it cumbersome to reach. On its way the procession stopped, as it had in the days of Baruch, for the traditional ceremony of the Jews' homage to the Pope. Again the rabbi and the elders stood on a platform decorated with symbols and flags. Again the Pope paused long enough to receive the Jew's assurance of loyalty and to hold the Scrolls of the Law which the rabbi presented. And again the Papal blessing for the ancient Jewish community of Rome was coupled with a sharp reprimand for their unyielding stubbornness in refusing to embrace the faith of the Church, a stiffneckedness for which their own Moses had taken them to task, no doubt the work of Satan himself. Nobody can doubt that Hildebrand repeated all these formulae, the blessings and the curses, unhesitatingly and even with conviction, knowing that his family in the old Ghetto of Trastevere had left the world of the Old Covenant and all the "superstitious and frivolous beliefs" of their former kin.

At five predetermined points the procession halted for the

rather mundane purpose of distributing money. (Rome was proverbially insatiable where money was concerned, and it was a well known medieval saying that if Rome could find a buyer, it would not hesitate to offer the city for sale.) At these points—St. Peter's basilica, the tower of Stephanus (where the procession had to come to a halt to receive the Jewish delegation), the place Cencii Muscae in Punga, St. Marcus and St. Hadrian on the Forum—the poor waited, having stood there for hours, pushing and cursing in the bawdy dialect of Rome's proletariat (the cockney of the time), the sick and the lame, the idlers and professional mendicants, prepared to do anything for ready cash. The Papal chamberlains were furnished with sufficient money, contributed mainly by the noble families so as not to burden the Papal treasury. The solemnity of the occasion was at these points abandoned in the mad scramble for money, shortly to be squandered in taverns and brothels which had been well prepared for the particularly profitable business on the occasion of a Papal coronation. These scramblings were worthy of Peter Breughel's caustic brush.

After what must have taken many hours, the procession arrived at the gigantic compound of secular and ecclesiastic buildings which is called the Lateran. There, on land which in ancient Rome belonged to the family of the Laterani, the Emperor Constantine had erected his great basilica. The church had once contained such treasures as the sacred ritual objects from the Temple in Jerusalem, which can be seen on the Arch of Titus—the seven-armed candelabra called Menorah, the golden trumpets of the priests, and vessels used in the sacrificial service. But these and other ancient treasures had long since been carried away by the Vandals, who in no wise realized what precious historical artifacts they had stolen in their one savage swoop on the city. Although Constantine's basilica formed the spiritual core of the complex and was its largest and most important church, many other buildings had been added through the centuries—chapel after chapel, monasteries, and hostels for the clerical and lay pilgrims who came by the thousands. When it became necessary to protect the holy places not only against the barbarians but against the warring factions of Rome, a fortified wall was erected around them; it has long since been reduced by earthquakes. Many of the early buildings have also been demolished, either by accident or design, notably during the Great Schism of the fourteenth century when the Popes moved to Avignon, and St. Peter's, Michelangelo's architectural monument, has since become the main church of Rome. Next to the Basilica (the Papal church) stood the Lateran Palace, the Papal residence. (The present Lateran Palace dates from the sixteenth century and is smaller than its predecessor.) The Pope was not considered canonically elected until he took possession of his property in a symbolical act of purchase which followed legal procedure laid down in the Roman law since the early days of the Papacy. It is this act of acquisition which now brought Gregory to the Lateran.

When the Papal procession reached the Piazza San Giovanni in Laterano, the riders dismounted and prepared to enter the great church. A multitude of curious onlookers, some of them still vainly hoping for handouts, ringed the periphery of the square as the invited guests began solemnly, albeit wearily, to climb the steps to the portico which contains Constantine's monument. There the Pope was ceremoniously seated on an ancient throne of Roman marble. The chorus, standing to the right, began to chant once more the liturgy of coronation. Then, as the Pope rose, the cardinals in unison intoned traditional blessings and a member of the Curia especially designated for this moment placed in the Pope's hand a small leather purse. The Pope opened it gravely and solemnly and held up for all to see three coins: one of gold, one of silver and a simple copper penny. Scattering these coins among those around him, he swore the oath of poverty: "Neither gold nor silver are mine. Whatever I possess I give to thee." (In the cases of Hildebrand and numerous other Popes—the Medici, for instance—this formality should not be taken literally; the personal fortunes of the Popes were not at all affected by the vow.)

Gregory now entered the church, where, seated on a throne placed on the altar for this occasion, he received the homage of the clergy. He then proceeded to the Chapel of St. Sylvester, dedicated to the Pope who had baptized Constantine the Great, and approached two magnificent chairs carved out of porphyry, identical in size and appearance. As he seated himself on the first, the prior of the church approached him in great solemnity, prostrated himself, and handed him the scepter of his pontifical office and the key to the Lateran. At this moment, Hildebrand formally seized the reins of government: he and he alone would rule over the realm of the Church—and even the world—from his Apostolic seat, the Holy See. Moving toward the second chair, he returned the symbols of power to the prior for safekeeping and was presented in turn with a red silk belt to which a purple purse was attached. The Pope arose and withdrew a handful of coins from the purse, scattering them among the assembled in a silent act of charity. The assembly rose as they watched the Pontiff descend the steps from the altar and enter the Chapel *Sancta Sanctorum*. This chapel, which pious Christians can enter only by gliding on their knees, contains the holy relics of the Apostles, stored in handwrought golden reliquaries, from which every worshipper expects healing for all the ills of his body and soul. Nobody stirred while the Pope knelt in the chapel, alone with his God and his thoughts for the first time, praying for strength to meet the coming struggles of the Church, struggles which he not only foresaw but had already planned and from which there was no escape. It was a long and fervent prayer. Then he rose and returned to the throne in St. Sylvester to permit the cardinals and prelates to pay homage to their Lord and Master, each of them kneeling and kissing the foot of the elected as prescribed by ecclesiastic custom. Each of them received as he rose the *presbetyrium*, a memento made of silver with the name of Gregory VII and the date of the coronation, June 29, 1073, engraved upon it. Presently it was the turn of the laiety, led by the Senate of Rome, to bow down and thus proclaim the majesty, the glory and the power of the new Pope.

Thus the ceremonies in the church came to an end and the gates to the palace were flung open. The Pope and the cardinals left through a small door leading into the Papal chambers for some moments of privacy and rest after their long ordeal, which had lasted for much of the day. The anticipated festivities were about to begin, and the large and illustrious crowd, relieved of the sobriety and reverence which had prevailed during the services and ceremonies, now milled about in the spacious anterooms until the banquet was announced. Then they joyfully entered the huge banquet hall, which was elegantly appointed in mixed styles dating from the fourth century. Much of Roman antiquity was still preserved here, as elsewhere in Rome: candelabra, tapestries, columns and much sculpture. Busts of Constantine were everywhere, remindful of the first great benefactor of Christendom. The hall had been rebuilt under Pope Leo III in the ninth century, but much of the earlier architecture and decor had been preserved. At the time of Gregory's coronation it still reflected the stern simplicity of the Romanesque world of kings and knights, Popes and saints. Many of the great Church councils took place in the Lateran church and palace, and some of the ecumenical pronouncements emanating from these halls were considered turning points in Church history. No one looking at the quiet elegance of the hall in 1073 could imagine that within a dozen years, Gregory was to be deposed in the Lateran and the hall itself would be sacked by the Normans.

No effort had been spared to heighten the dignity and splendor of the banquet. A famous icon of Christ, which was usually displayed at the altar, had been brought in for the occasion; it was said to possess the power of no other picture on earth, since according to legend it was not made by the hand of man. Long tables had been set up and adorned with golden plates, precious china, silverware and flowers; around them were seated the clergy, according to rank, then the noble families according to their status. As the Pope entered, everyone rose, and for a moment the pleasantries and small talk across the tables were interrupted. But when the Pope, who had replaced the formal, heavy robes of coronation with a light, white cassock, was seated, the conversation resumed and the meal was served. It was a heavy one consisting of many courses: various kinds of fish, roasted meats, all sorts of condiments, geese and chicken fried and stuffed with eggs, peppered game, trout cooked in ginger, and a variety of sweets as heavy as the main courses. The wines, which were not sufficiently cultivated at that time to be drunk alone, were mixed with some sweetener such as honey.

The Pontiff sat alone at a table far removed from those of his guests. Each course was brought to him by a nobleman, the honors having been distributed according to ancient etiquette, but as they served him not a single word was spoken. Course after course was presented at the Papal board, wine was poured, desserts and fruit were offered, but neither the Pope nor the nobles spoke. For sitting in utter isolation at his table, Gregory was meant to symbolize the awesome loneliness of the Pontifical office.

Hildebrand had adopted the name of Gregory in memory of his beloved master and relative John Gratian Pierleone—Gregory VI—whom he had escorted "beyond the Alps" and from whom he had inherited the large fortune which he administered with such care. For the cardinals had testified he was "moderate in prosperity." They had also noted he was "taught in noble fashion from childhood in the bosom of the Church," very likely referring to the fact that although he was a member of that noble family from Trastevere, he *was* born a Christian. At any rate, watching him as a Pope nobody could have doubted his deep Christian convictions and his passionate Christian zeal. Although he looked "more like a Jew or Saracen," his faith was unswervingly Christian. His remarks about the Jews betray no particular feelings for them. While his predecessor Alexander II had reprimanded Count Landulf of Benevento for his attempt to force Jews of his realm to convert to Christianity,[56] no similar document is known in Gregory's time. On the contrary, at the Roman Synod of 1078 he had the old warning repeated that Jews were not to be allowed to "rule over Christians." This prohibition was again expressed in a letter to King Alfonso VI of Castile, who was particularly lenient to his Jews: "But since we are bound not only to congratulate you upon the glories of your well-doing but sorrowfully to restrain you from unworthy actions," Gregory wrote in 1081, "we have to enjoin you no longer to permit Jews in your country to rule over Christians or have power over them. For to place Christians under Jews or to subject them to their jurisdiction—what is that but to oppress the Church of God, to exult the synagogue of Satan, and in aiming to please the enemies of Christ to throw contempt upon Christ himself?" [57]

•

At any rate, the Jews were not Gregory's main concern. His agenda had been prepared for decades: the cleansing of the Church and its Declaration of Independence. He addressed himself to the clerical Reform first. At his first synod, in 1074, he decreed that : 1) a cleric who had acquired his office by payment loses his office and parish, for ecclesiastic offices are not for sale; 2) a priest or bishop guilty of simony (purchase or sale of office) is herewith declared unworthy of his position; 3) a priest guilty of fornication loses his right to function in the Church; and 4) the people who avail themselves of the services of any priest guilty of any of these offenses are themselves guilty.

The decree met with disastrous consequences. In many churches the priests who in the performance of their duty read the decree to the people assembled for Sunday service were dragged from the pulpit and chased out into the street. The archbishop of Rouen, after reading the decree in his cathedral, was stoned by his own people. Henry IV did not react at all, but his clergy refused to read the decree. In England and Scandinavia the bishops were afraid to inform the people. In France the clergy at the Synod of Paris declared the Papal decree null and void and absurd. Simony and marriage had been part of Church life for such a long time that it seemed unrealistic to expect any radical changes. Furthermore, since the kings knew that the Pope's next step would be directed against them, they were loath to encourage their clergy to obey the Pontiff. The Church remained impure, and the dance around the Golden Calf was still the most widely observed ritual in Christendom. Religion, absolution and forgiveness could be bought, the cathedral was the marketplace, and its priests were the most eager hucksters; these customs were to survive until a renegade monk, Martin Luther, led a successful religious revolution against them. Celibacy was to prove equally difficult to impose upon the clergy, as we know from court claims for alimony in cases involving priests and bishops.

Failure evidently did not discourage Gregory, for he soon proceeded to his next step. He issued the most radical decree in Church history, the *Dictatus Papae*—the Papal Dictatorship. It was not merely a proclamation of independence, but a declaration of Papal superiority which derives its authority from God Himself. The style is arrogant, the content preposterous. Its consequences must have been fully known to Gregory. He had now publicly and irrevocably declared war. To modern man, who has become sensitive to any kind of dictatorship religious or political, it makes fantastic reading. Here (with my italics) is the full text:

> It is decreed:
> That the Roman Church was founded by God alone,
> That the Roman Pontiff alone can with right be called universal,
> That he alone can depose and reinstate bishops.
> That, in a council, his legate, even if a lower grade, is above all bishops, and can pass sentence of deposition against them;
> That the Pope may depose the absent;
> That, among other things, we ought not to remain in the same house with those excommunicated by him.
> That for him alone is it lawful, according to the needs of the time, to make new laws, to assemble together new congregations, to make an abbey of a canonry; and on the other hand, to divide a rich bishopric and unite poor ones.
> That he alone may use the Imperial insignia.
> That of the Pope alone *all princes shall kiss his feet.*
> That *his name alone* shall be spoken in churches.
> That *this is the only name in the world.*
> That it may be permitted to him *to depose emperors.*
> That he may be permitted to transfer bishops if need be.
> That he has the power to ordain a clerk of any church he may wish.
> That he who is ordained by him may preside over another church,

but may not hold a subordinate position; and that such a one may not receive a higher grade from any bishop.

That no synod shall be called a general synod without his order.

That no chapter and *no book shall be considered canonical without his authority*.

That a sentence passed by him may be retracted by no one; and that he himself, alone of all, may retract it.

That *he himself may be judged by no one*.

That no one shall dare to condemn one who appeals to the Apostolic Chair.

That to the latter should be referred the more important cases of every church.

That the *Roman Church has never erred; nor will it err to all eternity*, the Scripture bearing witness.

That the Roman Pontiff, if he has been canonically ordained, is undoubtedly made a saint by the merits of St. Peter; St. Ennodius, Bishop of Pavia, bearing witness, and many holy fathers agreeing with him. As is contained in the decrees of St. Symmachus, the Pope.

That, by his command consent, it may be lawful for subordinates to bring accusations.

That he may depose and reinstate bishops without assembling a synod.

That he who is not at peace with the Roman Church *shall not be considered Catholic*.

That he may *absolve subjects from their fealty to wicked men*.[58]

This decree, originally a Papal memorandum, was the prelude to the great medieval drama in which the German king, Henry IV, then thirty years old, and Gregory played the leading roles. Never before and never since had the Pope acted with such desperately aggressive courage, as though all were at stake—not merely the Papacy, but Christianity itself. In the course of his battle with the king, the Pope was obsessed with his role, to which he claimed to be inspired not by history, but by St. Peter, Christ and even God himself. If this was mere play acting, he overplayed the role badly—and, in the end, lost. But it was more than this. In his zeal for ecclesiastic power, he imagined himself as the rightful successor of those two great Old Testamentarian zealots who were not simply protagonists in the eternal battle between spiritual and secular power, but his great idols: Samuel and Elijah. Henry was Saul and Ahab, the kings against whom they had fought. Samuel the Prophet had demanded obedience from the king not in the name of an institution, but in the name of God, whose representative he was. Thus he took the sword in his own hand and killed in the name of God King Agag, whose life Saul had spared. But for all his fervor, even Samuel was too meek an example for Gregory to follow. He felt much closer to Elijah, the man of the desert, the raging Prophet, the disturber of complacency and peace, the avenger of God who was prepared to see hundreds of Baal's priests killed in that daring contest on Mount Carmel. So certain had he been of God's partnership that he could command fire to descend from heaven. This great ascetic of the Old Testament, this early exemplar of monastic living, became Gregory's ideal. No wonder his contemporaries called him "the holy Satan."

Gregory was indeed a man obsessed. His fury and passion seemed inconsistent with the small, frail figure of the man who sat almost lost in his high Papal throne. No picture of him has been preserved, no sculpture. On his tombstone in the Cathedral of Salerno there is no inscription, let alone one of those full-sized statues which can be found on so many Papal tombs. We know of an engraving which claims to be a portrait of Gregory, but it is hardly contemporary. The illustrations in the chronicles of Freising are even less convincing. Thus everything is left to our imaginations.

Needless to say, it may not be entirely accidental that a Pope so closely linked to the Pierleoni should have elected as his personal heroes figures from the Old Testament and that he should have emulated their examples so faithfully and so naturally. So real was his identification with the Prophets that he sometimes dared to foretell the future. During the Easter services in 1080, at the height of his war with Henry, he proclaimed solemnly that within a year's time Henry would be dead were he not to obey the Papal command, and should this prophecy not come true, he himself, Gregory, would cease to be the Pope. (Henry did not die, and Gregory did remain Pope.) Such rash prophecy would be impossible in a man who calculated political risks and moved prudently toward the defeat of his enemy. But there was nothing of that in Gregory. Writing to Henry "with the understanding that he obeys the Apostolic See as becomes a Christian king," Gregory expects "that the fear of God, in whose hand is all the might of kings and emperors, may impress this upon you more than any admonition of mine; bear in mind what happened to Saul after he had won victory by command of the Prophet, how he boasted of his triumph, scorning the Prophet's admonitions, and how he was rebuked by the Lord." [59] This was said to a king who had just won a smashing victory over his most formidable enemies, the Saxons, and was now ready to take on the Pope, a much more dangerous adversary.

The battle between Gregory and Henry divided all of Europe into hostile camps, providing a spectacle unparalleled in history. Two utterly unequal forces faced each other: on the one hand a mighty king, the commander-in-chief of a powerful army, by right and tradition the head of the Roman Empire of the German nation, a monarch whose ancestors had received their crowns and titles from the Popes; on the other, a man so meek and unassuming in appearance, armed with little more than the mystique of his office. This office, however, provided Gregory with a power greater than that of kings and armies: the power to bless and to curse. The battle was to be between sword and anathema. Nowhere in history has this battle been fought more dramatically. It held all of Christendom in suspense and forced aristocrats and simple folk, clergy and laity to side with either king or Pope.

●

The struggle began with an exchange of documents. The first, a letter of September, 1073, only a few months after Gregory's election, was written tongue-in-cheek by a young and as yet untested monarch pretending loyalty to a Pontiff whom in his heart he despised and was already preparing to confront: "To the most watchful and best beloved Lord, Pope Gregory, by divine will invested with the Apostolic dignity, Henry by the grace of God, King of the Romans, presents his due and faithful service. Kingdom and priesthood, if they are to be duly administered in Christ, need His continual support and, therefore, my beloved Lord and father, they must never be in dissension, but must inseparably cleave to each other in the bonds of Christ. For in this way and no other can the harmony of Christian unity and the institution of the Church be held in the bond of perfect love and peace. [This formulation of the Church-State relationship could not have satisfied Gregory, to whom both *sacerdotum* and *imperium* were in Papal hands, making the Church the superior force. But the next sentences of the young king were to convey a spirit of contrition and were bound—or calculated—to move the Pope.] Alas for me, guilty and unhappy that I am. Partly through the impulse of my youth, partly through deceitful advisers, I have sinned against heaven and before you with fraudulent disloyalty, and am no more worthy to be called your son. Not only have I encroached upon the property of the Church, but I have sold churches to unworthy persons, men poisoned with the gall of simony, men who entered not by the gate but by other ways, and I have not defended the churches as I ought to have done." [60] This full confession by a humble servant of the Church continues in asking for forgiveness and inviting the Pope's "fatherly support in all my interests." The tone was soon to change.

Two events accelerated the dramatic confrontation. In the spring of 1075 Gregory restated his principles against lay investiture at the second Synod in Rome and suspended three German bishops from the important Sees of Bamberg, Strassbourg and Speyer. These suspensions added new unrest and disaffection among the German clergy, who had never been too happy about Gregory's election. The king, so unsure of himself when he wrote Gregory in 1073, had since fought his victorious battle against the Saxons and no longer felt forced to placate the Pope. He now openly backed the bishops of Ravenna and Milan, who were eager to declare their independence from the Pope. In Rome he relied heavily on the nobleman Cencius, a leader of the pro-German party which bitterly opposed

Gregory, his Pierleoni and Frangipani supporters, and his plans for Papal supremacy.

A letter sent by Gregory to Henry formally opened the hostilities. "We warn you," he wrote at the beginning of December 1075, "with a father's love that you accept the rule of Christ, that you consider the peril of preferring your own honor to His, that you do not hamper by your own actions the freedom of that Church which He deigned to bind [to] himself as a bride by a divine union, but that she may increase as greatly as possible, you will begin to lend to Almighty God and to St. Peter, by whom also your own glory may merit increase, the aid of your valor by faithful devotion." The letter was delivered by three German legates. They were to inform the king that any act of disobedience would force the Pope to excommunicate him. Gregory's next response would be: anathema.

It was but a few weeks later, on Christmas Eve, that Gregory celebrated mass in Santa Maria Maggiore, according to the ancient Apostolic tradition that the Pope read Christmas mass in three churches in Rome. The church was filled with worshippers. The Pope knelt before the altar in preparation of the solemn occasion. As he was about to rise, there suddenly appeared a group of armed mercenaries. A few women screamed. The people turned, frightened and amazed, as the intruders proceeded swiftly toward the altar, where Gregory was still unaware of the sudden interruption. Within moments he was seized by the hair, his tiara having fallen to the ground, and dragged out of the church. That the intruders and their accomplices standing guard at strategic places in the church were in the pay of Cencius, everyone was aware, since they wore the coat of arms of the family. Making no apparent effort to hide the identity of those responsible for the conspiracy, they took Gregory directly to the towers of Cencius, where, bleeding profusely, he was subjected to humiliating treatment by Cencius himself, but more particularly by his sisters, who screamed obscenities and insults at the prisoner. Gregory, it is said, preserved his dignity by complete silence, bolstered by the knowledge that his family would know where to find him. Messengers had indeed been sent to the Casa Pierleoni, the Theatre of Marcellus and all the other Pierleoni towers, and soon a huge crowd of militia and townspeople, outraged by this sacrilege, moved toward the Cencius tower. With the help of machines and men, a breach was soon made, and the Pope was found in one of the rooms, surrounded by his tormentors. With the realization that his end had come and that the mob would soon cast him into the Tiber, Cencius fell upon his knees and asked Gregory for forgiveness. Gregory, who had suffered similar experiences prior to this one (and would again), quickly remembered his role as the protector of the weak, the compassionate forgiver of the penitent sinner. Hastily he moved between Cencius and the angry crowd and pronounced the Papal verdict of forgiveness for his persecutor, who knew not what he was doing. The penalty imposed upon him by the Pontifex Maximus of the Church, which should also be Cencius's church, would be a pilgrimage to Jerusalem. (I thought of this scene when, walking along the Tiber in Rome, I discovered that for a few blocks in front of the Ponte Fabricio, the entrance to Trastevere, the quay is called *Lungotevere dei Pierleoni*, while bordering on this monument to the memory of the Pierleoni for another two blocks or so the quay is called *Lungotevere dei Cenci*. The former enemies have thus become peaceful neighbors in the twentieth century.)

There is little doubt that the attempt to kill Gregory on that Christmas Eve was undertaken at the behest of Henry IV. An assassination of the Pope would have been the easiest way out of so many problems. But it was too easy to succeed. The Pope, still bleeding around his forehead, returned to Santa Maria Maggiore, where he was applauded wildly by the crowd which followed him. The church was filled to capacity with enthusiastic worshippers who marvelled at Prandellus, the great little Pope, ugly and swarthy and yet so impressive, as he stood at the altar on Christmas Eve of 1075, celebrating the mass as though nothing had happened, as though he were not in pain. It was an hour of dignity and victory. God had clearly demonstrated on whose side He was. It was He who had rebuked Cencius and Henry, and all those who would not obey. The prophet had been saved by God's will. The road he must follow was never clearer to Gregory than on that Christmas day. Gregory now recognized that his only logical, decent and dignified reply to Henry would be excommunication.

●

The anathema followed a few months later, in the "year of the Incarnation 1076" in the month of February. The synod was held "in the church of our Saviour which is called the Constantiana [that is, San Giovanni in Laterano], and a great number of bishops and abbots and clergy and laymen of various orders were present." As a preliminary, Siegfried of Mayence was excommunicated, he "who has attempted to cut off the bishops and abbots of Germany from the Holy Roman Church, their spiritual mother." Then came the great, fateful step, the first and only step of its kind in the history of Church and Papacy, when the might of the Church came down upon the powerful king of Germany. The text which follows is slightly abridged: "For the honor and defense of the Church, in the name of Almighty God, Father, Son and Holy Spirit, through thy power and authority, I deprive King Henry, son of the Emperor Henry, who has rebelled against thy Church with unheard of audacity, of the government over the whole kingdom of Germany and Italy, and I release all Christian men from the allegiance which they have sworn or may swear to him, and I forbid anyone to serve him as King. For it is fitting that he who seeks to diminish the glory of thy Church should lose the glory which he seems to have. And, since he has refused to obey as a Christian should . . . I bind him in the bonds of anathema in thy stead . . . that the nations may know that Thou art Peter and that upon thy rock the Son of the living God has built his Church and the gates of hell shall not prevail against it." [61]

The excommunication was not merely a response to the events on Christmas, but also a reaction to proceedings at Worms in which the king and twenty-four German bishops prevailed upon the Pope to abdicate. There is no more arrogant letter than that in which

Henry proclaims himself *"non usurpative, sed pia Dei ordinatione Rex"* (King not by usurpation but by God's ordination) to Hildebrand *"iam non apostolico, sed falso Monaco"* (no longer Pope but a false monk.) The letter continues: "You have deserved this salutation, you who stirred up unrest, you who instead of blessing continue to curse. Let me be brief: you have degraded archbishops, bishops and priests and made them into slaves without will. All of them you call ignorant, while you claim to be all-knowing. All this we tolerated out of respect for the Apostolic office. But you considered reverence, fear; you rose against the royal power, given to us by God, and threatened to withdraw it from us, as though rule and realm were not in the hands of God, but in yours. Christ has called us to the kingdom, but not you to the Papacy. You obtained it by cunning and fraud; despising your monkish garb, you obtained grace by money, and through it weapons, and with naked power have you gotten to the throne of peace from which you have destroyed peace. You arm the people to fight against authority and preach disdain for the bishops ordained by God. You permit even laymen to damn and depose them. You want to depose me, an innocent king who can only be judged by God, as the bishops left the judgement over Julian, the Apostate, to God. Does not St. Peter, the true Pope say: revere God and fear the King? Because you do not fear God, you try to dishonor me. St. Paul's anathema is meant for you. Condemned by all our bishops I say to you: descend from the Apostolic throne which you have usurped so that some one may occupy it who will not violate religion. I, Henry, by God's grace King, say to you in the name of all our bishops: descend, descend." [62] The letter, a unique document of insult addressed to the head of the Roman Church, was carried to Rome by Roland, a simple cleric who addressed the Council assembled at the Lateran Church in the following speech, the directness and impudence of which show that the king's messenger was a rather naive man: "My Lord and Master, the King, joined by the bishops beyond the Alps, commands you to descend from your throne immediately, for without the King's and bishops' consent nobody is permitted to occupy it. To you, my

164

brothers [addressing the clergy], I extend an invitation to appear before my Lord, the King, at Whitsuntide when he will give you a new Pope. For this one is not a Pope, but a raving wolf." The Cardinal of Portus called for an immediate arrest of the man; the Prefect of Rome drew his dagger and stormed toward the simpleton, who had evidently expected applause; but Gregory once again chose to save the offender's life. This incident took place at the same meeting in which Henry's excommunication had been proclaimed. The Empress Agnes, the king's mother, was present when the document was read. She listened respectfully and not a muscle in her face nor a tear in her eye betrayed for an instant that she had heard her own son's Papal condemnation.

The Council in Worms was indeed held at Whitsuntide, but instead of being the synod of a triumphant king it proved to be one of utter defeat. Henry was alone. The Papal decree of excommunication superseded his own. Clergy and nobility deserted him. Saxony found new allies, and the problem which Henry believed solved was very much alive again; Rudolf of Suabia was named anti-king, for Henry was not considered a fit ruler as long as he had not received the Pope's forgiveness. Furthermore, Gregory was invited to preside over a new council which would be held in the Bavarian city of Augsburg to examine the king's worthiness and, if he were found guilty, to name his successor. While the German princes met at Tribur, Henry was in Oppenheim, alone, desperate and almost a prisoner, deprived of power and glamor. He had ample time to muse about the fact that once at Sutri his father had sat in judgment over Hildebrand's kinsman, Gregory VI, and sent him into exile; now this very same Hildebrand, who had become Pope Gregory VII, had sat in judgment over King Henry and sent him into exile in his own country. Toynbee goes so far as to claim that Gregory's "nobler motives were allayed by a desire to exact vengeance from the Imperial power for the humiliation that it had inflicted on a degenerate Papacy at the Synod of Sutri in 1046. This last impression is strengthened by the fact that Hildebrand on assuming the Papal tiara took the name of Gregory which had previously been borne by the

Pope deposed on that occasion." [63] (If this were true, we would be dealing with a Pierleone embarking upon a vendetta for another Pierleone to whom he was deeply attached.) It was clear to Henry that he could not afford Gregory's meeting with the German nobles. There was only one way to prevent it: he had to meet Gregory first, not as a king demanding his rights, but as a repentant sinner asking for absolution from the sin of disobedience.

•

By this time, Gregory had gone to Lombardy to meet an escort which would accompany him to Germany. When the escort did not arrive, he decided to wait at a more suitable and friendly place, the fortified castle of his "beloved daughter in Christ," Matilda, the young countess of Tuscany, the richest, most powerful woman of the time. Matilda and her mother Beatrice, the widow of Boniface of Canossa, had inherited property which spread from the valley of the Po southward across the Apennines into the valley of Arno to the very border of the Papal States. In addition to these lands they had accumulated possessions in Lorraine and estates all over Italy. When Boniface died, his widow had married her cousin Godfrey, Duke of Upper Lorraine, and it seemed expedient (though to us it seems almost incestuous) that her beautiful twenty-three-year-old daughter should be married to her stepbrother Godfrey, who was a hunchback. The partners in marriage were unequal not merely in age and appearance, but in interests. Godfrey preferred Lorraine and German politics to home life and conjugal duties, and the couple remained childless. As a matter of fact they hardly saw each other. In time her husband and her mother died, and Matilda became the sole heiress of a vast fortune and enormous tracts of property. While her husband had chosen Henry and Germany as his political interest, she chose Gregory and the Papal Reform movement. There had, predictably, been rumors that the beautiful young Matilda and Gregory were united by something more than common interests and pious convictions, but there is little doubt that this was part of the vicious campaign against Gregory; few Popes have been so wickedly maligned during their lifetimes. Although Matilda was still young and childless, and therefore a woman with much love and passion to spare, there is not the slightest proof that anything but the purest motivations made her the great benefactor of the Papacy. (She was, incidentally, altogether unlucky in matters of love; at the age of forty-three she was persuaded to remarry, this time with a young Guelf, age seventeen, because it was politically expedient. The great novel about her still remains to be written. Only a great poet would be able to interpret the heart of this medieval woman, for documents, correspondence and clumsy portraits reveal little more than the significance of her role in Papal affairs and her complete devotion to Gregory.)

In her financial support of the Papal Reform, Matilda found herself in partnership and friendship with the Pierleoni, Gregory's family. "In all the aspersion of the anti-Gregorians concerning the Pope's financial dealings," writes the Jesuit Zema, "there may be said to be this kernel of truth: that the money of Pierleone, whether by way of gift or by way of banker's loans, was in time of need placed at the Pope's disposal, though our sources mention no specific sums." [64] So effective was the partnership of wealth and devotion between Matilda of Tuscany and the Pierleoni and so sacrificial were their donations to the Church that, as Zema notes, "the finances and influence of this convert family [the Pierleoni] contributed to the saving of the Reform in a decisive degree [and] were effective in turning the tide against every anti-Pope that raised his head in Rome during that period." The relationships were surely more than just financial: in the case of the Pierleoni the bonds were family ties, in that of Matilda they were those of genuine and abiding allegiance to a great man and a sacred cause. It was therefore natural that Gregory chose to sojourn at Matilda's Apennine stronghold at Canossa to await there the events which he could not have foreseen.

He arrived with a large entourage, among them Cencius Frangipani and Alberic Pierleoni, whom Matilda mentions in her will as Gregory's intimates. He found there waiting for him Hugh of

Cluny and Matilda's spiritual adviser and father confessor, Anselm, Bishop of Lucca. Matilda, young and radiant, completely behind Gregory, the militant Deborah of the Papacy ready to fight for the cause of Cluny which was now the cause of Rome, had watched Gregory's battle with more than casual interest. She had, in fact, attended the sessions of that great synod in 1074 at which Gregory announced his first clerical reforms. No doubt the discussions at Canossa turned immediately to the next step in the Battle of the Investitures, but these discussions were soon interrupted by dramatic news: Henry was journeying to Canossa. Although that month of January in 1077 was remembered as one of the most severe in the memory of contemporaries, Henry had taken the most difficult pass across the Alps, that of Mont Cenis. His queen and her young son had had to be sewn into fur hides and let glide across the glaciers, while the king himself and a small entourage of servants literally crawled across the formidable pass until they reached Italy. The pro-German noblemen and bishops of Italy had greeted the king jubilantly under the impression that he had come in a mood of defiance, ready to call them to battle against the Pope whom they hated even more now that anathema had been proclaimed against the king. Little did they know that Henry's mood was one of penitence. It must be noted that some historians view the famous surrender at Canossa —which in Bismarck's time became a political slogan against the French: "*Nach Canossa gehen wir nicht*"—with a more critical eye. These observers think the pilgrimage of the seemingly abject sinner, costume and all, was but a cleverly contrived masquerade meant to conceal a shrewdly calculated political move in the guise of humility and penitence. There is much to be said for this unsentimental interpretation.

At any rate, the king, with his wife, child and servants, did appear before the fortress of Canossa, a supposedly invincible stronghold surrounded not by one but by three walls, moats and all the other trappings of medieval defense. Henry requested admission not as a king, but as a sinner and suppliant. For three consecutive days beginning with the 25th of January, he stood penitently in front of the castle wall, wearing the woolen shirt of the sinner over his fur coat, his feet shod in simple sandals. (It is unlikely, as some romantic writers claim, that he should have remained there for three days and three nights wearing nothing but a shirt with his bare feet in the snow; in subzero temperature he surely would have frozen to death.) It was largely a symbolic act, but, nevertheless, the mighty king of Germany *was* standing out in the wintery cold, asking his Pope for forgiveness. If it was planned as a political chess game, the next move was up to the Pope, and that move was predetermined: whatever Gregory's personal emotions or suspicions, he had to yield. The Pope of the Christian Church must show mercy and forgiveness to the sinner, for who can look into a man's heart to prove his contrition insincere? That the king had to wait for three days proves that inside the castle there was hot debate. It appears that Matilda joined Hugh of Cluny and Anselm of Lucca in trying to persuade Gregory to yield; a twelfth century miniature portrait depicting the life of Matilda, which can be seen in the Vatican library, shows Henry asking Hugh and Matilda to intercede on his behalf, but whether this incident took place is unknown. On the fourth day, the 28th of January, Gregory succumbed and Henry was admitted into the castle, where he was received in the presence of the entire Papal company.

The scene has often been described. As the Pope entered, the king solemnly prostrated himself before him and lay there convulsed by constant and loud eruptions of tears as though his contrition were giving him tremors. In the sight of such evident subjugation, the Pope, it is said, was so moved that he too shed tears. But there was no embrace. (Efforts to compare the scene with the meeting of Jacob and his brother Esau, who had sought to kill him and met him at the river Jabok in that great Biblical scene of brotherly reunion, are absurd.) Gregory was now in complete control over himself and the situation, and, mindful of the historic importance of the meeting (it was less an encounter between two men than between two institutions), he asked the king to rise. The king stood before the diminutive Gregory—probably taller by more than a foot but nevertheless inferior in rank—now purely a petitioner and not a ruler. Gregory asked that a host, the consecrated wafer used in the Holy Communion, be brought to him. With a majestically defiant gesture, he took it, broke it in half and said: "Should the accusations flung against me, should but one of them be true, I pray that God may turn this wafer into poison, so that I may die." He placed the host slowly and solemnly into his mouth, inviting the divine judgement just as his idol, Elijah the Prophet, had once entered into a contest with the pagan priests. After he had swallowed the wafer and waited an appropriate moment for God to strike him down, those around him broke into jubilant applause, looking at him with admiration and pride—their Pope and master who defied the judgement of men and surrendered to no one but God himself. When the applause abated, Gregory took the other half of the wafer and handed it to Henry. To accept it would be to absolve the excommunication. That the king hesitated, as we are told, for a long while, tormented by the possibility of divine punishment, makes this whole episode such a typical medieval event. Even fifty years later, in the skeptical and rationalistic twelfth century, such a scene would probably no longer be possible, at least not among the upper classes; but in the eleventh the whole gamut of hell and damnation, so graphically represented in medieval paintings and sculptures depicting the horrible day of judgement, was still very real. The king swallowed the wafer. Nothing happened. The Pope had forgiven, and God evidently concurred in the act of atonement and absolution. There was no applause. Soon the king and his family departed from Canossa.

"When he left the castle," writes Gregorovius, "where he had left the dignity of his realm and the grandeur of his ancestors, he was like a man awakening from a nightmare. He was greeted with utter silence in Lombardy. The Lombards, still fully armed, turned away from him. The counts and the bishops turned their backs or received him coldly. The cities where the republican spirit was already growing refused him refuge and fed him grudgingly outside their walls. A wave of ill will had swept northern Italy. The king had betrayed his own crown. The people would have been prepared to join him in

fighting the common enemy had he not concluded such a humiliating peace treaty with him. It would, they thought, be better to depose Henry and elevate his young son Konrad as king in his stead, and march under his command to Rome, chase Gregory out, and elect a new Pope." [65]

The king had signed this declaration in Canossa: "I, Henry, king, within the term which our lord Pope Gregory shall fix, will either give satisfaction according to his decision, in regard to the discontent and discord for which the archbishops, bishops, dukes, counts and other princes of the kingdom of Germany are accusing me, or I will make an agreement according to his advice—unless some positive hindrance shall prevent him or myself—and when this is done I will be prepared to carry it out.

"If the same lord Pope Gregory shall desire to go beyond the mountains or elsewhere he shall be safe, so far as I and all who I can constrain are concerned, from all injury to life or limb and from capture, both he himself and all who are in his company or who are sent out by him or who may come to him from any place whatsoever—in coming, remaining or returning. Nor shall he with my consent suffer any hindrance contrary to his honor; and if anyone shall offer such hindrance, I will come to his assistance with all my power." [66]

After all the tears, the solemn kneeling and the praying, this seemed a rather sober and matter-of-fact declaration between two powers. The tone of contrition had disappeared. No wonder Canossa impressed the contemporaries much less than the historians and playwrights of the nineteenth century. After Henry's dramatic excommunication, it was an anticlimax.

Three fateful years now elapsed during which Gregory hesitated and Henry acted. Before he returned to Germany, Henry succeeded in mollifying the disappointed Lombards and making them once again his allies. The old anti-Gregorian groups in the nobility and clergy became active again; convinced by Henry that his oath in Canossa had been little more than a temporary accommodation and that he was still opposed to the Pope, their common hatred of Greg-

ory united them in a common goal. Henry returned home, every inch a king and not at all humiliated by the events. He made everybody understand that he was now free from the Papal ban and was prepared to build his realm. The situation was complicated by the fact that dissident nobles had succeeded in electing Rudolf of Suabia as king and now considered Henry deposed, but Henry decided to ignore them. Gregory's indecision during this, the weakest period of his life, could not last forever. He finally made his choice and recognized Rudolf, the anti-king. The battle had begun anew.

At the Roman Synod of March 1080, Henry was excommunicated for a second time. Gregory's long and strange document is an attempt to justify his actions as well as to interpret the events before and after Canossa. "In confusion and humiliation he came to me in Lombardy begging for release from his excommunication. And when I had witnessed his humiliation and after he had given many promises to reform his way of life, I restored him to communion only, but did not reinstate him in the royal power from which I had deposed him in a Roman synod." Then follows the usual formula of anathema, now grown stale by its repetition, and finally these threatening words: "And against the aforesaid Henry send forth your judgement so swiftly that all men may know that he falls and is overwhelmed, not by chance but by your power, and would that it were to repentence, that his soul be saved in the day of the Lord." [67]

Henry, the deposed and excommunicated king, did not fall, but Rudolf, the recognized and blessed anti-king, did. He succumbed in battle against the Saxons, bleeding to death. (The black skeleton of his handless arm, which he is supposed to have lifted as if swearing an oath, can be seen in the cathedral of Merseburg.) Gregory's curse had lost its power. Furthermore, Henry now named Wilbert of Ravenna, a man of vision and great learning, as anti-Pope. Everything, as a historian of the time remarked before Rudolf's death, was now double: two kings, two Popes, two sets of bishops. Henry, the excommunicated, was by this time ready to march across the Alps. His goals were Rome and the Papacy.

The next three years, which we are about to recount in all their horror, are among the most dramatic in history. The leading actors of the tragedy were Gregory, Henry, the Norman leader Robert Guiscard, and the faithful Matilda. Who, if any, were the victors is difficult to ascertain, for what developed after Henry crossed the Alps constitutes a great series of historic events in which, in a very real sense, everyone lost. Henry beleaguered Rome for three years but never conquered it. The city itself was put to the torch by the very Normans whom Gregory had summoned to rescue it; thousands of inhabitants died or were sold into slavery. What was left of Rome's ancient glory was in ruins, and the magnificent columns and ancient statuary which had graced her public squares were sold and sent to be used in buildings all over Europe. Gregory was held in protective custody by the Pierleoni in an ancient Roman fortress, a monument of the pagan world which the Popes had tried to defeat; sick of contemplating the sack and burning of his beloved Rome, he was to die in exile not long afterwards. There was death, destruction, frustration, betrayal by both friend and foe, bitter disappointment for all. In the end, the Imperial crown was placed on the head of the emperor, but it was made of paper; for the superiority of secular power had come to an end. Although the Pope may not have won the battle, the Papacy did.

The tragedy began when Henry arrived with his army—a sizable army, but not one large enough to win. His military and political support came, as always, from anti-Gregorian Lombardy, where his candidate for the Papacy, Wilbert, was formally proclaimed Pope Clement III. Such a proclamation, naturally, had no canonical validity whatsoever and was in clear violation of the election act of 1059. How the enemies of Gregory could have had the audacity to accuse him of illegal election maneuvers, and at the same time simply proclaim a man Pope without the approval of the College of Cardinals, is totally perplexing; it is no surprise that Clement remained very much Henry's private Pope. It is noteworthy that when Gregory VI had abdicated, his successor, who was presented to the Romans by Henry III, was also named Clement, an indication that Henry IV was endeavoring to identify his role with that of his much-respected father, just as Gregory VII was always associated with Gregory VI.

The Romans, aware that the German army would soon approach, were preparing for battle; the Leonine City provided the defenders with their stronghold and was to prove of great value. Gregory, as we have suggested, was by this time leaning heavily on the Normans as his allies. (He had even permitted William the Conquerer to carry the Papal flag into England.) But Robert Guiscard, the Norman leader who had once captured Leo IX at Civitella, was off on an adventure in Greece and was able to send only small detachments to join the Roman militia and the Tuscan defenders supplied by Matilda to help man the ramparts of Rome. The fortified places of the nobles were bristling with private armies; the Frangipani and the Cenci (now loyal to the Pope) were particularly important among these, as, of course, were the Pierleoni, who were so heavily entrenched in Trastevere that they never yielded it to the enemy. Henry, realizing the military strength of the defense and the tenacious loyalty which the Romans now gave to Gregory, did not yet dare attack the city; his own party in Rome, once powerful enough to kidnap the Pope, was now leaderless and substantially weakened. (Cencius had since died, or, as his enemies commented, gone to hell.) So Henry set up his court outside the walls of Rome, where his parades, processions and assemblies, in which the shadow-Pope Clement played the part of holy comedian, provided much-needed entertainment for the Roman soldiery watching from the parapets.

After forty days of utterly futile siege, Henry withdrew to Tuscany, where Lucca, Pisa and Siena became so impressed with the Imperial glamor that they joined his camp. Florence remained loyal to Matilda, whose fortresses, scattered all over the north, proved then as later to be more than annoying to Henry. The campaign against Rome was resumed in the spring of 1082, but was equally unrewarding. Gregory was in full control of Rome, and although Henry's soldiers plundered and pillaged the countryside around the capital, the city itself remained untouched. Matilda continued, meanwhile, to prove herself an irritating adversary as she incited various little wars from her fortresses. Seven months of renewed siege on Rome followed without any success.

It is true that the Romans began to murmur, and the only cure for such popular unrest was, as always, money. The Normans had sent money in lieu of much needed military help. Matilda melted down the vessels and plates of gold and silver which adorned her chapels and sent the precious metal to her friend. And of course the Pierleoni, Gregory's own family, also helped in large measure. For the time being, a popular riot was averted, and there was as yet no disaffection on the part of the noble families. In the month of June, however, Henry had a partial, but not unimportant, victory: he conquered the Leonine City. Gregory held out in St. Peter's, but this became much too dangerous, and his family insisted that he establish himself for the duration of the siege (for everybody was convinced that the Normans under Robert Guiscard would eventually come) in the family's prize possession, Hadrian's vast mausoleum, the invincible fortress of Rome, the Castel Sant'Angelo. Whether the family had purchased this building outright or whether it had come into their ownership by some other means is not known. They certainly did not have possession of it for the same length of time as their other great fortress, the Theatre of Marcellus, which remained in family hands for three hundred years, but that they owned it at the time when it was most needed is well documented.[68] The fortress was so huge that the entire Papal bureaucracy could be installed in but a part of the building. As a matter of fact, Gregory continued to govern the Church from Sant'Angelo.

The Pope's transfer from St. Peter's soon proved sound, for shortly afterwards the ancient basilica was taken by Henry. "Thus Henry entered St. Peter," observes Gregorovius, who writes about this period with great emotion and partisanship, "after long and futile attempts while his terrible enemy was hiding in Sant'Angelo, looking through the ramparts and watching the former penitent sinner of Canossa, surrounded by knights, bishops and Roman nobles, escorted by his anti-Pope, walking over the smouldering ruins toward the cathedral of St. Peter. The sound of Te Deum might have soothed him a bit. Revenge was sweet, but it did not satisfy him fully. His Pope, he knew, was a puppet (albeit a useful one for the present), not yet ordained and rightfully elected; his much coveted Imperial crown was not yet on his head. . . . He still hoped that some day the great Gregory might crown him." [69]

The coexistence of war and Papal business must have presented a strange contrast in Sant'Angelo. The castle had been built with such great skill and excellent craftsmanship that even today it seems to be practically untouched and, indeed, untouchable. The walls are of such thickness that they could withstand any kind of attack, and certainly by the standards of medieval warfare the invincibility of the building was no mere legend. There is a secret subterranean tunnel between Sant'Angelo and St. Peter's which had been excavated for the very sort of situation in which Gregory found himself. If it was in existence in the eleventh century (I have found no proof either way), it served the good purpose of maintaining contact and transferring valuables, ritual objects and manuscripts even during a siege by an enemy just a few hundred feet from the church. Since it was kept secret, it might even have been used after Henry had already breached the wall. At any rate, the castle was fully equipped for the Pope to attend to his daily business of praying and governing. When one walks today through the almost endless number of dark, vaulted rooms and halls, which now house a museum, one cannot help but try to visualize how it must have looked when it served as a combination of Papal church and secretariat. No doubt some of the altars had been transported from St. Peter's, along with paintings, statues, handsomely carved Romanesque reading stands, books and liturgic manuscripts finely written and beautifully illumined by the monks of Monte Cassino. In one of the halls, which had become the Papal chapel, Gregory celebrated the mass every day at certain hours for the clergy and nobility and at other times for the militia men who attended church, probably unwillingly, dressed in their makeshift uniforms, bows and arrows always ready in the event of an attack. There was probably a chorus to intone the sacred songs (which often had to compete with the rough and coarse voices of the soldiers outside and in the hallways.) Today one can sit in a little cafe high up on the roof and look down on the vast and inspiring panorama of Rome, with St. Peter's in the background. (Michelangelo's church, of course; the church was much less imposing in the Middle Ages, nor did it then boast Bernini's magnificent colonnade.) One is reminded of Gregory watching the city from the same point, peering anxiously at the Germans and Lombards whose heads were visible as they stood guard on the walls around the Leonine City and later, when the breach was made, walking through the streets across the Tiber, not more than a stone's throw away. But no stone was thrown, no arrow struck the fortress prison. One can almost envisage Gregory staring out into the distant plains encircling Rome, anxiously awaiting a sign of the approaching Normans who were his only hope, and who would surely come to his rescue as soon as Guiscard had settled his Greek affairs. He who was once the enemy of the Popes was now Gregory's great and mighty ally.

It was from this fortress prison that Gregory penned some of his most appealing letters. Written in anguish, they reveal more of the man than those from his days of undisputed power. His enemies and those who did not know him often spoke of his stubbornness, but it was his fortitude of faith and dedication of purpose that made him so unbending. Much of the manliness and courage which remained his characteristics until the very end are in evidence in these letters. Gregory knew that he was writing history. The following example, undated but belonging to the period of the siege of Rome, is addressed to "all loyal subjects of the Apostolic See."

"We are sure, beloved brethren, that you sympathize with our sufferings and trials and that you bear us in mind in your prayers to God. Nor can you have any doubts that we have the same mind toward you—and with good reason; for the Apostle says: 'If one member suffers, the other members suffer with it.' We desire one thing: that Holy Church, now trampled upon and in confusion and divided into parties, may return to its former splendor and unity. . . . Be not surprised, beloved brethren, if the world hates you; for we ourselves provoke the world against us by opposing its desires and condemning its works. What wonder if princes and mighty ones of this world hate us, Christ's poor, when we resist their evil doing, and rage against them with a certain indignation. . . . And yet, up to the present time, very few of us have withstood the wicked to blood. . . . Consider, beloved, consider how many soldiers of this world, enlisted for filthy lucre, give their lives daily for their lords. And we, what do we do or suffer for the Supreme King and for our eternal glory? Lift up your hearts then with strength; keep your hope alive, having before your eyes the banner of our leader, the King Eternal, with his device: 'In patience possess your souls.' " [70]

It was with the man who could write such a letter in times of hopeless distress that the nobles of Rome now began to negotiate. Cencius Frangipani, Gregory's childhood friend, and Alberic Pierleoni, his kinsman, headed the delegations that ventured back and forth to find some peaceful solution by which the dignity of the Pope, the prestige of the king and Rome itself could be saved. It is understood that Henry was willing to accept a compromise provided his coronation would take place with the participation of the rightful Pope. He was not pressing for a formal acknowledgement of the anti-Pope; he would, he said, be fully satisfied if Gregory, from a window inside the castle, were to hand him the crown on a long stick. The noblemen, on their part, were only too much aware of the mood of the people, the dwindling supplies of food, the general stagnation and demoralization of the population, and the high cost of maintaining the armies and bribing the mob; neither Matilda's nor the Pierleoni's treasuries were inexhaustible. With these considerations in mind they went to Gregory. But they found an unyielding man. Now at the end of his days (for he already felt the effects of exhaustion), he was not of a mind to sell out to the enemy whom he had pursued all his life, thus abandoning the principles of the *Dictatus Papae*, in which he intended to prove to the world that it is the

Pope before whom the princes must bow in homage. Gregory believed that for the Pope, the reincarnation of the Apostle Peter and the Vicar of Christ, to compromise with the German king under the threat of arms would be a betrayal of the Apostle, if not of Christ himself, and no worldly argument could shake his determination to persevere. The nobles departed downhearted, for they knew only too well that even if *they* could understand and respect the Pope's motivation, the man in the street would not. And the whole resistance of Rome depended not upon the nobles or even the militia but, ultimately, the people. A civil war would be catastrophe.

Meanwhile, Henry, disappointed with his limited military success and the complete failure of his negotiations, left Rome in the hands of but four hundred soldiers and headed for Canossa. Just as Gregory had applied pressures on Henry at Canossa, now Henry would do the same with Matilda. The latter had become the general of the armies spread over the north, harassing Henry and sending help and encouragement to her friend Gregory, more like an Amazon now than a Biblical heroine. All her energies, passions and resources were channeled into one purpose: the defeat of Henry and the re-establishment of Gregorian power. Under pressure from every side, she had waivered momentarily, but after regaining her strength in prayer and meditation she acted like a fury who had committed herself and everything she possessed to her single goal of victory.

Henry returned to Rome at Christmas of 1083. There he discovered that although most of his soldiers had died of fever and Gregory was still unbending, the situation had changed decidedly. In the minds of the Romans, it was no longer Henry who caused them hunger and deprivation, the long hours of watch and the disruption of their normal lives, but Gregory alone. For who among the ordinary people could imagine the Pope as anyone but a stubborn old man who cared little for the populace, but only for himself. High-minded and complex arguments, historical considerations and the long range planning of the Church were of little concern to them. Hunger was a more tangible argument. And so the Roman rabble opened the gates of their city (at least those to which they had easy access) and Henry and his army marched in. By the 21st of March, all of Rome, or at least the most significant parts of it, were in Henry's hands. Gregory was in Sant'Angelo and the Pierleoni held the left bank, but everything else belonged to the Germans. On Palm Sunday Henry called a "Parliament of the Romans" to which the nobles and the clergy were invited. Gregory, who of course did not appear, was summarily declared deposed as Pontiff, and Clement III was declared the rightful Pope. Although such a declaration meant nothing in the canonic law, it was sufficient for Henry, and on Easter Sunday his supporters assembled in St. Peter's (with Gregory probably watching from the turrets of the castle) and Henry and Queen Berta were crowned by Clement as Emperor and Empress of the Holy Roman Empire.

Just a few weeks later, on May 24th, Roman watchmen observed some strange movements down in the valleys: helmets and spears were visible in the distance, glimmering brightly in the sun, rolling like waves endlessly and relentlessly against the shore. Soon the plains were covered with soldiers on horseback and on foot. The Normans had arrived: Guiscard, his young son Roger and a huge army of six thousand cavalry and thirty thousand foot soldiers. They all were under Norman command but they hailed from many parts of the world. Most of them were Saracens from Sicily and Arabs from every corner of the Moslem world, a huge motley crowd, well-armed, hungry, hell-bent, undisciplined and very eager to take Rome. Henry, knowing his weakness and now wearing the long-desired crown, still not victorious but also not entirely dissatisfied, beat a quick retreat northward with his little army. Guiscard, now the great liberator, entered the city and proceeded to Sant'Angelo, where the Pope embraced and kissed him, a sentimental but strange scene if we think of Leo IX at Civitella. Nevertheless, Rome would now be free. The Papacy had found a powerful protector in whose presence even the German king trembled. Guiscard represented the power of tomorrow: his kinsmen had conquered England and his Empire was the new political phenomenon in medieval life. Such a man had come to liberate the Pope, and with him the Church. After many months and years in virtual captivity, it felt good to be free again, and the procession to the Lateran was a demonstration of victory and even triumph. As Gregory knelt down in the *Sanctum Sanctorum* of the great church, as he celebrated the mass, he gave thanks to God in the most personal prayer of gratitude. The Church was no longer in chains.

Unfortunately, Gregory was wrong. The first contacts of the Romans with the Normans were as bearable as relations with a foreign army can be, but it took only a few days for Rome to discover it was dealing with savages. Rape, murder, arson, robbery and every conceivable act of brutality had been committed, and the patience of the Romans came to an end. At first the Normans and the Romans were involved only in ordinary tavern and street brawls, but soon battle weapons were put into use. There was no doubt who would be the victors. The losers were, of course, the people; as I have noted, thousands died needlessly and helplessly in the streets, while thousands of others, the members of noble families among them, were sold into slavery. Rome burnt fiercely. Buildings, walls, villas and gardens either went up in flames or were wantonly torn down. Homes were ransacked, women violated, ancient and Christian monuments reduced to piles of rubble. Later poets who remembered the destruction described the debris of Rome in moving lamentations. To add insult to the carnage, Mohammedan soldiers penetrated the Church of St. Peter, and for the first time in history the prayers of Islam were chanted like a chorus of victory (to the Romans it sounded like a dirge of mourning and shame) in the sacred halls of Christendom.

Just as Jerusalem, which Gregory had been planning a crusade to liberate, lay in the hands of the Turks, so was Rome, the Jerusalem of Christianity, reduced to wasteful ruin by the heathens. No word has been handed down, not even in the letters of his loyal friend Matilda, to describe Gregory's thoughts and emotions as he surveyed the city in which he had spent his youth, labored for the Church long before he was elected Pope, and finally reigned over the people he knew and loved. Rome was empty and void; Rome was desecrated. The Norman army had mustered its men and left. Smoke rose from many buildings. Thousands lay unburied, and the stench of death hovered over the town. There was nothing but desolation, destruction and human misery as far as the eye could behold. Gregory became a stranger in the town of his childhood, isolated, hated and despised by the people. It was no longer Henry whom he had to fear, but his own subjects. Apparently realizing that it would be safer for him under Guiscard's protection, he set himself up in a palace in Salerno. Guiscard eventually left him, however, and died soon after while occupied in his old plans against Constantinople. Gregory lived on for a while and continued to govern the Church. He even called a new synod to be held in Salerno. But, however unbroken he was in mind and determination, his body was too weak to leave its sickbed. On the 25th of May, 1085, at the age of sixty-three, he died. It is said that his last thought was devoted to this concept which he had repeated frequently throughout his life: "I have loved justice and hated iniquity," he said, "therefore I die in exile." It was a paraphrase of an Old Testamentarian psalm. He lies buried under the altar of the cathedral of Salerno.

●

Although Gregory had named four bishops as possible successors, it took more than a year before the new Pope was elected. The final choice was sound by every possible consideration, but the candidate was and remained reluctant to assume the Papal office and to exercise any power. He was rich, pious, monastic and scholarly. He had been cardinal of Santa Celia in Trastevere, Gregory's home district, but his love and devotion belonged to the monastery of Monte Cassino. Nevertheless, Desiderius of Monte Cassino, as he was called, was proclaimed Pope in the late spring of 1086 as Victor III (1086–87). To a man of greater energy or ambition, the demands facing the Papacy at that point might have seemed challenging. Victor found them only discouraging and even appalling. Again and again when problems of the Curia seemed to overwhelm him, he simply retired to Monte Cassino.

Rome was now practically dominated by the Imperialists. Although the administration of the city was firmly in the hands of a Frangipane-Pierleone coalition (we find both names on several contemporary documents), St. Peter's was in the hands of their enemies and even Castel Sant'Angelo had to be abandoned by the Pierleoni. Henry's anti-Pope, Clement III, who at first seemed so insignificant, was not merely in possession of St. Peter's and the Lateran, but was recognized by many countries, including Hungary and England. Henry IV, who at first appeared to have recovered from his constant battles with Gregory and his domestic enemies, was soon to be faced with a tragic struggle with Konrad, his oldest son, who later forced him to abdicate and had himself proclaimed King of the Lombards.

This situation, unpleasant for the Curia and the Reform party, made the island in the Tiber more valuable and the Pierleoni an even greater power than previously. Their loyalty to the legitimate Papacy remained unabated. Their possession of Trastevere and the island now proved indispensable. Since the legitimate Popes could not live in St. Peter's, they stayed with the Pierleoni in the tower which can still be seen today. The island, interestingly, has retained its Jewish flavor. Where the Pierleoni had their stronghold, a hospital for the Jewish poor is now maintained by the Jewish community of Rome; its sign reads "*Ospedale Israelitico e Ricovero Israeliti Poveri Invalidi.*" There also on the island stands the medieval tower which is presently known as the tower of Matilda of Tuscany. Its rooms are inhabited by poor Roman families, but the tower itself, tall and impressive, commanding a view of the left bank of the Tiber and the whole of Trastevere, is still, after eight hundred years, in good repair. It was here that the Pierleoni played hosts to the Popes who succeeded Gregory, their kinsman.

Victor, the reluctant Pope, died in 1087, and the second name on Gregory's list of desirable successors was chosen. He was Otto of

Ostia, who took the name of Urban II (1088–99). His choice was to prove of enormous historic importance. In view of the chaotic situation in Rome, Urban's election took place in the outlying town of Terracina, but it was canonical in every respect; the new regulations for Papal elections were scrupulously observed, with forty cardinals, bishops and abbots forming the Collegium. Although Urban and Gregory had been lifelong friends (and there can be no doubt of Urban's closest relationship with the Pierleoni), the two men were strikingly dissimilar in background and character. Gregory's alleged rustic nature is said by some to reflect peasant origins, although it seems to us that his stubbornness, his lack of diplomacy, his onesidedness and his uncompromising battles with the Emperor need not be the traits of a peasant; to us they are the characteristics of an Old Testamentarian prophet—and Isaiah cannot possibly be called a peasant. Otto, who despite his Germanic name was born to a noble French family in Chatillon (not far from Rheims), was wealthy, well-educated, refined, cosmopolitan and handsome. Gregory, small and ugly, impulsive, sputtering forth his abrupt sentences of condemnation and curses, contrasted with the tall and imposing Urban, who by his very appearance dominated the people with whom he came in contact. In his dealings with bishops and royalty, Urban used the most refined manners and language, winning them over by persuasion rather than force. Yet he did not compromise on principle, however conciliatory his language. A former prior of Cluny, he was a man whose convictions were as strong and unbending as those of Gregory, whose disciple he was. In communicating with the masses he used a talent which few Popes possessed: he was an impassioned, fascinating preacher. His sermons were not in the spirit of Peter Damian's exhortations or, much later, Savonarola's; instead his rhetoric was as elegant as his appearance, and his eloquence (probably unparalleled in the Papacy) was greatly helped by his voice, a deep baritone which carried his burning message to the last pew of the cathedral. It was his ability as a speaker as much as his message which was to make history.

By the time of Urban's ascendancy, the situation in Rome and

Germany had become even more confused than earlier. Henry IV, betrayed by his son, had entered into a new marriage with the Russian princess Adelaide. When the marriage proved unsuccessful, Adelaide fled to Matilda, to whom she revealed the most scandalous intimate stories, some even hinting that she might have had an affair with her stepson. Henry, forsaken and isolated, a prisoner of his son, tried to commit suicide. Rome remained in the hands of Clement III, the anti-Pope, until at long last the Lateran was conquered by the Reform party—"by the use of money rather than arms"—and Urban took over his official residence. But Clement was not Urban's greatest problem. Christianity was by this time hopelessly fragmentized, and diplomatic skill, Urban realized, would not be enough to reunite it. Something dramatic was required to engage Christendom in a global undertaking that would give it a common goal. When Clement died, Urban, now the unchallenged Papal sovereign, acted on Matilda's advice and called a Council in Piacenza, the city where Henry III had received Gregory VI before he was deposed. It was an unexpected success. Urban immediately announced that he would call an extraordinary session to be held in Clermont at which he would proclaim to all of Christendom a plan, yet secret, his own great design for Christian unity. After such a dramatic announcement, it is small wonder that the large cathedral in Clermont proved too small when two hundred and five bishops, thirteen archbishops, numerous royalty and noblemen and thousands of the faithful assembled. Although it was a cold November day, the throng moved to a field outside the eastern gate of the city, where they huddled together for protection against the wintery weather. Then the great moment came.

Urban, tall and handsome, mounted the platform and delivered his startling oration. The text, alas, has not been fully preserved, but from the reports which have been transmitted through various sources, we know that he called for an end to fratricide in Christendom. "Rise," he began, "turn your weapons now used against your brothers against your enemies, the enemies of Christianity. You oppress orphans and widows, you indulge in murder and rape, you rob your own people on the highways of your country, you accept bribes to kill your fellow Christians and unashamedly shed their blood. You are like carrion birds attracted by the stench of human corpses, victims of your greed. Rise then, no longer against your fellow Christians, but against your enemies who have taken the holy city of Jerusalem. Fight under the banner of Christ, your only commander-in-chief. All of you, guilty of every possible crime, redeem yourselves. *Deus le volt:* God wills it." [71] *Deus le volt* was now repeated by thousands of voices, and the aged Adhemar de Monteuil, Bishop of Le Puy, stepped forward, knelt before the Pope and received his blessing to lead the great Christian movement. Thus began the First Crusade, a movement which gave Christendom a new goal, dangerous in many respects, rarely maintaining the high spiritual level of Clermont, appealing to the basest instincts of lust, robbery, greed, land hunger and political and military ambitions, but also exciting the true religious passions of many a believer.

●

Although the Crusaders were pledged to fight the Moslems in the Holy Land, some found a more immediate target in their own towns: the Jews. Characteristically, massacres of Jews were restricted to Germany; neither in France, Italy nor Byzant did Jews suffer. It was left to three German contingents under Emich of Leisingen, Volckmar and Gottschalk to murder thousands of Jews "under the banner of Christ." [72] For centuries to come, the bloodbath remained unforgotten by the Jewish people; many of the prayers and *piyutim* of the High Holidays remember this great collective nightmare, and the stories of martyrdom, heroism, desperation and bloodshed are repeated even in our own days when the Jewish people assemble for those solemn Days of Awe. It must be said that Henry IV, who had proven his friendship for his Jewish subjects before the Crusades, sent warnings to his vassals to prevent the bloodshed which he anticipated. They were in vain, as also were the warnings of the Jews of Rouen, who sent messengers to their brethren in the Rhineland. There was little that could be done. The fury of the holy hordes soon descended upon the ancient Jewish communities. Their only defense was the hope that bribes could avert the catastrophe: the Jews sent five hundred pieces of silver to Godfrey of Bouillon, a prominent military leader; the bribe was accepted but, then as later, the money was spent to no avail.

The prelude to the Crusade in Germany was an attack on the Jews of Speyer on May 3, 1096. The bishop of the city (again accepting large sums of money) decided to protect "his" Jews in his episcopal residence, but not all of them had time to reach the refuge and many were ambushed on their way to their protector; since they steadfastly refused conversion, all of them were massacred. A Jewess, assaulted by pious Crusaders who wore the Cross on their coat-of-mail committed suicide to protect her virtue. On May 18th the German Crusade moved to Worms, where the Jewish community (whose Romanesque synagogue was built in 1036 and survived until Hitler's crusaders razed it in 1938) was accused of having poisoned the wells. Hundreds were murdered; five hundred fled to the bishop's palace, but their hopes vanished when the gates of the palace were forced opened, and all of them died miserably. Five days later (onward Christian soldiers) these disciples of Christ, the Prince of Peace, reached Mayence, where Bishop Rothard ordered the closing of the city gates. A Jewish delegation appealed to the Crusaders, paying seven pounds of gold to Emich; it was accepted as usual. Promises of asylum were made and broken. The good burghers of Mayence opened the gates from inside the city, but the Jews, trembling in the bishop's palace, were certain of the bishop's promise of protection. When the Crusaders set fire to the palace, however, the good bishop fled, leaving the Jews to the Crusaders' "mercy." All of them, more than a thousand, perished. Rabbi Kalonymos of Mayence, knife in hand, had made a brave and daring attempt to force the bishop to adhere to his solemn oath of custody, but, needless to say, he died with his people. Not a single person converted for the reason of escaping death. When the murderers moved on to Cologne, where the Jews had erected their first synagogue in 324, no

Jews could be found; they had taken refuge in homes in villages surrounding Cologne, where good Christians offered them safe shelter.

The recitation of the exploits which followed begins to sound monotonous. In Trier, on June 1st, Emich's band drove the Jews into the river; in Metz they murdered all of them. From June 24th to June 27th they spent their time in the land of the Moselle. All the Jews of Neuss, Eller, Xanten and Wevelingshofen were exterminated. Volckmar, the second German leader, had marched to Prague —one of the oldest and noblest Jewish communities, where the medieval Alt-Neuschul (part Romanesque and part Gothic) and the ancient cemetery still exist—and massacred all the Jews. Gottschalk, the third of the heroes, slaughtered them in Ratisbon in the meantime.

Fortunately, all three German contingents were soon to meet their masters. Pillaging, robbing and raping their way along the road to Constantinople, where they were to assemble with the Crusaders from other countries for the journey to Palestine, they marched into the plains of Hungary hoping for new bloodbaths among the Jewish communities. Heretofore they had never encountered resistance, either from Jews or Christians. But when Gottschalk, the first to arrive, reached Hungary, he and his men were met by well-armed burghers and not a single Crusader escaped death. Emich came next; he too died with all his men. "The collapse of Emich's crusade deeply impressed western Christendom. To most good Christians it appeared as a punishment meted out from on high to the murderers of the Jews." [73]

In spite of the German debacle, the main force of Crusaders succeeded in taking Jerusalem and occupying Palestine. (Jews died there too, but they died heroically in battle as the tenacious defenders of Haifa and as combatants in the Holy City.) Thus the First Crusade came to a successful conclusion. It took several months, communication being what it was in those days, for news of the victory to reach Urban in Rome, and even then it was not received as joyously as we might expect. For Rome was not intimately involved in the Crusades; there were no knights in the city, and the population remained aloof from such secular events. The Jewish community there was in no way affected by the happenings. Furthermore, Urban, who had begun the Crusade in Clermont remembering that his great master Gregory had once dreamed of such an enterprise, had lived to see his great spiritual idea of Christians united in a great fight for Christian ideals sullied and degraded. Urban spent his last days with the Pierleoni. He died on August 24, 1098. Only a year before his death the Pierleoni had regained possession of Sant'Angelo, and it would have been fitting for the great Pope Urban to have died in that same building where once Gregory had hidden from the enemy, protected by his own family. Instead he died in "*S. Nicolai in carcere, in domo Petri Leonis*"—in the House of Pierleone.[74] The house no longer stands, but in a vacant space between the Church and the Theatre of Marcellus there are still some ancient columns which may once have been part of the "domo Petri Leonis." Urban's funeral cortege rode slowly through Trastevere until it reached St. Peter's, where Urban lies buried.

•

The Pierleoni were now so well established as to be considered unofficial members of the Curia. They were no longer merely Papal bankers and financiers: their monetary contributions were by this time taken for granted. Their castles became chateaux, the social gathering places of clergy and nobility, the salons of medieval Rome. They became the trouble-shooters and confidants of the Popes. When Rainer, Cardinal of Clemente, succeeded Urban as Pope Paschal II (1099–1118), his intimate friend and advisor Petrus Leonis became his permanent representative during Paschal's many absences from Rome. Almost automatically, the Pierleoni acquired the status of actual regents of Rome. The appointment became a simple formality; it was expected by everyone.

The old problems which had dominated the reign of Gregory VII—the relationship of Pope to king and, specifically, the question of investiture—were inherited unsolved by Paschal. Henry V, who now reigned while the body of his father, still under the Papal anathema, lay unburied in a German cathedral awaiting Papal permission for a Christian burial, had no intention of yielding; in fact he announced his intention to march on Rome to employ all his influence and power to force his coronation. A new drama was about to unfold in Rome, and in order to understand its significance it is necessary to appreciate two important factors. The first is the enormous power which was inherent in the mystical act of coronation in St. Peter's; although it is difficult to fathom it in our day, much blood had been spilled over it by Paschal's time, and much more was to flow. The second is the fact that the political power in Rome at this time was entirely in the hands of the noble families, notably the Pierleoni, who symbolized the power of all of the aristocracy. Militarily, the Pope had become utterly dependent on the militia of the nobles, bolstered by alliances with the Normans. Papal contracts with secular agencies, including kings, were being signed by the noblemen. Invariably these nobles included "Petrus Leonis et Leo duo Petro Leonis"—the latter of whom was destined to become the last of the Pierleone Popes. Thus when Paschal journeyed to France to enlist the king's help in his struggles (he failed, incidentally), it is not surprising that he left Petrus Leonis to rule in his absence, as he did later when he spent some months in Benevento.

In 1110, Henry V commenced his move toward Rome at the head of some thirty thousand German knights and thousands of mercenaries. In order to forestall new violence, it was decided to seek a peaceful settlement under the terms of which Henry's coronation could be granted honorably. A group of negotiators, with Pierleone as the Pope's representative met, in Santa Maria in Turri, not far from St. Peter's. That Pierleone should have signed the resulting compromise does not speak well for his diplomatic skill; but that the king should have agreed to it demonstrated his desperate desire for the crown, or at least for the Papal benediction. According to this fantastic record, the bishops invested by the king (this meant in reality all the bishops of Germany and many in Italy), were to return their land holdings and other properties which they had received at the hand of the king, and were from this time forward to live on meager incomes derived from the payment of the tithe. This meant simply that the bishops who had been living the lives of rich nobles were to be degraded (socially and economically) to clerical paupers. Although this was in keeping with Christian ideals, the monastic oath and the ancient Christian rules of poverty, it was hardly to the liking of the pampered clergy. Furthermore, the bishops were to renounce all rights not only to their property, but to all the other secular privileges which they had received and enjoyed, such as market rights, special jurisdiction and the right of minting. In short, they were to give up the privileged status of capitalist clergy which had given them their power and luxurious comfort. The king would promise solemnly that he would forever renounce his right of investiture. Pierleone's signature guaranteed the Pope's agreement. The king and his nobles swore solemnly (with tongue in cheek) to uphold the terms of the contract, and two separate documents, one containing the king's promise, the other comprising the Pope's pledge, were painstakingly written. Then the armies moved on toward Rome.

Messengers had already informed the nobles, the populace and the Pope of the successful negotiations, and all were prepared for the traditional festivities of coronation. As the king entered the city on horseback, surrounded by a large, dazzling retinue of military, noble and judicial rank, he was greeted with the jubilant salute: "HENRICUM REGEM SANCTUS PETRA ELECIT" (St. Peter has elected King Henry). It is unnecessary to examine the sincerity of the enthusiasm exhibited by the people if money was, as usual, lavishly distributed. The king halted at the little bridge before St. Peter's and swore solemnly to uphold the laws of Rome (another formality), then passed by the various groups representing the *scholae* of Rome. We are told he greeted the Greeks "condescendingly" and listened "with a contemptuous smile to the recitations of the Jews." As he entered the Leonine City he was greeted by a chorus of monks and nuns holding candles in their hands, chanting the official salutation:

"HENRICUM REGEM SANCTUS PETRA ELECIT." Signifi-
cantly enough, the king had premonitions of trouble in spite of all
the fanfare and pomp, and before crossing the threshold of St. Peter's
he sent secret-servicemen into the church; they immediately ordered
several army contingents to occupy and guard it while Henry approached.

What followed was first a burlesque, then a blood bath. King
and Pope were seated on their thrones, each of them holding the
parchment which contained the "agreement." When the Pope asked
the king to confirm the yet unsigned contract, the king asked for
permission to retire with the German nobles and clergy for consultation. The solemnity of the occasion by this time was gone, and the
noise within and outside the church almost drowned out the Papal
pronouncement that he would not crown the king unless the document was signed. This was too much for the Germans, a people
known for making short shrift of legalistic delays, and they decided
to solve such tedious problems with sterner means. "Enough of waiting," they shouted, "and enough of talk. Our Lord wishes to be
crowned now and without delay, as were Charlemagne and Louis."
Either to quiet the boisterous crowd or to delay the decision, the
clergy began to celebrate the mass. Minutes passed. The Eucharist
was lifted above the congregation, forcing them to kneel. Then
word spread among the soldiers that their master, Henry, was being
held prisoner in a building next to St. Peter's, and, swords drawn,
they surrounded the altar. There was just enough time for the Pope
and sixteen cardinals to leave by a side door before bedlam broke
loose. Clergy and worshippers alike were slain, left bleeding on the
altar and throughout the church, and the cathedral was looted. Two
bishops managed to escape to the Pierleoni-held Castel Sant'Angelo,
and soon the militia and the mob were informed.

During the middle of the night, the Romans marched toward St.
Peter's. But Henry, still in his nightclothes, managed to escape;
mounting a horse, he sped away with drawn sword, killing five men
who stood in his path. The Pope and his sixteen cardinals were
forced bodily into carriages and taken into custody. For the next

sixty-one days Paschal was the king's prisoner in Castle Trebicum.

Under a threat of death (which would not have compelled a man of the stature of Gregory VII) Paschal crumbled and signed a new agreement which submitted to the king's demand. A coronation was promised and the right to investiture granted with the understanding that the rights of Rome were to be respected. The text of the document was extremely humilating for the Pope. "God's wisdom has decided that your realm be particularly closely bound to the Church, and your predecessors, by power and wisdom, have demanded the crown of the city of Rome and the dignity of the Emperor. . . ." A Christian burial for the remains of Henry IV was also one of the conditions for the release of the Papal prisoner.

Wisely, Henry decided not to return to Rome for his coronation, and it took place in an open field outside the city. When Paschal returned, he was greeted as a martyr. But Pierleone was to soon realize that his tragic role in these negotiations was not to be forgiven. This was the fate of his family, as it has been the lot of other Jewish converts: in times of good fortune they were tolerated and even forgiven; in days of defeat and humiliation they were made to remember they were Hebrews from the old Ghetto after all, and that they had to prove themselves until the third and fourth generation, else the wrath of the people would be awakened. Then they would be reminded of that Easter day in 1030, just two generations before, when a Jew named Baruch became Benedict the Christian. Their Pierleoni faces, olive-colored and Oriental, betrayed their origins. Romans since days immemorial, they were strangers nevertheless. Again the baptism in Santa Maria in Trastevere proved to have been just so much water, and neither pelf, nor power, nor piety could erase the shame of the Jewish beginnings which they took so many pains to forget.

Nevertheless, when the Prefect of Rome died and the Imperialist noble families presented his son as their candidate to succeed him, the Pierleoni proposed one of their own sons, bright, very young and very arrogant. To become the Prefect of Rome was one of the dreams of noble families. For the Imperial party, it was a symbol of their own power, since the Prefect, confirmed by the Emperor with the Imperial insignia of sword and eagle, was considered the Emperor's vicar in Rome. (Henry had since returned home.) Although Papal confirmation was desirable, it was largely ceremonial. For the Imperialists, it was the right moment to take control; for Petrus Leonis it was a time to bolster the Papal power by electing a Pierleone. It was Easter and the Pope was celebrating the mass in the Church of the Lateran when a mob, bought and incited by the Imperialists, broke into the church presenting their candidate dressed in the silken robes of a Prefect, and demanded Papal confirmation. The Pope, having committed himself to Pierleone, his most trusted friend and defender, postponed the decision. He was never known to be a fighter, and when the people threatened to storm the Lateran he withdrew. They then turned and marched toward Trastevere, and began to stone the Pierleone towers. Windows were broken, fences torn down. But the Pierleoni had withdrawn to their main fortress, the Theatre of Marcellus. The people stood helplessly staring at the gigantic building, realizing the futility of storming an edifice which even today looks invincible. A few angry thrown stones could relieve their anger but do little to the Pierleoni. For hours they remained there, yelling obscenities against the powerful "Jew barons," before they went home. The Pierleoni were clever enough not to send their militia against the crowd. They were also clever enough to withdraw their candidate.

•

The events of the following years did nothing to alleviate the turbulence which had now become a regular part of Roman life. Soon after the abortive Pierleone thrust at the prefecture, Paschal died during another of the frequent street riots of Rome. His death was followed by that of Matilda, the great ally of the Reform, the defender of Gregory VII and the devoted friend of the Pierleoni; long resigned to the changing times, or in any event hopeful that even if skirmishes and battles are lost the great wars of history are won in the end, the once glamorous and militant heroine closed her eyes at seventy. (She left her entire property and fortune to the Curia, but her will, loosely drawn, was to involve the Church in litigation for generations to come.) The new Pope, Gelasius II (1118–19), was to experience nothing but hardship. The alignment of forces in Rome had changed, with the Frangipani, comrades-in-arms of the Pierleoni for generations, now siding with the Imperialists. When the Pope was abducted and taken in chains to the tower of Cencius Frangipani, Petrus Leonis called the Trasteverines to arms and freed him. Trastevere and its island had by now become almost a city within a city, an independent borough with its own fortifications and a population fanatically devoted to the Pierleoni. When Henry returned to Rome, Gelasius fled to France, with Petrus Leonis at his side. He died in Cluny, never actually ruling as the Pope; prison, strife and exile were his fate during his one year reign. His successor, Calixtus II (1119–24), a relative of the king of France, was elected on Pierleone's island, where the nobles assembled in the family's castle under Pierleone's undisputed leadership and confirmed the election. Calixtus was never to forget this event; some hold that his benevolent attitude toward the Jews of Rome and his solemn declaration guaranteeing their freedom in trade and worship were the results of agreements he had made with Pierleone, the latter acting in behalf of his former kinsmen.

But Calixtus' main interest lay elsewhere, for he was destined to be the Pope who would bring the Contest of Investiture to its conclusion. He announced his intention to do so in the presence of four hundred and twenty-four bishops at a council in Rheims, where, true to his royal blood, the tall and regal Pope towered over the assembly. He returned to Rome (where Pierleone "opened Sant'Angelo and St. Peter's with a key made of gold" and Calixtus publicly singled out Petrus Leonis and his brothers as the most loyal of his backers) and continued to lay the groundwork for the last act in the Church-State struggle. Finally, in 1122, the Concordat of Worms, one of the most splendid church gatherings of the century, hammered out the great compromise which laid the investiture problem to rest. Under its terms, Henry and his successors gave up the right to name bishops and abbots, but retained the right to prevent the election of the Pope's candidates when they were not to their liking. Thus ended one of the most bitter struggles of the Middle Ages.

Calixtus died of Roman fever shortly before Christmas of 1124, comforted in knowing he had made an end of the struggle between Pope and Emperor. The new peace was no longer based on the old Gregorian formulae of the *Dictatus Papae*. It could not be. Both powers, Church and Empire, were a reality and both had to be acknowledged and recognized; it was a matter not of mutual exclusion but of mutual respect. This agreement had been reached in the Rhenish city of Worms, in the great Romanesque cathedral which had been completed just a few years before. Petrus Leonis had accompanied the Pope to Worms for the conclave. He might well have passed by the synagogue of the city's old Jewish community, a Romanesque structure to which a Gothic chapel was later added. Did he pause to remember that not far away, in Cologne, his ancestor John Gratian Pierleone—Gregory VI—had spent two years in exile together with his kinsman Hildebrand? Did he notice the graves of the Jews who had been mercilessly slaughtered during the Crusades, just a quarter of a century earlier? The relatives of those victims were still alive. But they probably knew little and cared less about the Pierleoni—the noble converts who had turned their backs on their own people and had preferred to rule rather than to suffer.

4 ANACLET II, ABELARD AND BERNARD OF CLAIRVAUX

Petrus Leonis had nine sons. None of them was to play a greater role than Peter, who was destined to become Pope Anaclet II. Peter was systematically and deliberately trained for the office from the first years of his childhood. In appearance very much a Pierleone (his Jewish physiognomy is described in several contemporary reports), he had the bearing and the habits of a Roman nobleman of the twelfth century. He was altogether a child of his time: intellectually alert, widely read, open-minded, rational and with a philosophical bent of mind.

Small wonder then that he was attracted to that great and controversial teacher of Paris, Peter Abelard, who taught at the college of St. Geneviève and whose lecture hall was filled to capacity with students from France and far-away lands. They listened eagerly as the man who was the sensation of the twelfth century brought not merely a breath, but a veritable storm of fresh air into classrooms where orthodoxy and stale theology were usually taught. Thus historians record that among his students there was "a future Pope"— young Peter Pierleone, who never missed a class. The spirit of Abelard was so much like Peter's that Abelard seemed the embodiment of Peter's own restless mind. Furthermore, Abelard's extraordinarily unconventional life enthralled the young listener as much as his outrageously new philosophical theology. No figure of the Middle Ages was so passionately adored and so deeply hated as Abelard; there seemed to be no middle ground. He challenged the most sacred convictions and respected none of the widely accepted theological axioms. His was not merely a challenge of ideas, but a defiance of the whole establishment of ecclesiastic theology and church institution. All the doubts and questions of the young generation were asked and answered by him, or at least acknowledged as legitimate, permissible and even creative skepticism. He dared to define openly and fearlessly the hidden and forbidden thoughts of the age, and what had theretofore been considered heretical was now taught from the most celebrated platform in Europe.

To Peter Pierleone's delight, his own doubts had become respectable. Although he had not yet been made a cardinal, Peter was high in ecclesiastic circles. Whether he himself shared the great ambitions his family had for him during his years in Paris must be doubted; he was too intelligent not to realize that for a future Pope to be Abelard's most ardent disciple might prove fatal. The Papacy was the very symbol of the Establishment, and Abelard's radical theology was so much in conflict with official interpretation of dogma that he hardly provided a desirable preparation for the high office. Nevertheless, Peter stayed in Paris for several years, unable to tear himself away from the beloved teacher who was soon to involve himself in the most scandalous love affair of his time. Although that affair caused an outcry of indignation and disgust from the Church authorities, it made him even more attractive to his young students; he had become their idol and his breach with conventional chastity seemed but the logical consequence of his unconventional teachings. The consequences for Pierleone's career were all too clear to his family, however. Messenger after messenger arrived with his father's urgent request to leave Paris for a more wholesome climate. He finally yielded and went to Cluny, where for several years the atmosphere of the monastery and the teachings of the order conditioned him for his future life. Cluny was indeed the proper antidote to Abelard's deviations from tradition and a more suitable place for somebody who was destined and trained to become the shepherd of Christendom.

Peter dressed carefully and splendidly, as befits the scion of a wealthy family. Much of what we know about him comes from the poisonous pens of his opponents, but some of it sounds plausible and fits well into the colorful background of this Pierleone. We cannot believe the often repeated calumny that when travelling in England as a papal legate he had a young lady among his retinue dressed as a man. When in Oxford, it was said, he spent much of his time in the bawdy houses of the city, where his purse, filled with gold pieces, bought him all the pleasures and favors he desired. Such charges were probably exaggerated for use in the bitter battle which ensued after he became Pope, but they are not impossible.

The twelfth century, the most extraordinary period of the Middle Ages, has been called the medieval Renaissance.[76] The change from the Dark Ages of narrowness and brutality, of dogmatism and theological obscurantism, to the concept of an open and free society was refreshing in the extreme to those who welcomed it. Peter was very much a man of this new society and a new type of cleric, and given a chance he might have become a new type of Pope: financially independent, well educated, a gourmet and a lover of life. Alas, it was not to be. The powerful forces which conspired to prevent the new society were still too strong in the Church, and Peter Pierleone was to become their carefully selected target and victim. In the great and dramatic battle between Peter Abelard, the symbol of the new era, and Bernard of Clairvaux, the ascetic "Doctor Mellifluous" and the most powerful ecclesiastical figure of the time, Peter Pierleone was forced to succumb.

•

Although the awakening of the twelfth century seemed to have come suddenly, its antecedents are clear. The Crusades, usually viewed primarily as military and religious phenomena, had also brought Europe into contact with the Oriental world and roused it from its provincialism. The French knights and their comrades-in arms from other countries came back after years of adventures among unfamiliar cultures and nations with a new outlook on life. They brought with them not only the material products of this fascinating world—Oriental damask, muslin and silk; Persian rugs for their castles; new spices and recipes for their cuisine; fanciful ornaments for their armor; a new writing material called paper now widely manufactured by the Arabs in Spain—but, most important, a new universal spirit. Peoples which had been separated by nationalism had learned to know and respect each other's differences. Men from various classes who had fought together, now lived together. Upon their return home a period of leisure and affluence began. The cultural intercourse between the Oriental lands, Islamic Spain and the rest of Europe supplied new dimensions to their lives.

The medieval world which had divided society into *Sacerdotum* (the Church and the Papacy) and *Regnum* (the Empire and the King) now added a new and independently potent group: *Studium*, the world of the University. The word itself expresses the revolution: *universitas* does not merely mean the universal scope of learning, but also the universal character of teachers and students. They came from many countries, many nations and every walk of life. Learning was no longer restricted to the sons of noblemen. In Toledo, Arabs, Jews and Greeks worked with Spaniards, Germans, Frenchmen, Englishmen and Balkans. In Salerno, the university specialized in medicine and was dominated by Jewish scholars; the medical works studied there came mainly from Jewish and ancient sources. Altogether, the Renaissance of the twelfth century would have been impossible without the active role of the Jews as translators and interpreters of the scientific and philosophical literature of antiquity. Aristotle, whose works formed the very foundation of university training and intellectual speculation, was brought to the western world through the works of Arab and Jewish philosophers, most notably Ibn Gabirol and Maimonides among the Jews and Averroes (Ibn Rushd) and Avicenna (Ibn Sina) among the Arabs. Some combined medicine with philosophy. Maimonides practiced medicine in Spain and Egypt and wrote his Jewish philosophy, the *Guide for the Perplexed*, in Arabic. Ancient Latin and Greek texts had to be translated from Arabic and Hebrew. Aristotle, who in the days of Thomas of Aquino was to be pronounced infallible, was the symbol of the new medieval rationalism (which prepared the way for Martin Luther, Descartes and even the French revolution.)

The Church, although it still dominated religious life, was no longer monolithic, and numerous sects sprang up in spite of severe trials against heretics. Nor was thinking and discussion restricted to theology. The new goal was to reconcile religious doctrines with philosophical thought. The curriculum called for studies in grammar, rhetoric, dialectic and logic and—in another course of studies—arithmetic, geometry, music and astronomy. The sciences were taught at separate schools. The first university to encompass the whole curriculum was Paris, the cathedral school of Nôtre Dame which became famous through Abelard. Thousands of students, the sons of noblemen and peasants, began their studies at the age of fourteen and remained in school for sixteen years, crowding into the primitive dormitories and boardinghouses. The structure of our own universities was established at that time: campus, dormitories, the degrees of Bachelor, Master and Doctor and other rudiments of humanistic education stem from the twelfth century. When, a hundred years later, Robert de Sorbon added the famous college in Paris named for him, he was able to build upon the solid foundations of the earlier schools. In 1500 Paris had sixty colleges. In addition to Salerno and Paris, there were Bologna and Oxford and the many universities of the Arab world and Asia Minor, a veritable empire of learning.

The doctrine of the Church was no longer accepted without critical analysis. A new spirit of rationalism and even skepticism prevailed in spite of violent Church opposition. The monastic schools and their asceticism seemed to be out of step with the times. In the urban centers (though not yet in Rome) the new way of thinking developed new intellectual and social forms. It seemed that all over the western world the literary and musical creativity which had been held in bondage by the Church now began to flourish. Remote places such as Iceland, where the sagas of the North were told and written, became seats of learning and literature. In the south of France, the land of the *langue d'oc*, troubadors and *jongleurs* chanted ribald new songs which spoke of wine, women and song in a new meter and with secular boldness, establishing the tradition which two hundred years later produced a *chansonnier* by the name of Villon. Cycles on new themes revitalized the medieval tale, the medieval "novel" and the education of the masses: the tales of King Arthur, the Nibelungenlied, Parsifal and the Holy Grail sang of unflinching courage in adversity, of fate and loyalty, and brought this newly discovered world of fairy tales and heroic stories to the motley crowds which assembled in the square, eager to hear the message of the new century. Poetry, no longer purely the property of the rich and noble, now spoke in the vernacular, some of it vulgar and obscene. The ordinary people welcomed a medium which addressed them in their own language, and the new verses and tunes were sung and whistled in the streets.

The feudal castle, once martial and masculine, began to assume the appearance of the chateau. The male society of knights permitted the lady of the manor to play the central role in the new world of *jongleurs* and storytellers. Drinking parties became the subjects of reliefs and paintings. The whole gamut of a new way of life, the *amour courtois*, found its expressions. Plays were performed in this new society of wealth and leisure, and were it not for the fact that crinolines and perukes had not yet appeared, one might associate the period with the eighteenth century, when the "Marriage of Figaro" was presented and chamber music played. As a matter of fact, the monotone of early medieval music gave way to the polyphony invented by the masters of Nôtre Dame.

As society grew free and critical, bold anticlerical talk began to be daringly expressed. The satire, which sprang up as a refreshing new form of literary expression, was no respecter of religion. Rambaud of Orange, for instance, declared openly and without fear that "my girlfriend's smile causes me more happiness than that of four hundred angels." Even the Holy Scriptures were lampooned. Particularly popular was the "Gospel according to Mark Silver," a critical parody of clerical avarice which contains this disrespectful variation of the Sermon on the Mount: "Verily, thou wilst not enter into the

joys of the Lord, unless you spend every last penny for the Church."
This impudence, impossible but a few decades before, was now accepted as the *esprit du temps*. No wonder that serious theologians began to express skepticism toward accepted and revered religious mores. Wibert of Nogent doubted the efficacy of relics, those tremendously popular objects of reverence which were reputed to work miracles, and Abelard disputed the whole concept of the miraculous.

The new rationalism which expounded critical thought and brought together people from various backgrounds also bred a new spirit of tolerance. It is interesting that the parable of the three rings which Gotthold Ephraim Lessing used in his famous dramatic poem, "Nathan the Wise," the prelude to the emancipation of the Jews in the eighteenth century, was written in the twelfth century. It tells the story of a father who gives to each of his three sons a ring. Only one of them is genuine, but nobody knows which. Thus it is with religious truth: who knows which of the three religions—Judaism, Christianity or Islam—is the true religion? This spirit of tolerance was applied not only to relations between Christians and non-Christians, but also within the Christian society itself. The nobility admitted a constant flow of new members from the socially inferior ranks, notably the moneyed aristocracy which had previously been considered so ignoble in origin and descent. New nations with little claim to ancient nobility, such as the Normans, produced their own upper classes, and these became part of European society without any fuss or fanfare. This open aristocracy had its parallel in the clergy. Until then, only those of noble rank could achieve any prominence in the Church hierarchy, but now even the humblest son of a peasant could rise to the rank of ecclesiastic prince. As the clergy was often indistinguishable from the people in secular habits, so was there a process of equalization within the Church. "The open Church of the older Europe," writes Friedrich Heer, "was a living union of mighty opposites: heaven and earth, matter and spirit, living and dead, body and soul, past, present and future. Reality was seamless, there was no chasm separating created from redeemed mankind; all men were of one blood, from the first man to the last. This open Church was served by bishops and lower clergy who led boisterous, cheerful lives, accepting tears and laughter as they came. They were full of savoir vivre. The tolerance ceased only when the Church discovered that it was so deeply and widely undermined by heresy and skepticism that it had to become rigid and uncompromising." [77]

Considering the vast knowledge which the Greeks, Jews and Arabs had accumulated and which had only now come to the attention of the western world, it is no wonder that Bernhard of Chartres exclaimed: "We are dwarfs standing on the shoulders of giants." It was said that in Chartres theology was turned into mathematics and geometry and that "to theologize means to philosophize." Mathematics and geometry were only the scientific symbols of a general curiosity in numbers as the key to the mysteries of the world, and it is no coincidence that the Jewish mystical science of numbers, the Kabbalah, became more than but a pastime for many alert students.

Some believe that this preoccupation with logic, order and numbers was directly responsible for the new architectural style which Italians contemptuously called Gothic, because it looked barbarian to them. It is easier, however, to associate the new style with the awakening of the spirit which found the Romanesque church too small, too severe, and even oppressive. Today we go from church to church in the classical land of the Romanesque, the south of France, and find Nîmes, Arles, Orange and Moissac so overwhelmingly beautiful just because of their regal simplicity, their solid faith and the artistry of their statuary. But the twelfth century found it all too sombre. It did not reject solemnity, but it did call for more grandeur in halls of worship—for the spires, vaulted roofs and stained glass windows which replaced the mosaics and frescoes of the Romanesque. The science of engineering was so advanced in those days that it was able to give us the great cathedrals of Chartres, Paris, Rheims and Canterbury, to name just a few. The great figures which stand at the tremendous portals of the cathedrals in Chartres, Naumburg, Strassburg and Bamberg were no longer merely ornaments; they told the stories of the people of the New and Old Testament in most moving and human terms. In front of the portals of the cathedrals of Strassburg and Bamberg there stand large figures representing Church and Synagogue: the Church, a queen wearing a crown on her head and a victorious smile on her lips, standing as it were on the very top of the world and looking defiantly and triumphantly at the Synagogue, depicted as a young woman holding a broken spear, unable to look at the queenly Church for her eyes are blindfolded, the book of the Law gliding from her hands. Although the Church is portrayed as the victor and the Synagogue as the vanquished, there is no attempt at caricature or contempt. Both are great ladies. Though the Synagogue should be the mother, being the older of the two, she is here shown as the daughter, younger, slender, and much more appealing. Perhaps no monument is more eloquent testimony of the place of Judaism and the Jews in the twelfth century. Had the secular spirit of the universities and the newly awakened quest for rational inquiry prevailed, the story of the Jew in the western world would have been one of respected and even honored differences. Alas, Europe had to wait for the Italian Renaissance and the French philosophy of reason to resume its aborted course. The intervening centuries brought narrowness, blind faith and unreason into the world. It was not Abelard and the spirit of St. Geneviève which prevailed during these centuries, but the monastic schools under Bernard of Clairvaux, the ascetic and restricting schools of the Cistercians. Heretics and Jews were punished, and the hope for a more understanding and compassionate world was postponed.

The merciless battle in which Peter Abelard and Bernard of Clairvaux were locked symbolized the turbulent state of all European thought. No longer was the battle between Pope and Emperor; the Concordat of Worms, though not entirely satisfactory, was a treaty of peace, or at least a truce. The battle was now within the Church. Was there to be a new ecumenical spirit, tolerant of others and truly catholic? Or were severity, stringency and intolerance the only means of coping with the growing number of heretical Christian sects unwilling to conform to the official doctrines of the

Church? Could the Church survive critical inquiry? Or was the *auto-da-fe*—burning at the stake—the only answer? History chose the latter course, and Bernard (who was later beatified) was the victor. Liberalism and its representatives were to experience excommunication and ban. Books were burned, scholarly findings rejected. The Church Militant ruled Europe, and was to continue her rule until mankind triumphed in the new philosophies of humanism, of the worth of the individual and the affirmation of the human mind—the *"cogito ergo sum"* of Descartes—as the criterion of human experience. It was not until our own century, in fact, that a blood bath and radical world changes forced the Church to postulate a new Credo of the ecumenical spirit.

But all this was unforeseeable to Abelard and Bernard as their titanic battle raged on in the lecture halls of Paris and the monastic cells of Bernard's Cistercian order. Anaclet, who as that "Jew on the throne of Peter" was to make his own contribution to the new century and, in the end, become its victim as inevitably as the protagonist of a Greek tragedy, was one of Abelard's most brilliant and promising students, but this very fact identified him with the losing side in the new era. Had the new spirit prevailed, his Papacy might have gone down in Church history as the first attempt of medieval Catholicism to adapt itself to the new intellectual revolution of the angry young men of Europe and to identify itself with their restive hopes and aspirations. Until Abelard, it had been a world of mature and old men, but now it could have been the world of the young men. Peter Pierleone was one of them, but his beloved teacher (he was only loved, not revered) ended his life in condemnation. Bernard's victory was not merely Abelard's undoing, but also Anaclet's doom.

In order to understand the struggle of the schism of 1130—the battle between intellect and blind faith, between the passion of life and the monastic denial of its values—the man of Paris and the man of Clairvaux must be understood. Abelard held that if Christianity were to survive in a new world standing at the threshold of a new age of reason, then faith and dogma must be reinterpreted. To Bernard, no one could really be a Christian in the true sense and still share in any kind of normal life; monasticism, strict and unbending, was the only answer.

●

No figure of the Middle Ages has a more immediate appeal to modern man than Peter Abelard. His enemies claimed that he was the "son of a Jewish father and an Egyptian mother." (They attached such pedigrees to others as well; Joachim of Flora, for instance, was supposed to have been the son of a notary, an unfree peasant or a Jew, each of which would have disgraced him, but all this was idle gossip of which there was a great deal in the Middle Ages.) Of course, Abelard was actually the son of a nobleman from Brittany, that northern province of France which has given many extraordinary people to the world. Brittany, a strange country little changed even in our own time, is a land of curious and unique people who have preserved their Celtic origin and language until this very day. There at the stormy coast around Finistère they dye their home-woven linen suits with lobster juice, wear wooden shoes, and fear the witches and demons just as they did in the olden days. The churches, thatch-roofed as are the houses, are neglected, for Christianity is not at all accepted. On the altars of the simple churches one can see rabbit feet put there by the faithful as sacrificial gifts to the gods who now have Christian names, but are in reality the old pagan saints of the pre-Christian era. Gaugin and the other Fauvists who painted here in the nineteenth century caught something of the savage spirit of Brittany. The women are not pretty in spite of the lace headgear they don on Sundays, and when the men put on their Sunday finery they look like characters on some timeless theatrical set. They are independent people, not easily swayed. Their prehistoric forests of unhewn *pierres de justice*, the French Stonehenge, do not stand as isolated as their English counterparts; they appear instead to be organically linked not merely to the landscape, but to the stark lives of the Bretons themselves. Many of the men go out every day at dawn to fish for sardines and do not return until evening, their silvery loot shining in the timid setting sun like the old heirlooms in their wooden huts.

Of such people, though he himself was noble and rich, came Peter Abelard. He had left the security of his home full of new longings and ideas, a medieval Dylan Thomas or Brendan Behan out to remake the world in his own image. There was something compulsive about Abelard and in the moods which caused him to spell out the ugly truth in an autobiography in which nothing is made smooth, beautiful or easy. *"Historia Calamitatum,"* he called his book, and of calamities, misfortunes, uneven battles and tragedies he experienced all too many. His active career began when he was in his early twenties and ended when he was sixty-three. It is amazing that it should have lasted that long. His mind should have burned out long before, and it probably did, though the body which kept it captive succumbed to complete exhaustion only in 1142. No novelist has ever invented a greater story of vices and virtues. There in the midst of the twelfth century, the period of the great ferment, lived this restless spirit whose unsettled mind made him a roving, raving philosopher and whose impotence made him a monk. No one was so brilliant and at times so intellectually reckless, so vain and so painfully eager to find truth. He disgraced his teachers with contempt, dethroned the platitudes and the accepted cliches, and substituted for them the embarrassing and painful question of *"sic et non,"* yes and no, which he applied to all accepted doctrines. Where he could not find the affirmation which rooted a doctrine in the fertile soil of reason, he dared put a question mark. At a time when the elders were horrified at uncertainty in the realm of faith and had the temerity to claim *"Credo quia absurdum est"* ("I believe, *because* it is absurd," which means beyond proof and obviously improbable), he looked for that which the German-Jewish philosopher Hermann Cohen later called "religion within the limitations of reason." His approach was almost Kantian. He applied Aristotelian terms to the realm of irrational faith. The young people roared approval: at last the great rebellion had come. Wherever he taught—in Mount St.

Geneviève near Paris, in the Cathedral School of Nôtre Dame on the Isle de France, or even in the wilderness—he was surrounded by thousands of devotees. He was the founder and saint of an intellectual sect such as the world has never seen before or since.

Among his students was a seventeen-year-old girl of good family who was not merely beautiful, but bright and learned, a serious scholar of Greek and Hebrew, as lovely as Botticelli's Flora, and completely dedicated to Abelard's new philosophical theology. At first she sat at his feet in adoration. In time they found each other as lovers in Abelard's bed. She was Héloise, whose pure and passionate love has become one of the great paradigms of selfless merging into a man's very being. When a son was born of this consuming love, her uncle, a canon named Fulbert, surprised Abelard in his sleep and castrated him as punishment for transgression of law, custom and Christian virtue. That Abelard, in a mood of conformity, married Héloise hardly mattered; the family had been disgraced, although Héloise hardly thought so. She surely shared Abelard's thoughts when he said: "It was more becoming to her to be called my mistress, so that affection alone might keep me hers and not the binding power of any matrimonial chain. And if we should be separated for a time, our joys at meeting would be dearer for their rarity." [78] They were to become rare indeed, for he became a monk and she a nun; he was no longer a man, and she had learned to sublimate the passion of her flesh into compassion of the spirit. She was an extraordinary abbess. "The bishops loved her as a daughter, the abbots as a sister, the laity as a mother; and all wondered about her piety, her wisdom and her gentle patience in everything. She rarely let herself be seen, that she might devote herself more to worthy prayers and meditation in her cell; but all the more persistently people sought her spiritual counsel." [79]

No love was ever more passionately and more tenderly expressed than theirs was in that famous letter written by a woman who, though she had taken the veil, did not cease to love as few have loved before or since. I cannot resist quoting a paragraph from that great document written more than seven hundred years ago: "I endured," she writes, "to wreck myself at thy command. Nay, more than this, love turned to madness and cut itself off from hope of that which alone it sought, when I obediently changed my garb and my heart too in order that I might prove thee sole owner of my body as well as of my spirit. God knows, I have ever sought in thee only thyself, desiring simply thee and not what was thine. I asked no matrimonial contract, I looked for no dowry; not my pleasure, not my will, but thine have I striven to fulfill. And if the name of wife seemed holier or more potent, the word mistress was always sweeter to me, or even—be not angry—concubine or harlot; for the more I lowered myself before thee, the more I hoped to gain thy favor, and the less I should hurt the glory of thy renown. I call God witness that if Augustus, the master of the world, would honor me with marriage and invest me with equal role, it would still seem to me dearer and more honorable to be called thy strumpet than his empress." [80] No man deserves so much love. Abelard, brilliant, articulate, original, a great teacher and a fascinating man, was also vain and self-centered; his was not the love of self-denial and all-consuming passion. He died some twenty years before Héloise. In tender respect of their love they were buried together in Père-Lachaise in Paris.

Abelard's love affair, the great and famous scandal of the time, is not unrelated to the story of Peter Pierleone, who studied under him in St. Geneviève and Paris. If the private life of the great teacher was considered sordid, so was his philosophy as it applied to the teachings of the Church. Just as the great conflict between him and St. Bernard, into which Anaclet was to be drawn, was based not merely on interpretation of Christian doctrines but on personal behavior as well, so the tragic battle against Pierleone was, as we are going to see, based not on canonical law or even dogma but on the evaluation of his life and character. In the eyes of Bernard of Clairvaux, anyone who came into contact with the great sinner Abelard had contaminated himself, and the very fact that Peter Pierleone had sat at the feet of so unworthy a teacher was grounds in itself for condemnation. Since Abelard's method, which was later accepted by

Thomas of Aquino and others, was an attempt to philosophize theology and thus elevate philosophy to the position of controlling science, it reduced theological doctrine to the role of servant of reason rather than queen of faith. Instead of a clear, unequivocal affirming "yes," Abelard had admitted the possibility of applying a "maybe" and even "no" to hallowed tradition, and thus he had sinned. Disregarding the teachings of the Church, he had taught that the differences between good and evil cannot be discerned in the *deed* but in the *intention* of man. Such ethical relativism could lead to endless investigations into the psyche of the sinner rather than the sin itself. But was not man burdened with the sin of Adam, the original sin, from which there is no escape? There, too, Abelard denied tradition. It was not really guilt that was inherited but punishment. In a theological system which was based on guilt, which preached guilt to a world of sinners yearning to be forgiven not only for their own transgressions but also for the inherited guilt of Adam, a world redeemed only by the blood of Christ, such teachings were sheer heresy. As if this was not enough, Abelard taught with deep conviction that not merely theologians but also philosophers shared in divine revelation. How could he in good conscience exempt Plato and Aristotle from divine grace? But how, on the other hand, could the Church, which distinguished the faithful believers from the pagans, the perfidious Jews and the Moslems, grant such grace to mere philosophers—heathens and sinners to boot?

Abelard, then, was the iconoclast, the tradition-breaker. His popular songs, written in the vernacular, appealed to the people in the streets of Paris. He was impertinent enough to debate his own teachers and, being more brilliant than they, to lower them in the eyes of their students. He had taken over as the master of the famous School of St. Geneviève at the age of twenty-two. Banned and condemned to burn his own book on the Trinity, he was forced to retire to Nogent-Sur Seine, a deserted spot, only to find that thousands of his students followed him and built their simple dormitories around him. There they erected a lecture hall, the Paraclet, where he, humiliated in the Christian world, continued to teach with brilliance and wit and disdain for respectable views. Chased from pillar to post, he was a monk who because of his castration could not officiate at the altar of God, a man maimed in body and, in the end, broken in spirit. His last days were spent in Cluny, where there were still people who respected his originality and his intellectual integrity.[81]

●

    Bernard of Clairvaux, the "white monk" who had brought about Abelard's exile and his misery, is supposed to have rushed to his bedside at Cluny, and Peter the Venerable reported having seen the two men embrace in a kiss of peace. Alas, it was too late. From the first years of Abelard's teaching career, Bernard watched in holy anger and revulsion as his influence seeped into and beyond Paris. Abelard represented all that Bernard fought against with relentless zeal and bitterness.

    A Burgundian nobleman, Bernard had joined the Cistercians, the "white monks," who frowned on Cluny, where art and science were respected and cultivated. The monasteries of the Cistercians were shabby and threadbare, and the monks subsisted on a meager diet of barley bread and boiled nettle leaves. Bernard, accustomed to the lavish cuisine in his father's chateau, was nauseated at the very sight of the wretched food, but he ate it heroically. He lived to overcome temptations. Often overwhelmed by desires of the flesh, he found it necessary to plunge into icy water to combat them. "His pale visage, emaciated by fatigue and fasting, seemed almost ethereal and so impressive that the mere sight of him convinced his hearers before he even opened his mouth," reports Wibald, the abbot of Stavelot. At the age of twenty-two, when he left his father's estate to become a monk, he was "filled with ardor, impatience and the impetuosity of desire. That force, that vigor, that hot boiling blood, like a heady wine, allows him no rest or relaxation." At Clairvaux, the monks slept in dormitories that resembled rows of coffins, and Bernard, their abbot, slept on a hard board under a staircase. Beauty was a forbidden departure from his ascetic rule: "The enormous height of the churches," he said in a sermon against the new Gothic style, "their extraordinary length, the useless width of their naves, the richness of polished stone, the paintings which distract attention. Vanity of vanities, nay, worse than vain. The church's wall may shine, but her poor go naked; she covers her stone, but leaves her children unclothed." He was constantly ill, yet travelled under the most difficult circumstances, traversing the Alps on horseback, journeying to Rome and even Sicily, driven by the fanatic desire to annihilate himself in order to serve the Church. She was his mother. Although he adored the Virgin Mary (he was the first to call her Our Lady), he refused to call anybody mother but the Church. That his main work should have been a commentary on the *Song of Songs*, the book of love between man and woman, might be an interesting key to the psychology of this gigantic man, Christ's most valiant knight.

It was only natural that such a man should have hated Abelard. The affair with Héloise profoundly disgusted him; he was too much aware of his own temptations, and he lived solely to root them out. He had a deep loathing and contempt for women because he was fearfully afraid to love them. Even clerical vanity was to him feminine conceit. "Why do you get yourselves up like women if you do not wish to be criticized like women? Be known for your works, not for your fur capes and embroideries. You think to shut my mouth by observing that a monk should not criticize the bishop? Would to heaven you might shut mine eyes also. But were I to remain silent, others would speak—the poor, the naked, the starving. They would rise up and cry: Your luxury devours our lives. Your vanity steals our necessities." Such were the fervor, charity, uncompromising zeal, profound faith and dedication which made him easily the most powerful ecclesiastic figure of his age. His clash with Abelard was not merely one of personalities, but of deep convictions as well. To Abelard, who called philosophy into service for a closer and more critical examination of theology, he simply said: "What does philosophy matter to me? The Apostles are my masters. They have not taught me to read Plato or to unravel the subtleties of Aristotle, but they have shown me how to live and, believe me, that is no mean science." There was no room for understanding: faith was set irreconcilably against reason. When the two men met at Sens in 1141, it became obvious that there was simply no common basis for discussion. Bernard ruled reason out of order; it had no place in the consideration of faith. Thinking itself was considered rebellion. How could the *anima curva*, the bent and disabled soul of man, undertake any rational examination of a matter of faith? Faith has no eyes, no ears and no brains. It has to be believed, accepted and lived. "Peter Abelard," he said, "is trying to make void the merit of Christian faith when he deems himself able by human reason to comprehend God altogether. He ascends to heaven and descends even to the abyss. Nothing may hide him in the depths of hell or in the heights above. The man is great in his own eyes—this scrutinizer of majesty and fabricator of heresies."

We side with Abelard, for he is the man of the future and Bernard the man of the past. But in the twelfth century Bernard was very much the man of the present. The Abelards were in a hopeless minority, and when Bernard preached in Mount St. Geneviève twenty of Abelard's students followed him into the misery of Val d'Absinthe, a Cistercian cloister. A great preacher and prolific writer, he published three hundred and thirty-two sermons and fourteen treatises, and more than five hundred of his letters—fiery, angry and erudite—are still extant.

Bernard was, first and last, a monk. Strict obedience to the rules of self-denial, austerity, continence and poverty met all his personal needs and expressed his deep and sincere convictions. He claimed to have no will of his own, only submission to the will of God. Although God the Father was acknowledged by him, his religious union was with the Son. He awed his listeners with minute descriptions of Christ's suffering on the cross. Every state in the development of what he called God-man was significant. Even the pitiful swaddling clothes of the Christ baby had profound meaning to him. His fervor was so great that he became brilliantly effective as a missionary. Though he said of himself "I light my fire at the flame of meditation," it was a blazing flame indeed; for the "conscience of Christendom" was neither meditative, nor timid, nor even humble. In a speech against Arnold of Brescia, Abelard's brilliant disciple, he used these words. "Arnold of Brescia, whose speech is honey, and whose teaching is poison, is the head of a dove and the tail of a scorpion. What Brescia vomited forth, Rome abhorred, France repelled, Germany abominates, Italy will not receive." This is not the language of a monk given to reason and saintly patience but of a zealot ready to tear down and destroy. No wonder his critics claimed that even his emaciated face was calculated to sway and impress people, an ability which helped immeasurably when he entered ecclesiastic affairs, involved himself in world politics, and negotiated with kings and princes. All this he accomplished for the sake of the Church, to be sure. In his dealings he was not given to any kind of compromise and never yielded one iota of his conviction. Nevertheless, the metamorphosis of the monk of Clairvaux into the *de facto* ruler of the Church (much more powerful than the Pope) was a turning point not only in his personal life but in the life of the Church.

The immediate cause of this change in the Church's power structure was the elevation of Peter Pierleone to the Papacy. It is important to understand the colorful historic background of the events which led to Peter's election and, consequently, to the schism of 1130. When Calixtus II died in 1124, his successor, Lambert of Ostia, was hastily and uncanonically elected with the help of the Frangipani, that family which had formerly allied itself with the Pierleoni but was now prepared to act on its own. A consultation with the Pierleoni proved fruitless: the Frangipani insisted on their candidate, and with their assistance Lambert became Honorious II (1024–30). The election decrees of Nicholas II, which prescribed the procedure of Papal election in great detail, were thrust aside, but Honorius was in fact confirmed. The Frangipani had won their first victory over their erstwhile allies.

Petrus Leonis, the head of the Pierleoni, was now an old man, ill and not strong enough to resist. He had submitted the name of his own son Peter, but he was rejected. Some four years afterwards, on June 2, 1128, the old friend and close collaborator of Hildebrand and Urban II breathed his last. He was buried with great pomp in the Church of St. Paul Outside the Walls. His richly decorated Roman sarcophagus, the only Pierleone tomb which can be seen today, was placed near the altar of the church, a great honor for a man who, although a leading nobleman and a Roman consul, was still remembered as *"originaliter precedente de Judaica congregatione"* [82] (a man originally connected with the Jewish congregation.) After the church burned down in 1823, the sarcophagus was moved to its present location in the beautiful cloisters, where it is the largest of the many memorials. It is almost entirely intact (a little corner on the upper right is loose). The inscription[83] reads:

TE PETRUS ET PAULUS SERVENT PETRE LEONIS,
DENT ANIMAN CIELO QUOS TAM DEVOTAS AMASTI,
ET QUIBUS EST IDEM TUMULUS SIT GLORIA TECUM.

MAY PETER AND PAUL PRESERVE YOU, PETRUS LEONIS,
MAY THEY GIVE YOU THE HEAVENLY SPIRIT WHICH
    YOU LOVED SO DEVOTEDLY.
AND THUS MAY THE SAME LIGHT OF GLORY BE WITH
    YOU.

He died surrounded by his nine sons and his daughter, members of the noble families and the clergy. Cardinal Peter closed his father's eyes—eyes which had been so eager to see him enthroned on the Papal chair. Although it is only natural for any cardinal of the Church to consider himself a potential candidate for the Papacy, few, as we have noted, were so carefully prepared for the office as was Peter. The family had given John Gratian to the Church. His rule as Gregory VI had proven abortive, but he had, after all, ended the disgraceful Papacy of a worthless and immoral young man and cast the lot of the Church with the movement of Cluny, the purifiers and reformers who had welcomed him jubilantly as one of their own. The fact that he was a Pierleone, the son of a Jewish mother and father, did not matter. He had become a devout Catholic and his sincerity was doubted by no one. The great triumph of Hildebrand as Gregory VII had brought the family of the converts into the very center of Church affairs, not merely as Papal bankers but as the protectors of the Popes, the most faithful and powerful of the Papal party, rulers of Trastevere, owners of the great strongholds of Rome. Hildebrand was a relative perhaps by marriage only, an indirect descendant of Baruch the Jew. But Peter was a direct descendant, Baruch's great-grandson, Leo's grandson and the son of Petrus. In his veins flowed the blood of the converted Jews. More than any other Pierleone was he considered a Jew by friend and foe. He looked like the most Jewish of the Pierleoni. Although baptized and the great-grandson of a convert, a member of a family that played an extraordinary role in Papal history, he was considered a Jew and was to be constantly reminded of this fact.

Rome at the time of the death of Petrus Leonis was curiously outside of the intellectual mainstreams of Europe. Honorius, who was still Pope, devoted his reign primarily to political problems in southern Italy and Sicily. He was neither a great nor a bad Pope. He showed little spiritual creativity, but then Rome at that time demanded little. Of all the great centers in the twelfth century, Rome benefited least from the medieval Renaissance prepared in France. It was altogether intellectually stale: the great universities were elsewhere; moral and theological battles were fought between Paris and Clairvaux; even the new architecture did not come to Rome, witness the fact that there is no Gothic church there and the few Romanesque churches are unimpressive. It seems as though the times had bypassed the Eternal City. The Papacy, the Lateran and the Leonine City, although connected with the whole Catholic world and the very heart and center of the Church, led their own insular life. Bulls and decrees were issued, synods and ecumenical councils were called, kings were crowned, pilgrims came on their journeys, Peter's pence reached the Papal treasury, Papal messengers and legates travelled throughout the world—but Rome, the city, lived its own life, dominated by the factions of the nobles who provided the consuls as well as the Popes. After the Concordat of Worms, the king no longer had a voice in the election of the Pope, and though the nobles did, they were not free and unlimited in their actions. The laws governing Papal elections had been laid down, and they were to play a central role in the years to come, during which the conflict between the Frangipani and Pierleoni led to dramatic events.

During the celebration of Christmas mass in 1129, Honorius II became ill and fainted. As he was being carried to the Papal bedchamber it was quite obvious that this was not an ordinary case of exhaustion, for he ran a high fever. Among the diseases of the Middle Ages, the Roman fever—caused by the ever-polluted water—was one of the most dreaded; it nearly always proved fatal, and from the first day of his illness the Pope was considered to be in mortal danger. From time to time he would fall into unconsciousness, and the spells would sometimes continue for days. The necessity to appoint someone to carry on the daily business of the Curia soon became apparent, and the choice fell naturally to Haimeric, who had served Calixtus as chancellor and had continued in that post under Honorius. A man of great political astuteness, he found the position of chancellor to a weak Pope very much to his liking. Just as Hildebrand had consented to serve in the same position for many years under Popes of lesser stature than himself, so Haimeric believed that the real power lay in the hands of the chancellor.

In any event, Honorius' days were numbered, and it was now necessary to weigh carefully the choice of a successor. The situation in Rome had again become tense. Although the former political divisions of Imperialists and anti-Imperialists were blunted by the Concordat of Worms and the influence of Cluny had waned once the program of the Reform Papacy had large been fulfilled, the third power struggle—that for political and economic control of the city itself—was being fought more hotly than ever among the powerful noble families, most notably the Frangipani and the Pierleoni. The Pierleoni were clearly the stronger party, with a vast majority of the people beholden to them either through extended bonds of kinship or through the countless favors and exchanges of money which the seemingly unlimited resources of the family could provide. The proverbial greed of all Romans permitted the rich to buy not only support, but even the oath of loyalty to a new Pope. It was by this time taken for granted that the sum of 18,000 talents would be required to seat a new Pope, and bribery of the clergy, high and low, was accepted and expected as a matter of course. He who paid the most got the better service, and the rivalry between the Pierleoni and the Frangipani, which had so recently revolved around political questions involving the German emperor, was now to a great extent one of money. The Pierleoni, who had supplied prefects and consuls to the city since the days of Leo, Petrus Leonis' father, were so well established that it was naive to anticipate rapid changes. Their power was clearly visible in the city: they owned not only the strongest and largest of the five-hundred-odd fortified towers in twelfth-century Rome, including Sant'Angelo and the Theatre of Marcellus, but entire quarters of the city, particularly Trastevere and the left bank of the Tiber, which were fortified by their well armed militia and made more powerful by the possession of advanced machinery capable of storming enemy fortifications. Clearly, to choose a Pierleone as Honorius' successor would make this family the undisputed rulers of both Church and city.

There were, however, certain factors working against the Pierleoni. For one thing, Haimeric, who wanted to see a candidate who was of good character but nevertheless meek enough to be ruled by him, sided with the Frangipani. But more basic were certain psychological considerations. Though the Pierleoni could buy favors, they were not at all popular. The nobility distrusted them because they thought of them as upstarts. The people disliked them because they demanded service and servitude. But all hated them because they were Jews. The conversion was unforgotten and, strangely enough, unforgiven. To the enemies of the Pierleoni, the situation was dangerous and required speedy and determined action, especially since the family possessed a natural candidate in Peter, the Cardinal of Saint Calixtus, a brilliant and active member of the Curia. Sufficient money had already been distributed to make his candidacy and election more than likely. This was not the time for diplomacy nor observance of procedural minutiae; it was a time for cunning outwitting of the enemy. And as far as Haimeric was concerned, the enemy was Peter Pierleone.

But the time was not yet ripe. The month of January had come and gone. Honorius had been confined to his bed since Christmas. He was dying, there was no doubt, but he had not died yet. The rules of election laid down by Nicholas II, which could not be disregarded completely, required that when a Pope was seriously ill a council was to be held to discuss a possible successor. It was to be attended by cardinals, members of the Roman clergy and representatives of the noble families. Upon the Pope's death, the council would discuss the time and place of the funeral. It was rare, as we have noted, for a Pope to be buried on the day of his death; the usual time between death and funeral was three days. Under customary procedure, the election usually took place in the church where the Pope had been entombed. During the period of conflicts between the various noble families in Rome, the election was conducted in a fortified church close to the strongholds of the family sponsoring the Pope. The nomination of the candidate, called *denominatio*, became complicated when the Pope did not designate a successor. At times, several candidates were nominated. During a formal session, called *deliberatio*, the cardinals and the clergy discussed the merits of the various candidates. Specially designated cardinals asked for the vote. A two-thirds majority was required; the number of voting members by 1130 had grown to fifty. At first, the election of the candidate was in the hands of cardinal bishops only, but by the twelfth century their power had been considerably decreased, and deacons and presbyters participated in the election. Nevertheless, the theological quality, age, experience and reputation of the clergymen weighed heavily in favor of or against a candidate. The election was often disturbed by armed forces of opposing noble familes. But when, at the end of often turbulent sessions and the candidate was dutifully elected, he chose a new name and the immantation, the solemn ceremony of dressing the Pope with the Papal robes and insignia, took place. Following the adoration by clergy and nobles, kneeling before the Pope and kissing the Papal ring, the Pope was formally enthroned. Only then was he considered a canonically elected Pope.[84]

At the beginning of February, the Pope fell into a coma and his end was expected momentarily. Possession of the physical remains of the Pontiff now took on a grim significance: since the election of his successor could not take place until Honorius was buried, it was obvious that if the Pierleoni were to kidnap the Pope they would gain strategic control over the proceedings. Consequently, Honorius was hastily transferred from the Lateran to the Monastery of St. Andrew, which was located near a tower from which the Frangipani could quickly send their mercenaries in the event of an emergency. The bishops who escorted the sick Pope did not go their way unnoticed (no event, trivial or significant, could go unobserved in Rome, the city where gossip was always rife and where rumors spread like wildfire) and soon the people began to assemble in front of the monastery, watching and waiting for some news. Hardly had the Pope been taken to his new bedchamber when Haimeric called a meeting of the clergy to nominate a successor. However, the cardinals balked. There were some, like Petrus of Porto, who had remained independent and neutral and who objected to such a flagrant violation of the election rule that no nomination could be made before the Pope expired. He prevented an actual nomination, but he had to yield to the majority who demanded preliminary meetings. The mood of the mob was too obvious to leave anything to chance. Taking another tack Haimeric went to the Papal bed to persuade Honorius to nominate a successor. It would have made matters so much easier, for the Pope's wishes would have to be respected. He even went so far as to suggest names, but the Pope was far too weak to react one way or another. Another meeting was convened to discuss the situation, but it was interrupted during the evening hours by the thousands of people who had assembled outside St. Andrew's. Rumors that the Pope had died were spreading throughout the city, and the people demanded to know the day of the funeral. Haimeric, in desperation, had to prove to the wild mob that their Pope was still alive. A weird scene followed. The bishops moved the Papal bed to the window so that it could be visible to the gaping crowd, and lighted torches were brought to both sides of it. Honorius was hardly aware of what was going on. His tired eyes were half closed, but the din and the light helped to open them a little. Bewildered by all these unusual activities, he gazed around confusedly. Haimeric rearranged his pillows, and more were brought and placed behind the Pope's back so that he was now propped up in a sitting position. His face was pale and seemed even paler in the light of the torches. "Bless them, father," said Haimeric, "the people ask for your Apostolic benediction." The Pope moved his lips; he was too weak to raise his arms. Then a bishop on either side directed his arms upwards. Honorius had become a puppet. Three times did the arms move in this fashion so that to the clamoring populace outside it appeared to be the motions of the Papal blessing. The Pope was alive. The noisy jubilation of the mob continued long after the Pope had been returned to his bedroom. This strenuous ordeal could hardly have shortened his life considerably, however, for he was already more dead than alive; he fell into a coma which lasted for almost a week and from which he was not to awaken.

St. Andrew's now became the scene of the most feverish activity. The Collegium of Cardinals was hopelessly divided. Haimeric, driven by personal ambitions and influenced by the wishes of the Frangipani, was determined to elect his candidate: Gregorio Paparesci, Cardinal Deacon of Sant'Angelo, a man of good character who had served the Curia for many years. He was one of the authors of the Concordat of Worms and had been in the diplomatic service as legate in France, where he served with Cardinal Peter Pierleone, who was to be his opponent. There was no doubt as to Paparesci's excellent character. He was the son of an old Roman family, not a very strong man and certainly not a very colorful one, but upright nevertheless. Haimeric was anxious to have the election take place even before Honorius died. A committee of eight cardinals had been appointed, but it was soon clear that the majority would vote for Peter. Thus the "Battle of the Tiaras" was on. It was fought with such bitterness that neither party gave too much thought to legality and used every possible trick to win. Haimeric's candidate could be victorious only if his friends acted swiftly and even ruthlessly. When Honorius finally died during the night of the 13th of February, Haimeric rushed to his bedside and had him quickly removed from the living quarters of the monastery to the Church of St. Andrew. Everything was done with the greatest speed and in complete secrecy. Since the rules of election provided that the Pope must be buried before a successor is chosen, a temporary grave was hastily dug in the courtyard near the church and without more than a few hurried prayers, the body was there interred. The gates to the monastery were firmly bolted to prevent anyone leaving or entering.

The news of Honorius' death was concealed for as long as possible. When Peter Pierleone and his close friend Cardinal Jonathas wanted to rejoin the committee of eight of which they were members, they were not permitted to enter the building where the meeting was to convene. A minority of the Sacred College then elected Paparesci, who was to be known as Innocent II. The election was held in the dark of night. Nobody dared later to examine the legality of these proceedings for fear of having them declared canonically invalid. In the long arguments which were to follow during the next eight turbulent years, not even Haimeric could claim to have obeyed the rules. In order for the election of Innocent to have some semblance of lawfulness, the Frangipani mustered their mercenaries in the early morning and Honorius' body was placed on a hearse and taken to the basilica of the Lateran. "It was now day," writes Bernardi.[85] "The Frangipani, with whom Haimeric was in constant contact, had provided those people who had dug the grave and dragged the Pope into it. They now stood ready to protect those ceremonies which customarily surround a Papal election. The Lateran was not far away from St. Andrew and it had to be readied for this purpose. Now they removed the body from the fresh grave and carried it to the Lateran, followed by the new Pope, his electors, the Frangipani and some people who gathered quickly. The dead and the living Pope enter the Church simultaneously. Honorius is lowered into the grave as quickly as possible, while Innocent is being dressed with the Papal robes and insignia. He goes through the ceremonial motions prescribed by custom, in the basilica and in the palace. He is Pope." [86]

•

While all this was transpiring, the majority of the clergy waited in the Church of St. Marcus. They had not been informed of the Pope's death, nor of Innocent's election. In fact, everything had been done so surreptitiously and so few of the higher clergy were in Haimeric's retinue that their absence had not been noticed. There was a large number of clergy in Rome at that time—six cardinal bishops, nineteen cardinal prelates and fourteen cardinal deacons, thirty-nine in all—and most of them were at St. Marcus when they finally received the news of Innocent's election. They opened their formal meeting at noon. Angered by Haimeric's shameful disregard of canon law and the rules of election, they were determined to elect the new Pope with painstaking regard to law. Strangely enough, they forgot the most important legal point: they did not formally annul Innocent's election, though they had the power and the votes to do so. They simply overlooked it. Had they done so, Anaclet would have been the undisputed Pope and the schism which resulted could have been avoided. Instead they simply proceeded with the election. Cardinal Peter Pierleone was the first to rise and suggest a candidate: the Bishop of Porto. No doubt this had been prearranged to give the proceedings legality and respectability. The bishop was too advanced in years to serve, and he declined as was expected; but the maneuver had won over the conservatives for Peter. The bishop himself, who was to remain faithful to Anaclet until the bitter end, now proposed Peter Pierleone. Twenty-nine clergy, ranging from cardinal deacons to archpresbyters elected him unanimously. Assuming his new name, Anaclet II, he was ceremoniously dressed in the purple robe. (Alas, the ring and the crucifix were in Innocent's possession and substitutes had to be used.)

Needless to say, in the case of neither Innocent nor Anaclet was the election accompanied by the customary pomp. In fact, neither camp had cause for much jubilation. As for Innocent, although he had the prior claim to the Papacy—however illegal his election—his situation was not at all pleasant. Most of Rome was clearly against him. Only the Frangipani and their closest friends, together with Innocent's family, were present at his installation. No public banquet was held, nor were there any celebrations in the city. Innocent himself advised caution under the circumstances. As soon as he was enthroned, he was spirited away to the monastery of the Palladium, in the shadow of Frangipani fortresses, where he felt safer than in Rome itself. The hasty interment of the dead Pope, the indignities to which the body had been subjected in the second burial, and the unseemly urgency with which the ceremony in the Lateran had to be conducted must have burdened the conscience of all participants including the new Pope, the victim of Haimeric's cunning. It is generally agreed that Innocent was not a man of great stature, but nobody denies that he was a man of personal integrity. His retreat to a fortified monastery was sufficient proof of this bad conscience. Even Anaclet's enemies had to admit the irregularities at Innocent's election. "Comparing the election in the monastery of St. Andrew with that [of Anaclet] in the Church of St. Marcus, we cannot help but admit that the election of the contemptible Petrus Leonis was more in accordance with canon law than the elevation of the Cardinal Deacon of Sant'Angelo [Innocent]. The clergy who elected Anaclet consisted of the oldest, most experienced and tried civil servants of the Holy See." [87]

While there was little disagreement as to Innocent's character and personality, thoughts and opinions about Anaclet differed violently. Few voices speak quietly and without passion about him, for from his early youth he was considered a controversial figure. We have already mentioned his "Jewish" physiognomy. He looked *"nigrum et pallidum,"* a contradictory observation which seems to translate into "dark complexioned, but pale." His Jewish appearance was resented while he was yet a student in Paris and, later, a Papal legate in France and England. Even then he was called "the anti-Christ," which is a polite Christian phrase for "that cursed Jew." "The world suddenly remembered with contempt Pierleone's Jewish descent," writes Gregorovius, "and forgot the family's merits on behalf of the Church. The Jewish physiognomy of a Pope could not possibly be considered a detriment, if we remember that Peter and Paul and Jesus himself must have looked more Jewish than Anaclet." [88]

The criticism, however, was not really concerned with his looks, but with his character. He was suspected and accused of every crime under the sun. As a member of a family of Jewish converts, a family of piety, to be sure, but of money and power as well, he was hated. There was nothing monastic about him, and his short stay in Cluny was considered snobbery rather than acceptance of the monastic rule; Cluny was the Eton of the Middle Ages. The Pierleoni could afford for their son to be educated at the court of the King of France and in the study halls of Abelard, as well as in the spiritual and aristocratic atmosphere of Cluny. At any rate, he was not ascetic. "Anaclet was undoubtedly the more outstanding man [as compared with Innocent], educated in Paris, worldly, ambitious, eloquent and witty, in spite of his upbringing in Cluny, not without luxurious taste due to the wealth of his shrewd Jewish ancestors, altogether the type of an aristocratic Pope." [89] But this is a modern assessment. His contemporaries were less charitable. Hubert of Lucca called him "avaricious and ambitious"; Peter of Pisa described him as "that carrion bird which was either drowned or glutted with flesh." The Bishop of Mantua went so far as to accuse him of "violent attacks upon women and even nuns and incestuous carnality." Haimeric called him "a man given to greed, a lover of actors and comedians, a robber of the Church, a Godless oppressor of God's servants." Bernard of Clairvaux, the leader in the fight against him, was comparatively mild at the beginning when he restricted himself to this comment: "Anaclet is the abomination of desolation standing in the holy place, to gain possession of which he set fire to the sanctuary of God." According to St. Bernard: "If what they say about him were true, he would not deserve to serve as pastor of the church in the smallest hamlet; if it were not true, we must nevertheless insist that the head of the Church be not merely a man without blemish but must also enjoy a blameless reputation." [90] This is a rather strange argument: if his reputation were based on rumor and distortion of truth, it would have been the churchmen's duty to reveal the truth. But the arguments against Anaclet were merely smokescreens. "One argument, not publicly aired," says Bernardi, was an impediment: his Jewish origin." [91]

Nobody will ever know whether any of these moral allegations was borne out by fact, for there was no objective contemporary historian who recorded the events without bias. After the schism of 1130 Christendom had become hopelessly divided, with two bishops, two archdeacons, two abbots everywhere, the one representing Innocent, the other Anaclet; in such a situation objectivity is rarely found. But the fact remains that Anaclet was not a duly elected Pope. To his greatest enemy, Bernard, the election which took place at noon reminded him of *"the treason of the Jews who at that same hour nailed Jesus Christ to the cross."* The innuendo of this observation is all too clear; the anti-Jewish argument against Anaclet was to be repeated often in the course of the next bitter years.

Since most of the Roman churches were in the hands of the Frangipani, the Pierleoni would have to take them by force or not at all. Anaclet's brothers, Leo, Jordan, John and Guido, who had prepared the election with the greatest care, distributing money where it would help, negotiating and making promises where they would sway people in their brother's favor, now placed the entire military force of the Pierleoni at Anaclet's disposal. St. Peter's was taken —some say with the loss of many lives—and so was the Lateran. Anaclet had insisted that his enthronement take place in St. Peter's and the other ceremonies be held at the Lateran in accordance with custom and canonic law. He knew that Innocent's enthronement in the Church of Maria Nuova represented not more than "tenure of the Diocesan Episcopate of Rome whereas enthronement at St. Peter's represented tenure of the Papacy." [92]

Since the churches needed for the Papal installation had been taken by force, Bernard of Clairvaux, in an address to the bishops of Aquitaine, could later say: "It is not by reason of his good life or of his virtues that he attained his dignity or that he holds it; he usurped it by force, by fire and by bribery." But similar accusations can be made against many Popes, few of whom, at least during the early Middle Ages, abhorred force. Some of the greatest Popes, as we have seen, resorted to coercion and even bloody battle, often as veritable generals riding in the forefront of armed forces in battle array. While Anaclet actually left all this to his brothers, no one could possibly defend his actions by our modern standards. Nevertheless, it would be hypocritical to attack him while Innocent at the same time was in hiding, protected and guarded by the mercenaries of the Frangipani. It was alleged that Anaclet in his travels as Papal legate asked to see ruins "in Vezelay and Burgundy" and that he admitted to a strange and almost mystical predilection toward ruins. "I want it," he is supposed to have said ,"because I delight in the destruction of anything great, and it has been foretold of me that I shall be the cause of the destruction of the world." But this is obviously apocryphal. The only sane and unbiased observation came from the wise old bishop of Porto, who warned the clergy against distortions: "Both Anaclet and Innocent have lived in your, my and the Church's presence, wisely and honorably, and have fulfilled their duties arduously. It is not becoming of you to speak hatefully and reproachingly, for all this is based on rumors and hearsay."

The date for Anaclet's solemn enthronement was set for February 23. It was a day of celebration and gayety for the whole town. Never had Rome been more festively decorated, for it was the day of greatest triumph for the Pierleoni. That most secret, but most insistent, of their hopes had at last come true: the great-grandson of Baruch the Jew, *a direct descendant*, one who bore the name of Pierleone, the one who had knelt at his father's deathbed and been blessed with the benediction of Abraham, Isaac and Jacob, this same Peter, whom they called "that man from the Ghetto," was to be Pope. Decorations and ornaments abounded everywhere. Wine, food and money were generously dispersed among the poor. The array of high clergy was impressive. The Bishop of Porto, who had designated Peter at that dramatic session of the Sacred College some two weeks before, was to perform the rites of consecration in the great Church of St. Peter, assisted by bishops from many regions of the land. There could be no doubt as to the canonicity of this ceremony; all the fine details had been scrupulously and conscientiously considered. Hymns and psalms accompanied the long and splendid procession to St. Peter's. Upon his arrival at the Church, Peter Pierleone was lifted upon the throne and the golden tiara was placed on his head while the crowd broke into unrestrained applause. All the prayers were said, all the formulae prescribed by ancient custom uttered. Anaclet was now properly invested and ready for the long march to the Lateran, there to take possession of the Papal church and the palace. Mobs of people formed long lines in the streets and the various *scholae* stood at their assigned places to do homage to the new Pope. It would be interesting to know what went through the minds of the Jewish delegation as it waited in anticipation to present the scrolls of the Torah to a Pope from the Ghetto. Gregorovius ventures this interpretation: "As the tumultuous processions greeted the new Pope, we look at the Jewish delegation waiting at the fabulous palace of Chromatius led by their rabbi, carrying the scrolls of the Torah, and we can imagine that never in their history have they greeted a Pope with hymns so sincere, and yet so mischievous." [93]

At the Lateran there was the usual ceremony: the oath of office, the distribution of the coins to the people as an affirmation of the vow of poverty (coming from a Pierleone the words must have sounded hollow), the solemn symbolic seating on the thrones of porphyry, the silent prayer in the *Sanctum Sanctorum* and the solemn ceremony of homage by the clergy and the noblemen. Among the aristocrats kneeling before the new Pope were Anaclet's four brothers, who had done so much to make the old Pierleone dream come true. The banquet followed, probably more elaborate than ever, but the old custom was preserved: Anaclet sat at the great festive board in utter loneliness as each of the courses was served by a nobleman, his brothers again among them. Yet neither glamor nor gayety could conceal the fact that two Popes had been elected. Innocent was still in Rome with the Frangipani (who two months later were to recognize Anaclet), but since he could accomplish little in protective custody he soon sailed to Pisa. His removal from Rome did not, however, eliminate him as Pope; on the contrary, it was but the beginning of his career. Anaclet, far too brilliant a man to underestimate the many difficulties, surely must have anticipated the years to come with much apprehension and fear.

●

After the Concordat of Worms, the recognition of an elected Pope by secular powers would ordinarily have been a matter of course. But the schism of 1130 posed a complicated problem: which of the two Popes was to be the rightful Pope, recognized not merely by the ruling kings but by all of Christendom? Innocent was now journeying from Pisa to France, where he hoped to win over the spiritual power of Cluny and the French king. Anaclet, meanwhile, addressed urgent letters to kings and clergy. In a letter to the German king, Lothair, he described his election in these words: "Our brother cardinals, deprived of the solace of a Pastor [after Honorius' death], had with wonderful and stupendous unanimity on the part of the clergy and the people elected us to the supreme dignity of the Pontificate." Most of the thirty-eight known letters written by Anaclet deal with the schism. There was little time for other matters. No important ecclesiastic decisions were taken, no bull was written, no ecumenical council was called together. The schism thus deprived the Church of the creative services of a Pope carefully prepared for the office, one who had chosen the greatest theologians and philosophers as his teachers. Anaclet was compelled to devote the eight years of his reign to political and even military problems in an attempt to convince Christendom that he was the only duly elected Pope. The rulers did not respond to either his letters or the interventions of Papal legates. There was a conspiracy of silence which isolated Anaclet from the first moment. Rome was with him—of that there was no doubt—and so was the rest of Italy; he had, for instance, confirmed Milan's ancient prerogatives, and this powerful city and its clergy adhered to him almost until the very end. Even in France, where Innocent prevailed, he had such influential friends as Hildebert, the Archbishop of Tours, and Gerard of Angoulême, one of the great spirits of the time, who was convinced that Anaclet was the rightful Pope and who acted as his Papal legate with zeal and wisdom in a situation which was all but hopeless. The chief secular rulers who decided for Anaclet were William of Aquitania and Roger, the Duke of Sicily, who was eager to be the first Sicilian king and who was to become Anaclet's most powerful protector. There were also the Eastern churches: "The whole Eastern Church," Anaclet writes in 1130, "the churches of Jerusalem, Antioch and Constantinople, are with us and maintain friendly intercourse with us."

But obviously the decision did not lie with the Eastern Church, but with France. Louis VI sent royal messengers to Innocent upon his arrival in Arles, but withheld for the time being any formal recognition. More alarming for the Anaclet forces was Innocent's visit to Cluny, where he was warmly greeted by Peter, the abbot of the monastery—rather strange considering that Anaclet had been a student and even a monk of Cluny and had maintained a friendly relationship with the clergy. However, Cluny was no longer the decisive spiritual factor: the great power of the Church, still abiding in seclusion in the austere surroundings of Clairvaux, was its abbot, Bernard the White Monk. It was he alone who would determine the fate of the two Popes. His decision would be accepted by kings and clergy. Since he had not as yet spoken, no one dared commit himself to either Pope.

The emergence of this great ascetic from the solitude of Clairvaux into the world of public affairs was an extraordinary event. Before the schism he was a respected monk, an uncompromising believer in the monastic ideal of poverty and self-denial, an orthodox theologian who denied reason to play any part in the realm of faith, and a passionate preacher. This world was not his, because faith was not of this world. Christianity was not to yield one iota of its early teachings from the Sermon on the Mount and the theology of St. Paul. Looking around at his contemporary Christian world, he found nothing but betrayal of these early ideals. The traitors were in the clergy, high and low, in the Papacy, and even in the monasteries. Everything which constituted a deviation from the purest Christian ideals was to him an abomination, and even Cluny did not meet his extraordinarily high standards. The Papacy had chosen "velvet and silk" instead of the monkish habit of Peter and Paul, the golden tiara instead of the simple cap of the early Pontiffs. The Pope had become a ruler, surrounded by a Cabinet, courtiers, legates and the whole diplomatic apparatus of a monarch. This, too, was treason. The old Apostolic traditions of the Pope were forgotten; he was no longer the shepherd with the simple staff holding his flock together by piety and example. No, this whole world, clerical and secular, was not for Bernard.

Yet he also felt in his isolation of self-chosen austerity and even misery that he was the conscience of true Christianity. He was the yardstick with which all others must be measured. Whenever the very foundations of Christian belief became endangered, he was ready to fight to protect it. The devil himself had appeared in Paris in the person of Peter Abelard, to whom students flocked by the thousands, and it was Bernard's duty to defeat him. By 1130 he had not yet succeeded. It was to take another decade before Abelard succumbed. He thus remained dangerous in this new world of awakening reason and doubts. *The schism of 1130 was but another phase of Bernard's battle against Abelard.* For Anaclet was Abelard's disciple. Anaclet was in fact much like Abelard: an intellectual, alert, witty, even frivolous, partial to aphorisms, bored with mediocrity, impatient with boors, arrogant, and fond of those luxuries which his father's wealth could afford him. It was all of this that Bernard detested. After all, Bernard himself was born a nobleman, had lived in the castle of his rich father and had deliberately and often painfully deprived himself of all the comforts of an aristocratic life. Bernard was not of one piece, but this made him the more passionate. In fighting the Devil without he also fought the Satan within. Wealth to him was in itself a sin. And Anaclet was wealthy. It was reported that Innocent impressed Bernard most deeply on his visit to Clairvaux when he described the wealth of the Pierleone family and their distribution of gold among the people and clergy. It was ill-gotten through the crime of Jewish usury; thus Anaclet had bribed himself into the Papacy. Although there was no actual purchase, he said, as in the case of that early Pierleone, Gregory VI, the price for the Papacy had been paid by the Pierleoni to hundreds of people. As was their money ill-begotten, so was Anaclet's Papacy. The argument had to be against the person elected rather than the election itself. Even those who would not publicly recognize that Anaclet's election was *more* canonical than Innocent's, admitted that it was *at least* as canonical as his. There was no point in debating the issue in legal terms anyway. Bernard was not interested in legality but in morality. In almost every letter written by Innocent and his adherents, Anaclet was accused of the most heinous crimes. Anaclet spoke of his opponent in respectful tones and never once attacked him. There was probably no reason to do so, and it must be said to Anaclet's credit that he never resorted to the campaign of vilification to which he was exposed. Bernard, to whom the world of sin was the natural battlefield of his personal wars, listened attentively to the long register of Anaclet's alleged crimes. Innocent did not even hesitate to accuse Anaclet of attempted assassination against him.

But immorality, Abelardism and wealth were not the only, nor the most convincing, charges against Anaclet. In several documents Bernard referred to this greatest of crimes: Anaclet was a Jew. At a meeting in Salerno, he turned to Peter of Pisa with these remarks (my italics): "I know that you are a wise and learned man, Peter. Would that a party more discreet and of better credit had obtained your services. Would that a juster and happier cause could have your advocacy. Then doubtless no eloquence could withstand your reasonable contentions. . . . But now charity compels us to speak because *that robe of the Lord which at his passing neither the Gentile nor the Jew could tear, Peter Leonis with the approval of the*

233

Jew, his master, tears and divides. There is one faith, one Lord, one baptism. We know neither two Lords, nor twin faiths, nor two baptisms. To go back to the old days: in the time of the flood there was one ark. On this eight souls escaped the flood; the rest perished. No one doubts that this ark was a symbol of the Church. Of late men have built a second ark; and there being two arks, one is of necessity a counterfeit doomed to be lost at sea." [94] "To Bernard, Anaclet was Judas, the betrayer of his master," [95] Williams writes, but Judas in a most literal sense: he was Judas because he was a Jew. After Anaclet's death, Bernard wrote jubilantly to Peter the Venerable (again my italics): "The winter has passed; the rains have abated; flowers have appeared in our land. He, that wicked one, *I mean who made Israel to sin,* has been swallowed up by death." [96] "The mad fury of the *lion* [meaning Peter *Leonis*] is stilled; wickedness has come to an end; the Church is at peace." The theological propriety of such jubilation over the death of a Pope is questionable; but Bernard's passionate hate of the enemy needed no theological justification.

The most violent anti-Jewish remark against Anaclet is contained in a letter from Bernard to King Lothair. Roger had been crowned King of Sicily and Lothair had appeared in Rome with a small army. Bernard the monk asks for more effective warfare. The argument against Anaclet is again purely anti-Jewish. "At Rome you attained most gloriously the height of Imperial dignity"—he was referring to Lothair's coronation—"and, what is more, you attained [it] by the aid of no great material force, just in order that the greatness of your mind and of your faith might be more plainly manifest. But if the earth trembled before an insignificant little army like that, what sort of terror are we to expect to possess the hearts of our enemy when the king goes forth with a mighty arm? While it is not for me to be stirring up strife, I am certain that it is the duty of an advocate of the Church to ward off the fury of schismatics who attack it. . . . *For even as it is undeniable that it is an injury to Christ for the spawn of a Jew to have usurped the throne of Peter,* so it is beyond doubt that a man who makes himself a King of Sicily injures the Emperor." [97] When Bernard left the solitude of Clair-

234

vaux to spend eight long years almost uninterruptedly in France, Germany and Italy, it was in the service of a personal crusade against Anaclet the Jew who had usurped the throne of Peter, whose Jewish family of usurers had desecrated the Church and who would serve Abelard the heretic to dignify his diabolic teachings with the authority of the Roman Pontiff.

●

Dramatic events proceeded to unfold with great rapidity. The French king and clergy assembled in *Étampes*, a city between Paris and Orléans, where Bernard appeared for the first time at the side of Innocent, whom he now considered the only true Pope. No investigation into the legality of the election was attempted. A report was presented according to which those who elected Innocent were morally more weighty than those who chose Anaclet. Although this was a subterfuge rather than a fair appraisal, Bernard not only agreed but began to claim that the electors of Innocent even formed a numerical majority. This was untrue, but nobody contradicted him. France had decided against Anaclet. Those who doubted the fairness and even legitimacy of the decision preferred to remain silent. Bernard was now Innocent's constant, indefatigable companion. Together they went to Clermont, where once the call to the first Crusade had been sounded, and where now a synod was held in November. Due to Bernard's influence, it decided to prohibit the study of jurisprudence and medicine for any member of the clergy. It was an anti-Abelard decision, quite in place at a synod which also decided against Anaclet, his disciple.

An assembly called by Lothair, the German king, was held in Liége in the spring of 1131. Lothair made an attempt to cancel the agreement of Worms as a condition of his recognition of Innocent, but Clairvaux wanted no part of it and Lothair yielded. So it was also in England, where Anaclet had yet some influence since the days when he had been Papal legate: whatever hesitancy there was to acknowledge Innocent, it soon dissipated. The battle was lost. Anaclet was isolated. He had understood it long before all these meetings were held. However, his position in Rome and Italy remained strong. Since Germany and France had rejected him, he had to look for a new military and political ally. He found it in Roger, Duke of Sicily. In September of 1130 Anaclet invested Roger as King of Sicily. On Christmas Day of the same year the solemn coronation took place in the presence of the Papal legate (Anaclet did not attend in person) and several of the Pierleone brothers. (It was said that Roger married Anaclet's sister, but there is no document to verify this.) The next ten years were a decade of wars between Roger and the forces of Lothair and Louis, combined with those Italians who always feared the Normans. Some battles were lost to Roger, but in the end he proved victorious and even Innocent had to acknowledge him as *Rex Siciliae*, ruler over Sicily and much of southern Italy, one of the most powerful kings of Europe and the founder of Norman Sicily as the leading maritime power in the Mediterranean.

It mattered little that Innocent could come to Rome for the promised coronation of King Lothair, restricted in festivities but nevertheless valid. It was of just as little consequence that Lothair himself came with his army. Anaclet remained the only Pope in Rome, despite the facts that anathema had been pronounced twice, that he had been declared anti-Pope and that he had lost his power in most of Western Christendom. He watched the military invasions from his family's old possessions: Sant' Angelo and the Theatre of Marcellus. But his physical safety was less important to him than the fact that Rome, the people, the clergy and the nobles remained faithful to him. He ruled that part of Christendom which had acknowledged him: Rome, Italy and the Eastern churches.

In December of 1137 King Lothair died in a small hut in the Tyrolean Alps. Roger II now assumed the role which Lothair had once rejected: to decide the schism based on documents and legal arguments. He met with Bernard in Salerno and listened patiently to the arguments of both sides. But his decision was never made. On January 28, 1138, Anaclet died. No document tells of the circumstances surrounding his death. There was enough grief, disappointment and heartbreak in the eight years of his reign as the last Pope from the Ghetto to exhaust even the strongest. Peter Pierleone, great-grandson of the banker Baruch who had taken the name of Benedictus Christianus in 1030, the ardent hope of those great money aristocrats, was dead. Nobody reports about his funeral. The family decided to bury him in Santa Maria in Trastevere, the church in which their ancestors had converted to Christianity and which Peter himself had served as archdeacon. There they must have erected a suitable tombstone for him bearing the name of *Anacletus II, Pontiff of the Roman Catholic Church from 1130–1138*. Soon after Anaclet's death, Innocent II entered Rome as the *only* Pope, and the people of Rome, including Anaclet's brothers, paid homage to him. He decreed that the walls of Santa Maria in Trastevere, where his enemy Anaclet had been buried, be torn down and that a new church be erected in its place in the ancient Ghetto of Rome on the Via San Franciscus d'Assisi. With the old church, Anaclet's tombstone disappeared. Where Anaclet had been buried, there is now the tomb of Innocent II.

•

During the reign of Anaclet, a new synagogue was built in the Ghetto on the Via dell'Atleta, where it can still be seen today. Could it be that the same Jews who had greeted him so fervently on the day of his coronation at the Palace of Chromatius said the ancient prayer of *El Male Rachamim* for him—the Jewish prayer for the dead?

Genealogy of the Pierleone Popes

The discovery of the Pierleone roots of Gregory VI and Gregory VII must be credited to the lifelong work of Pietro Fedele, who, in his *Le famiglie di Anacleto II e di Gelasio II*, has laid the scholastic foundations for a discussion of the origins of the two Gregorys and Anaclet II.

The Pierleone origin of Anaclet has never been doubted. In his election the Pierleoni played a leading role, and there are numerous documents of the time to prove his kinship beyond doubt. Fedele, however, undertook to supply contemporary Latin documents to prove the family relationship of the other two. It was to be expected that his contentions would meet with resistance. The German medievalist Max Tangl, in his lengthy essay *Gregor VII Juedischer Herkunft?* (1905) claimed to be outraged by the very suggestion that the great Hildebrand could be of Jewish origin; his piece has some anti-Semitic undertones, but it must still be taken seriously. The Italian medievalist G. B. Borino, with his *L'elezione e la disposizione di Gregorio VI*, entered the fray largely on the side of Fedele, while G. B. Picotta in his *Della supposta parentèla ebraica di Gregorio VI e Gregorio VII* (1942) disagrees violently. The great English medievalist Reginald Lane Poole, after a thorough investigation, summarized his findings in the Proceedings of the British Academy in 1917. He said:

> "We find (1) a modern statement that Gratian (Gregory VI) was of the house of Peter Leonis; (2) an inscription, probably also modern, asserting that he was Peter's uncle; (3) his great wealth, which implies that he belonged to a family of capitalists; (4) his close attachment to Hildebrand (Gregory VII), whom by one dubious

account he made his heir; (5) that Hildebrand was later on reputed to be connected on his mother's side with Peter Leonis; (6) he was associated with Gratian in a way that suggests relationship; (7) he was reputed to have business relations with Peter Leonis; (8) when active in ecclesiastic affairs he enjoyed the steady adhesion of Peter Leonis."

As a result of these cautious considerations he suggests the following pedigree:

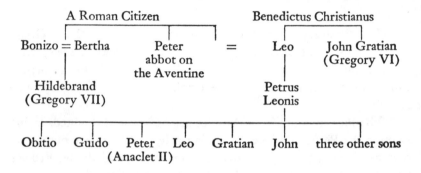

Although this scheme admits blood relationship only in the cases of Gregory VI and Anaclet II, Poole does not doubt that there was a family involvement of all three. Nevertheless, his family tree differs from that proposed by Fedele, which looks like this:

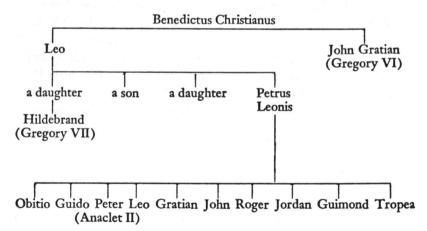

It is now generally agreed that the three Popes were connected with the Pierleoni, a family of Jewish converts. Even the conservative *Cambridge Medieval History* accepts it. As related in the book, the official Catholic list of saints mentions the Jewish origin of Gregory VII.

I am, frankly, not at all interested in racial "purity." It does not matter in the least to me how many ounces of Jewish blood a man has in his veins. Considering that Anaclet II was the great-grandson of a Jew but the son and grandson of mixed parents, the whole question of Jewishness is absurd. But he was, nevertheless, a Jew in the eyes of his contemporaries and was attacked because of it. We are not dealing here with the fact or fiction of "Jewishness," but with a remarkable family and its relationship to three Popes. There are no Jewish sources in eleventh century Rome, and the Jewish writers of the history of the Jews in Rome—notably Rieger and Vogelstein, who deal with the Pierleoni in their famous work—regret it. Poole remarks wryly that "these writers are not interested in converted Jews," but this is not altogether fair. There are many Latin medieval sources, and those interested in the scholarly aspects can find them listed in Gregorovius' standard work on medieval Rome (vol. IV) as well as in the other works pertaining to the Pierleoni listed in the bibliography.

Notes

Legend

1. Micha bin Gorion, *Der Born Judas,* one-volume edition of his famous collection of Jewish legends. Variations of the legend can be found in Rieger-Vogelstein's pioneering *Geschichte der Juden in Rom,* vol. I, pp. 296–298, for which the Hebrew source is Jellinek, *Beth Hamidrash VI,* 137.

Chapter One

2. Zazzera, *Della Nobilità Dell' Italia, Tome II,* Milano, 1621, pp. not numbered where the Pierleone coat-of-arms is reproduced and the relationship with the family of the Frangipani reported. Interesting, but historically not always reliable.

3. Harry J. Leon, *The Jews of Ancient Rome,* 1960, p. 137. Although this book deals chiefly with the ancient Jewish catacombs and pagan Rome, it contains excellent and most reliable material on Jewish life in early Rome.

4. *op. cit.* p. 47.

5. F. Gregorovius, *Geschichte der Stadt Rom im Mittelalter,* vol. IV, p. 350.

6. The story of the Jewish minters can be found in any of the many economic histories of the periods mentioned. For those interested in more details, the following are recommended: Lushim von Ebengreuth, *Allgemeine Muenzkunde und Geldgeschichte des Mittelalters und der Neueren Zeit,* 1904; for Jud Suess, as Oppenheimer was popularly and contemptuously called, the best and most reliable is Selma Stern's *Jud Suess;* for additional material, Werner Sombart's *Wirtschaftsgeschichte der Juden,* a work which, though pre Hitler, is anti-Semitic Nazi literature of a scholastic variety which was common during the period.

7. See R. de Rovier, *Money, Banking and Credit;* Siegfried Wendt, *Banken II* in *Handwoerterbuch der Sozialwissenschaften,* 1956; Julius

Lehmann, *Banking, commercial* in *Encyclopedia of the Social Sciences*, vol. II, 1930.

8. Quoted from Robert Lopez and Irving W. Raymond, *Medieval Trade in the Mediterranean World*, p. 31. For the whole problem of Jewish urbanization and participation in early capitalism, see Salo Baron, *A Social and Religious History of the Jews*, vol. IV, particularly chap. XXII.

9. Bernhard Blumenkranz, *Juifs et Chrétiens dans le monde Occidental*, p. 376.

10. The original text reads: "*De rebus edrum onos jure haereditario possident Judaei in areis, in casis, in ortis, in vineis, in agris.*"

11. See Salo Baron, *The Jewish Factor in Medieval Civilization.*

12. See the interesting essay by Irving A. Agus, *Control of Roads by Jews in Pre-Crusade Europe*, *Jewish Quarterly Review*, 1957, p. 93.

13. Peter Browe, S.J., *Die Judenmission im Mittelalter*, Rome, 1942. See also his *Die Kirchliche Gesetzgebung ueber die Behandlung der getauften Juden* (*Archiv fuer Kirchenrecht*, 121, 1941).

14. *Monumenta Germaniae Historica*, L866, Ep. 5, 200.

15. See S. Grayzel, *The Confessions of a Medieval Jewish Convert*, *Historia Judaica*, 17, 1955.

16. The text is taken from the 6th Council of Toledo (639) and quoted in Bernhard Blumenkranz, *Juifs et Chrétiens dans le monde Occidental*, as are the other texts of the ritual conversion (pp. 113–119).

17. John Coulson, *The Saints*, p. 202.

18. Wilhelm Bernardi, *Lothar von Supplinburg*, p. 314.

19. D. A. Zema, *The Houses of Tuscany and of Pierleone in the Crisis of Rome in the 11th Century*, *Traditio II*, 1944.

Chapter Two

   The purpose of this chapter is to provide the background without which the story of the Pierleoni Popes cannot be fully understood. The development of Christianity from its Jewish origins to a truly separate religion took the better part of a thousand years. The *Cambridge Medieval History*, a most reliable guide, has been a key source in the writing of this chapter. There are also, of course, countless other books on the history of the Church; some of those which I used are listed in the Bibliography. Since we are dealing with the story of a family of Jewish converts, and since the interpretation of events in this book is largely influenced by the Jewish viewpoint, many of the references cited are studies in Jewish history. The few notes for this chapter deal mainly with source material quoted in my text.

20. *Book of the Popes* (*Liber Pontificalis*) Vol. I. Translated with an introduction by Louise Rope Loomis, *Records of Civilization: Sources and Studies*, pp. 4–5.

21. James T. Shotwell and Louise Eppes, *The See of Peter*, pp. 673–4.

22. *Liber Pontificalis*, p. 47 (edition Loomis).

23. Sources and interpretations on the Councils of Arles and Nicaea are best found in *The See of Peter*, beginning p. 477 (where the issue of Donatism is explained) and the sources on Nicaea beginning p. 485. Our quotations are taken from these pages (edition Shotwell-Loomis 1947).

24. The Gelasian theory became the foundation of the early definition of the doctrine of separation of Church and State. It is quoted throughout the centuries as the undisputed authority. Of course, this doctrine must be understood in its medieval Catholic context and bears little resemblance to the American Bill of Rights. The Church proclaimed her independence from the secular rule only in matters of the Church, such as appointments of bishops. Emphasis is, however, on the superiority of the Church and her decisions. As we are going to see, the Emperor is the recipient of his authority from the hands of the Pope. The source is God. The Church is His agent.

25. The text of the Nicene Creed can be found in any authorized publication of the Episcopalian Church. It remains the main doctrine of all, not merely the Catholic Churches. See also: E. H. R. Percival, *The Seven Ecumenical Councils of the Undivided Church: The Nicene and Post Nicene Fathers.* 1900.

26. There is, of course, no history of the Middle Ages which does not deal with the monastic movement, nor can any history of Christianity overlook it. William Ragsdale Cannon, a Protestant, writes in the fifth and seventh chapters of his *History of Christianity in the Middle Ages* a lucid account of asceticism. So does C. W. Previte-Orton in Book V of his concise *Shorter Cambridge Medieval History*, beginning on p. 510. R. W. Southern in his *The Making of the Middle Ages* is very helpful as he treats with monasticism as part of what he calls the "ordering of the Christian life" as well as with the monastic orders and their contribution to the intellectual history of the times. On the artistic production in the monasteries, read the brilliant analysis in Arnold Hauser's *Social History of Art*, Vol. I, a short, but enlightening chapter (pp. 168 ff.).

27. Crane Brinton, *The History of Western Morals*.

28. Quoted in André Lagarde, *The Latin Church in the Middle Ages*, p. 85.

29. *The Rule of Saint Benedict* (translated by Cardinal Gasquet) 1936.

30. Quoted from G. G. Coulton, *Medieval Panorama*.

31. See Jacob Marcus, *The Jew in the Middle Ages*, a very useful albeit incomplete collection of translated sources.

32. From Coulton, *op. cit.*, who culled it from the classical medieval source, Migne's *Patrologia Latina*.

33. Marcus, *op. cit.*

34. R. W. Southern, *The Making of the Middle Ages*, p. 135.

35. Gregorovius, *Geschichte der Stadt Rom im Mittelalter*, vol. IV (my translation).

36. Gregorovius, *op. cit.*

37. *Vitae Pontif.* 1.781 edition 1677.

38. Horace K. Mann, *The Lives of the Popes in the Early Middle Ages*, p. 253.

Chapter Three

39. John William Bowden, M.A., *The Life and Pontificate of Gregory the Seventh*, 1840, vol. I., p. 126.

40. In his letter to Henry IV on March 7, 1080, published in *The Correspondence of Pope Gregory VII*, p. 150.

41. *History of the City of Rome in the Middle Ages*, German edition, vol. IV, p. 72.

42. In the German edition of his history, already quoted, p. 395, vol. IV (1906). The translation is mine. There Gregorovius also describes the fortified towers of the Pierleoni. The book was written in 1859.

43. *The Correspondence of Pope Gregory VII*, pp. 49, 63, 150.

44. Gregorovius, *op. cit.*, p. 90.

45. For a detailed analysis, see Demetrius B. Zema, S.J., *The Houses of Tuscany and of Pierleone in the Crisis of Rome in the Eleventh Century*.

46. Zema, *op. cit.*, p. 171. There is also this description of Hildebrand's face by Hugh of Cluny, who cannot be accused of malice: "*homuncio valde despicabilis parentelae exilis staturae.*" It is difficult to understand why this statement is not accepted, as it were, at face value. Since the closeness of the relation between Hildebrand and the Pierleoni is well documented and therefore accepted, why should the description of his "semitic" looks be discarded? It is understandable that the German historian, M. Tangl, (in his *Gregor VII Juedischer Herkunft?*), does not like it. But everybody agrees that his arguments are not very convincing. Is it so difficult to admit that the great Pope might have been not merely related by marriage to the converted Jews, but actually Jewish? What is so frightening about it?

47. Friedrich Heer. *The Medieval World*, see the chapter "The Crusade and the Conflict of East and West" which deals with both the religious and the political conflict between the Byzantines and the West.

48. For a comprehensive exposition of Norman history and particularly their role in southern Italy and Sicily, see *The Cambridge Medieval History*, vol. V., chap. 4.

49. *Cambridge Medieval History*, vol. V., p. 35.

50. Zema, *op. cit.*, p. 171.

51. *Cod. Vatic.* 1954; both lists from Gregorovius, *op. cit.*, vol. IV., pp. 120, 124.

52. The decree of 1059 is quoted from *Select Historical Documents of the Middle Ages*, pp. 361–364. There is an Imperial version of the decree which emphasizes the role of the cardinals and not merely the cardinal bishops. The text can also be found in the Select Documents.

53. Georg Caro, *Sozial- und Wirtschaftsgeschichte der Juden im Mittelalter*, p. 205 (my translation).

54. *The Correspondence of Pope Gregory VII*, p. 2.

55. *The Correspondence of Pope Gregory VII*, p. 1

56. The parts of his letter pertaining to Jews are quoted in Vogelstein-Rieger, *op. cit.*, vol. I., p. 216, from Jaffe Loewenfeld I 576 No. 4581.

57. *Correspondence*, p. 177 ff.

58. Quoted from *Select Documents*, p. 366.

59. *The Correspondence of Pope Gregory VII*, p. 89.

60. *The Correspondence of Pope Gregory VII*, 18 f.

61. *The Correspondence of Pope Gregory VII*, 90 f.

62. Gregorovius, vol. IV., p. 187.

63. Arnold J. Toynbee, *A Study of History*, 1947, p. 357.

64. Zema, *The Houses of Tuscany and Pierleone*, p. 173.

65. Gregorovius, vol. IV., p. 197 (my translation).

66. *Corresp.* p. 112 f.

67. *Corresp.* p. 151 f.

68. Gregorovius, *op. cit.*, p. 218.

69. Gregorovius, *op. cit.*, p. 219.

70. *Corresp.*, *op. cit.*, p. 188 f.

71. Gregorovius, *op. cit.*, p. 271.

72. For the Crusades, see Runciman, *A History of the Crusades*, 3 vlms.; for the special chapter on Jews during the Crusades, see vol. I., pgs. 134 ff. and any Jewish history such as Graetz, Dubnow, Roth or others.

73. Runciman, *op. cit.*, p. 137.

74. *"Urbanus—apud eccl. s. Nicolai in carcere in domo Petri Leonis IV. Kal. Aug. animam deo redidit, atque per Trastyberium propter insidias inimicorum in eccl. B. Petri—corpus ejus delatum est."* Pand. Pisan. p. 352, quot. in Gregorovius, p. 282, footnote 2.

75. Gregorovius, *op. cit.* p. 350.

Chapter Four

76. We cannot deal adequately here with the Renaissance of the twelfth century. In our context it serves only as background material. Friedrich Heer's *The Medieval World* is a fresh and sometimes daring approach to the problems and phenomena of the period. There are, of course, many other works, such as C. H. Haskins' *The Renaissance of the Twelfth Century;* R. W. Southern's *The Making of the Middle Ages;* and H. O. Taylor's *The Medieval Mind,* to mention but a few.

77. Friedrich Heer, *op. cit.*, p. 4.

78. Quoted in H. O. Taylor, *op. cit.*

79. For an analysis of Héloise, see Henry Osborn Taylor, *The Medieval Mind,* vol. II, "The Heart of Héloise."

80. See George Moore, the *Letters of Héloise,* 1926, and P. Gilson, *Héloise and Abelard,* 1953.

81. For Abelard's work, see Charles de Remusat, *Abelard,* and McCabe's *Life of Abelard.* A concise, reliable summary of his views can be found in Taylor, *op. cit.* p. 368 ff.

82. Quoted in Bernardi, *Lothar von Supplinburg,* p. 287, footnote 49.

83. Gregorovious, *op. cit.*, p. 394, footnote on the page, mentions another, much longer inscription which, however, was no longer in existence in his time. The brief inscription on the sarcophagus is a little disappointing, and something more must have been there before. The date, for instance, which is generally given as 1128, is missing. Gregorovius mentions an inscription on the tomb of what he calls "the last heiress" of the house of Pierleone to be found in Sta. Maria della Consolazione, but I did not find it there. Lucretia Pierleonia claims that the family was related to the Habsburgs. There are similar allegations in Zazzera and other books. The relationship is supposed to stem from a marriage between Roger II and Anaclet's sister. Of course, anti-Semitic encyclopedias were eager to accuse the Habsburgs of such "contamination" with Jewish blood and consider the famous Habsburg lip proof of their Jewish origin. But all this is now proved to be a legend.

84. See Zoepfel, *Papstwahlen,* for a detailed analysis of the election decree of 1059 and its development.

85. Quoted in Bernardi, *op. cit.* p. 298 ff.

86. The election of 1130 in all its legal and political ramifications has been dealt with by a number of Church historians. The two basic works are Zoepfel's *Papstwahlen* and Muehlbacher's *Die streitige Papstwahl des Jahres 1130.* Bernardi adds his own scholastic material to a critical analysis of these two essays. He also quotes the contemporary Latin sources at great length, and readers who are interested in the scholastic aspects will do well to consult the sources quoted there. Of course, Gregorovius has dealt with it as well, but since his is a large work dealing with the whole history of Rome in the Middle Ages, he does not deal with the details. Zoepfel, Muehlbacher, Bernardi and Gregorovius are no partisans and deal with the personalities and problems objectively. More partisan (in favor of Innocent and opposed to Anaclet) are those works which deal specifically with Bernard of Clairvaux's involvement in the "Battle of the Tiaras." Among those are E. Amélineau, *St. Bernard et le schisme d'Anaclet II;* E. Vacandard, *Saint Bernard et le schisme d'Anaclet en France;* and Williams, *St. Bernard of Clairvaux,* p. 100–154. For details consult the bibliography.

87. Zoepfel, *op. cit.*

88. Gregorovius, *op. cit.* p. 398.

89. Carl Hampe, *Abendlaendisches Hochmittelalter,* in *Propylaen Geschichte,* p. 432.

90. Bernard of Clairvaux, *Epistle 127.*

91. Bernardi, *op. cit.* p. 286.

92. Williams, *op. cit.*

93. *op. cit.* p. 398.

94. Quoted from *Vita Prima* in Williams, *Saint Bernard of Clairvaux,* p. 152.

95. *op. cit.* p. 154.

96. Bernard, *Epistles 147.*

97. *Epistle 139.* The anti-Jewish phrase reads in Latin: *"ut enim constat, Judaicam sobolem sedem Petri in Christi occupasse injuriam."* See also Newman, *Jewish Influences on Christian Reform Movements,* p. 248 ff. where Bishop Meinfredus of Mantua is quoted as having said of Anaclet *"jam nec Judaeus quidem, Judaeo deterior,"* that he was a Jew and even worse than a Jew.

Bibliography

AMÉLINEAU, ABBÉ E., *St. Bernard et le schisme d'Anaclet II. Revue des questions historiques* XXX.

ARMELLING, MARIANO, *Le chiese di Roma dal secolo IV al XIX.* Rome, 1941.

BARON, SALO W., *A Social and Religious History of the Jews.* v. III and IV.

————, *The Jewish Factor in Medieval Civilization: Proceedings of the American Academy for Jewish Research.* 1942. 12 v.

BARK, W. C., *Origins of the Medieval World.* 1958.

BAXMANN, R., *Die Politik der Päpste.* Elberfeld. 1869.

BELOW, GEORG VON, *Die Juden. Reallexicon der germanischen Altertums-kunde.* 1915. v. II. p. 617.

BEN YEHESKEL, MORDECAI, *Sefer Ma'asiyot.* 1958.

BERNARDI, WILHELM, *Lothar von Supplinburg.* Leipzig. 1879.

BLOCH, HERBERT, *The Schism of Anacletus II and the Glanfeuil Forger-ies of Peter the Deacon of Monte Cassino.* Trapitio. 1952. v. VIII.

BLUMENKRANZ, BERNHARD, *Juifs et Chrétiens dans le monde Occidental, 430–1096.* Paris. 1960.

BORINO, G. B., *L'Elezione e la Deposizione di Gregorio VI. Archivio Della R. Soc. Rom. di Storia Patria* XXXIX.

BROWE, PETER, S. J., *Die Judenmission im Mittelalter.* Rome. 1942.

————, *Die kirchliche Gesetzgebung über die Behandlung der getauf-ten Juden. Archiv für Kath. Kirchenrecht.* 1941. p. 121.

Cambridge Economic History of Europe, Cambridge. 1952. 2v.

Cambridge Medieval History, Cambridge. 1929. v.5.

CANNON, WILLIAM R., *History of Christianity in the Middle Ages.* New York. 1960.

CARO, GEORG, *Sozial-und Wirtschaftsgeschichte der Juden im Mittelalter und der Neuzeit.* Leipzig. 1908. v.I. 204f.

CARUS-WILSON, E., *Medieval Merchant Venturers*. London. 1955.

CASPAR, ERICH, *Roger II und die Gründung der romanisch sizilianischen Monarchie*. 1904.

COMAYRÉ, GABRIEL, *Abélard and the Origin and Early History of Universities*. 1893.

Correspondence of Pope Gregory VII., The, New York. 1932.

CURTIS, EDMUND, *Roger of Sicily and the Normans in Lower Italy*. London and New York. 1912.

DANIEL-ROPS, H., *Cathedral and Crusade, Studies of the Medieval Church*. London. 1956.

DAUX, C., *Le Denier de St. Pierre*. Paris. 1907.

DELARE, O., *Saint Grégoire VII: Dernières années de son pontificat*. Rev. Questions Historiques. *1885. v.XXXVIII.*

DEUTSCH, S. M., *Peter Abaelard—Ein kritischer Theologe des 12.Jahrhunderts*. 1883.

DOPSCH, ALFONS, *The Economic and Social Foundations of European Civilization*. London. 1937.

EALES, S. J., *St. Bernard, Abbot of Clairvaux*. 1890.

EHRENBERG, RICHARD, *Die Banken in der Volkswirtschaft vom 11.-17. Jahrundert*. Handwoerterbuch der Staatswissenschaften. 1925.

FABRE, P., *Recherches sur le Denier de St. Pierre en Angleterre au Moyen-Age*. Rome. 1892.

————, *Beiträge zur Geschichte des Peterspfennig vom 11.-15. Jahrhundert*. Zeitschrift für Sozial-und Wirtschaftsgeschichte. 1896. v.IV.

FEDELE, PIETRO, *Pierleoni e Frangipani nella Storia Medievale di Roma*. Roma. 1937. v.XV.

————, *Le Famiglie di Anacleto II e Di Gelasio II*. Archivio della R. Societa Romana di Storia Patria. 1899. v.XXII.

GERSTENBERG, OTTO, *Studien zur Geschichte des römischen Adels im Ausgange des 10.Jahrunderts*. Dresden Historische Vierteljahrschrift. 1936/37.

GIERKE, OTTO, *Political Theories of the Middle Ages*. Cambridge. 1958.

GIESEBRECHT, WILHELM VON, *Geschichte der deutschen Kaiserzeit*. 1869.

GIETMANN, FELIX, *Die Wahlanzeigen der Päpste bis zum Ende der Avignonesischen Zeit*. Marburg. 1931.

GOETZ, WALTER, *Die Entstehung der italienischen Kommune im frühen Mittalter*. Munich. 1944.

GOITEN, S. D., *From the Mediterranean to India*. Speculum. 1954. XXIX.

GOLDSCHMIDT, L., *Universalgeschichte des Handelsrechtes*. Stuttgart. 1891.

GONTARD, FRIEDRICH, *Die Päpste und die Konzilien*. München. 1963.

GORION, M. J., bin, *Der Born Judas*. Berlin. 1934.

GREGOROVIUS, FERDINAND, *History of the City of Rome in the Middle Ages*. v.IV.

GRISAR, HARTMANN, S.J., *History of Rome and the Popes in the Middle Ages*. London. 1912. 3v.

GUDEMANN, M., *Geschichte des Erziehungswesens und der Kultur der abendländischen Juden während des Mittelalters und der neueren Zeit*, 1880–88.

GUTMANN, FELIX, *Die Wahlanzeigen der Päpste bis zum Ende der Avignonesischen Zeit*. Marburg. 1931.

HAMPE, KARL, *Abendländisches Hochmittelalter* in *Propylaen Weltgeschichte*. Berlin. 1932.

HAUCK, ALBERT, *Kirchengeschichte Deutschlands*. 1896.

HEER, FRIEDRICH, *The Medieval World: Europe 1100–1350*. Cleveland and New York. 1962.

HENDERSON, ERNEST F., *Select Historical Documents of the Middle Ages*. London. 1925.

HOFFMANN, M., *Der Geldhandel der Juden im Mittelalter*. 1912.

HOMO, LÉON, *Rome Medievale 476–1420*. Paris. 1956.

JACOBS, JOSEPH, *Jewish Contribution to Civilization*. Philadelphia. 1919.

JELLINEK, A., *Beth Hamidrash*. Jerusalem, 1938. vs. V, VI.

JORDAN, KARL, *Zur päpstlichen Finanzgeschichte im 11. und 12. Jahrhundert. Quellen und Forschungen aus italienischen Archiven und Bibliotheken*. 1933–34. v.XXV.

KEHR, P., *Die Belehnungen der Süditalienischen Normannen Fürsten durch die Päpste 1059–1192*. Berlin. 1934. Preuss Akad. D. Wissenschaften. Phil. Hist. Klass.

KERR, P., *Diploma Purpureo di re Roggero II per la Casa Pierleoni*. Archivio della R. Societa Romana di Storia Patria. v.XXIV.

KÖLMEL, W., *Rom und der Kirchenstaat im 10. und 11. Jahrhundert. Abh. zur mittleren und neueren Geschichte Heft 78*. Berlin-Grunewald. 1935. p. 135.

LAGARDE, ANDRÉ, *The Latin Church in the Middle Ages*. Edinburgh. 1915.

LE FORT, GERTRUD VON, *Der Papst aus dem Ghetto*. Berlin. 1934.

LEHMANN, JULIUS, *Banking, Commercial, Encyclopedia of the Social Sciences.* N.Y., London. 1930. v.II.

LEON, HARRY J., *The Jews of Ancient Rome*, 1960.

LEWIS, ARCHIBALD R., *Naval Power and Trade in the Mediterranean A.D.500–1100.* Princeton. 1951.

LIEBE, GEROG, *Die Juden.* Stuttgart. 1902.

LOEB, ISIDORE, *Réflexions sur les Juifs. Revue des Études Juives.* 1894. v.XXVIII.

LOPEZ, R. S., *An Aristocracy of Money in the Early Middle Ages.* Speculum XXVIII.

—————, *A Propos D'une Virgule Revue Historique.* 1947.

—————, *Some Tenth Century Towns (Medievalia et Humanistica).* 1955. v.VIII.

LOPEZ and RAYMOND, *Medieval Trade. Jewish Quarterly Review XXXV.*

LUZ, PIERRE de, *Histoire des Papes.* Paris. 1960.

MANN, HORACE K., *The Lives of the Popes in the Early Middle Ages.* London. 1925.

MATHEW, A. H., *The Life and Times of Hildebrand, Pope Gregory VII.* London. 1910.

MILANO, ATTILIO, *Il ghetto di Roma.* Roma. 1964.

MUEHLBACHER, E., *Die streitige Papstwahl des Jahres 1130.* Innsbruck. 1876.

NELSON, B. N., *The Idea of Usury.* Princeton. 1949.

NEWMAN, L. I., *Jewish Influence on Christian Reform Movements.* New York. 1925.

NOONAN, JOHN T., JR., *The Scholastic Analysis of Usury.* Cambridge. 1957.

NUEBLING, EUGEN, *Die Judengemeinden im Mittelalter.* Ulm. 1896.

OELSNER, TONI. *The Place of the Jews in Economic History.* Yearbook Leo Baeck Institute. London. 1962.

OVERMANN, A., *Gräfin Mathilda von Tuscien und ihre Besitzungen.* Innsbruck. 1895.

PALUMBO, P. F., *Lo Schisma del 1130.* Rome. 1942.

PANNENBORG, A., *Studien zur Geschichte der Herzogin Matilde von Canossa.* 1872.

PARKES, JAMES, *The Jew in the Medieval Community.* 1938.

PERCHERON, RENÉ, *Itineraires Romains.* Paris. 1950.

PICOTTA, G. B., *Della Supposta Parentèla Ebraica di Gregorio VI e Gregorio VII. Archivio Storico Italiano.* 1942.

PIRENNE, HENRI, *Medieval Cities.* Princeton. 1949.

POLAZZO, TERZO ANTONIO, *Da Castel Sant'Angelo alla Basilica di S. Pietro.* Rome. 1948.

POOLE, REGINALD LANE, *Benedict IX and Gregory VI, Proceedings of the British Academy.* 1917–1918.

————, *Names and Numbers of Medieval Popes. English Historical Review XXXII.* 1917.

————, *Papal Chronology in the Eleventh Century, ibid.*

RASHDALL, HASTINGS, *The Universities in the Middle Ages.* 3Vs. 1936.

RENOUARD, Y., *Les Hommes des Affaires Italiens au Moyen Age.* Paris. 1949.

RORIG, FRITZ, *Die europäische Stadt im Mittelalter.* Göttingen. 1955.

ROTH, CECIL, *The Qualification of Jewish Physicians in the Middle Ages.* Speculum. 1953.

ROVIER, RAYMOND DE, *Money, Banking and Credit in Medieval Bruges.* Massachusetts. 1948.

RUNCIMAN, STEVEN, *A History of the Crusades.* Cambridge, 1953. 3Vs.

SCHAUBE, A., *Handelsgeschichte der romanischen Völker.* Munich. 1906.

SCHMALE, F. J., *Studien zum Schisma des Jahres 1130.* 1961.

SCHIPPER, IGNATZ, *Die Anfaenge des Kapitalismus bei den abendlaendischen Juden.* Vienna. 1907.

SCHULTE, ALOYS, *Geschichte des mittelalterlichen Handels und Verkehrs.* Leipzig. 1900.

SEIDLHEIMER, MICHAEL, *Currents of Medieval Thought.* Oxford. 1960.

SOLERO, SILVIO, *Storia dei Papi (I Papi del Medievo).* Torino. 1938. v.II.

SOUTHERN, R. W., *The Making of the Middle Ages.* London. 1953.

STEINDORFF, E., *Jahrbuch des Deutschen Reichs unter Heinrich III.* Leipzig. 1881. vs.I and II.

STORRS, R. S., *Bernard of Clairvaux: The Times, The Man and His Work.* New York. 1893.

TANGL, M., *Gregor VII, juedischer Herkunft?* Neues Archiv. XXXI. 1906.

TAYLOR, HENRY OSBORN, *The Medieval Mind.* Cambridge. 1959. 2vs.

THOMPSON, J. WESTPHAL, *Economic and Social History of the Middle Ages.* New York. 1928.

VACANDARD, L'ABBÉ E., *St. Bernard et le schisme d'Anaclet en France*. *Revue des Questions Historiques XLIII*.

——, *Vie de Saint Bernard, Abbé de Clairvaux*. Paris. 1895.

VOGELSTEIN, HERMANN, *The Jews of Rome*. Philadelphia. 1940.

—— and RIEGER, PAUL, *Geschichte der Juden in Rom*. Berlin. 1896.

WALKER, WILLISTON, *A History of the Christian Church*. New York. 1919.

WENDT, SIEGFRIED, *Banken II (Mittelalter)*. *Handwoerterbuch der Sozialwissenschaften*. 1956.

WILLIAMS, WATKIN, *Saint Bernard of Clairvaux*. Westminster. 1952.

WILL, CORNELIUS, *Die Anfaenge der Restauration der Kirche im 11. Jahrhundert*. Marburg. 1859. 1863.

ZAZZERA, *Della Nobilità dell' Italia*. Milano. 1621.

ZEMA, D. *The Houses of Tuscany and of Pierleone in the Crisis of Rome in the Eleventh Century*. Traditio II. 1944.

ZOEPFEL, RICHARD, *Die Papstwahlen. Die Doppelwahl des Jahres 1130*. Göttingen. 1871.